Narrative of Power

Essays for an Endangered Century

Margaret Randall

Common Courage Press   Monroe, Maine

ISBN: 1-56751-262-3 paper
ISBN 1-56751-263-1 cloth

**Library of Congress Cataloging-in-Publication Data is
available on request from the publisher**

Common Courage Press
Box 702
Monroe, ME 04951

800-497-3207

FAX (207) 525-3068
orders-info@commoncouragepress.com

See our website for e versions of this book.
www.commoncouragepress.com

First Printing
Printed in Canada

for my grandson
Martín Randall Carlevaro

thank you for allowing me
to see some of these issues
through your 13-year-old eyes

Contents

Introduction

We U.S. Americans[1] are living a lie, and governmental sleight of hand has most people doing so in relative complacency. I don't mean we are unaware of what our lives have become. Violence, massive corporate downsizing, overall economic crisis, reduced social services and ever so much less of that commodity known as opportunity-for-all are palpable for most of us. I mean we are living as if the downturn is inevitable. And too many buy into the idea that it's up to us alone to make it right.

With only 10% of U.S. military spending—about 40 billion, the amount initially requested to fund the attack on Afghanistan—the essentials of life for everyone on earth would be assured.[2] There is nothing right about the fact that this money is spent on death rather than on life.

Even many who have lost jobs, whose civil liberties and human rights are being eroded, who have no health care or pensions—even many who find themselves in the streets—seem willing to follow the president's rote imperatives. The general consensus is there's nothing to be done. If they ever did, many no longer have the feeling government has anything to do with them. Money speaks, not need. And money is power—in every electoral race, every story of corporate greed, every TV image or Hollywood human interest story. In seemingly irreversible increments, U.S. Americans are being conditioned to internalize and accept the situation in which we find ourselves.

One way this follow-the-leader apathy is being pushed upon the nation is through a profound cooptation of language. I am fascinated by the ways in which official rhetoric subverts our grasp of reality. Wrong is right. Expedient (or brutal) is moral. The danger of a country possessing weapons of mass destruction only refers to others, never to the United States which, after all, was the first and so far only country to drop an atomic bomb on a civilian population—twice. Previously unimaginable scenarios are specs to be flicked from our questioning consciousness.

Selling his Attack Iraq agenda, Bush vows to go it alone if necessary, but also claims that our allies, many of whom are visibly opposed to his doctrine, will eventually come on board. No doubt he assumes he can buy them with continued promises of aid. When the Turkish parliament voted against allowing a U.S. invasion of Iraq from its soil, a TV news analyst said this showed the Turks' lack of experience with democracy: They made the mistake of listening to the people in the streets, he explained.

The economy? It is basically sound, we are told. Even as it goes about raiding important social programs and greatly increases the national deficit, the administration allocates billions to defense.[3] Bush and company give lip service to education, public health, and a crumbling infrastructure, while promising "no new taxes" or, more absurd, a tax cut for the wealthy. Even to the least politically educated, the contradictions should be obvious. Yet, much like the pensioner who responds to the scam phone call and relinquishes his lifetime savings to the promise of the windfall he is told will be his reward, many U.S. Americans believe our government's insistence that it's up to us to get ourselves through an economic downtime by displaying more consumer confidence—spending what we don't have.

The group in power—and thus also the group that holds power over much of the rest of the world—relies on a complex double-speak to maintain the popular support the polls tell us remains high. Despite its glaring disregard for everything from national security to the economy, despite its failure to address urgent domestic needs and its criminal protection of corporate greed, vacuous phrases and bombastic bullying continue to stand in for analysis and reason. These phrases and actions tell us two and two is five, and too many of us seem to accept that this is so.

The first and biggest lie may be the notion that Bush/Cheney were elected to office. Most subsequent independent vote counts revealed Gore/Lieberman to be the winners in 2000. The Republican Party engineered the coup. It was judicial rather than military. No blood was shed, as it was in those military coups the U.S. supported in Guatemala (1954) and Chile (1973). Yet the outcome was similar. Through blatant electoral fraud in Florida and elsewhere, behind-the-scenes power trade-offs that may never be fully known, and the intervention of a Supreme Court already stacked in its favor, the Republican Party was able to put its man in office.

Language was important here as well. With the coup, democracy became a hollow concept. Yet this flagrant abuse of the electorate was spun as "democracy at work." And most citizens accepted it as such.

The United States has a long history of external and internal abuse. What's new is the reach of its power today, the impunity with which it exercises that power, and the fact that it is no longer necessary for it to operate covertly. Successive administrations have been able to put millions into influencing foreign elections, overthrowing democratically elected heads of state, invading and effecting regime changes in countries whose policies they didn't consider favorable to U.S. interests. Ten, twenty, thirty years ago, this gross interference had to be hidden, perpetrated under cover. Even George W. Bush, in campaign speeches and debates, claimed he didn't believe in nation building. We can't just go in and impose our way of doing things on others, he said.

Then a bloodless coup gave us the Bush administration. And the September 11ᵗʰ, 2001 terrorist attacks on New York and Washington provided it with a mandate, relieving Bush of any pretense at non-intervention. We will never know what kind of a president this limited, devious, and clumsy man might have become, because the horror of experiencing such death and destruction on home ground gave him a blank sheet of paper upon which to write his presidency. U.S. government bombast, policy, and the need to appear to be open about that policy turned an important corner on 9/11.

In a saner political climate this horrendous tragedy might have led to the sort of wise consensus capable of producing a deepened national awareness of the intrusive role the United States plays around the world. An attempt to understand why others hate us, or why this is even a question at a time when news from every corner of the globe is readily accessible, might have produced constructive change. Following such loss, people need time to grieve. But rather than encouraging grief to morph into self-examination and debate, the administration and its sidekick, the corporate press, have battered us with a repetition of images and phrases designed to keep us suspicious of dark-skinned men, fearful and focused on revenge.

The political climate created by this administration and immensely strengthened by 9/11 is fertile ground for dictatorship, in essence if not in name. It's not difficult to find parallels between the coercive policies of Bush, Cheney, Rumsfeld and Ashcroft and those enacted by Hitler and his cohorts in the mid to late 1930s. Here's a quote from Hitler's reichsmarschall Hermann Goering, made at his 1946 Nuremberg trial: "Naturally the common people don't want war ... but after all it is the leaders of a country who determine policy, and it is always a simple matter to drag the people along, whether it is a democracy, or a fascist dictatorship, or parliament or a communist dictatorship. All you have to do is tell them they are being attacked, and denounce the pacifists for lack of patriotism and exposing the country to danger. It works the same in every country."[4]

To those who may be offended by the analogy, I say consider just a few of Bush's post 9/11 policy initiatives: He launched a full-scale military campaign against Afghanistan that resulted in a regime change, social chaos, a large number of civilian deaths, and a country so physically devastated it will take decades to rebuild. Osama bin Laden lives and Al Qaeda remains operative. He disregarded the Constitution by demanding unilateral war powers, bullied Congress and then vilified and overrode the United Nations. When the 2002 Nobel Peace prize was awarded to ex president Carter, the president of the conservative Nobel Committee publicly declared the prize should be seen as a commentary on Bush's warmongering.

The Bush administration has consistently refused to enter into any of the important international agreements, ignoring other world leaders, and displaying bully tactics every time another government disagrees. Decades of open anger against the United States is now more clearly articulated than ever. And when the administration speaks through the World Bank or International Monetary Fund, its words are no less absurd. The former applauded privatization of Zambia's public health system: "It's a model for Africa; there are no more lines at hospitals," a World Bank spokesperson said. The Zambian Post completed the idea: "There are no more lines at hospitals because people are dying at home."[5]

Domestically there are many examples of areas in which what was once off-limits in a democratic society has now become acceptable. Under the pretext of national security, all manner of freedoms are being curtailed. Christian fundamentalist ideology informs our Department of Justice. Legal as well as illegal aliens, and also citizens, are being held without specific charges, denied their right to the confidentiality of legal counsel and access to visits. As it keeps the public fearful by releasing periodic threats of new attacks, the administration rolls back environmental protection, appoints judges whose only claim to fame is their conservative ideology, and challenges such international bodies as the United Nations to show its backbone (read: support for U.S. warmongering).

Arbitrary dichotomies are put forward, such as the idea that fighting terror requires that we give up our civil and human rights. There is no consideration of alternatives. Discussion is discouraged and those who would engage in it are labeled unpatriotic. Academics are attacked for promoting debate. Pacifists are attacked for being un-American. The racist, often fascist, ideas of radical conservatives are encouraged.

This squeeze on our lives causes dramatic rips in the social fabric. In the mid 1990s we saw a rash of workplace shootings by laid-off and frustrated workers. Later in that decade a similar madness began to claim middle and high school students, and we lived through a series of incidents in which young white males turned their murderous angst against fellow students and teachers. Both phenomena should have been warning signs, telling us a dangerous fear was running rampant in our society.

Government failed to grasp the roots of the problem: no solid preventative measures have been implemented, gun control has never really been on the agenda, nor has there been a serious effort to tone down the violence in entertainment, the media or our popular culture. The official response has been to increase funding for law enforcement, build more prisons (we are already the industrialized country with the most prisoners per capita), and use the threat of violence itself to further control the population.

In October of 2002 a sniper began murdering men and

women in the Washington area. One after another the victims
fell. Once again warfare was the response to individual madness,
this time surveillance planes were added to the usual arsenal.
Little has been made about the fact that there is a legal sniper
culture in this country. Freedom of speech, association and dissent are under attack, while freedom of action remains unchallenged for survivalists and other violent cults.

There are clear connections between international terrorism—real and supposed—as it is portrayed in our press, the state
terrorism employed by the U.S. government in Afghanistan,
Iraq and elsewhere, and the tacit permission our government's
policies give to other states that seek an excuse to do the
same—Israel in its war against the Palestinians, Russia in its
campaign in Chechnya, Colombia using the "war against drugs"
as an excuse to slaughter its civilian population and guerrilla
insurgents, to name a few.

Torture is one dramatic example of how our understanding of what is and is not off-limits has changed in recent
years. Although use of torture by our police, our CIA and other
covert operatives has been amply documented, we have been
taught that the practice of torture is incompatible with democracy. Under no circumstances do our forces of law and order
condone the use of torture, we are told, indeed its existence in
other countries is reason to punish or take their governments
down. The U.S. pretends to set diplomatic and trade policy
according to a country's use or curtailment of torture. Yet in the
spring of 2003 our media questioned the methods the administration considers acceptable when interrogating prisoners in the
war against terror. These include withholding food and light,
sleep deprivation, and other methods of psychological coercion.
It's not torture, we are told.

Now even this is changing. Several of our statesmen have
indicated that terrorists might better be interrogated abroad,

where torture is routine, or that we must begin to use torture here if we want results. Even liberal law professor Alan M. Dershowitz told Sixty Minutes' Mike Wallace that "torture is inevitable" and that he can conceive of "torture warrants" being useful in certain cases. On the same segment Human Rights Watch executive director Kenneth Roth disagreed, saying that "torture is against the Constitution, degrades humanity and the idea of democracy." Roth also pointed out that it is not reliable, that prisoners will confess to anything when torture is used.[6]

The growing amount of violence in Hollywood films, on TV, and in popular music; the stereotyping, racial profiling and assault upon Middle Eastern and Arabic men; the randomness and proliferation of individual acts of violence and our system's inability to control them: all are denounced by those in power. But all are a mirror image of the violence with which the Bush administration acts domestically and around the world.

Things are moving fast. We are frightened, by our vulnerability to outside attack as well as by our government's strategies for keeping us safe. It all comes down to the use and misuse of power. Who holds it? How have they usurped it? What alternative remedies are we left with? And, perhaps most importantly, how may those of us still searching for ways to implement social change be able to analyze the nature of power itself, so that we can develop more justice-oriented solutions?

I wrote these essays during a period whose principal characteristics are its deep shift in human expectations and the velocity with which what we once cherished seems to have become expendable. Since the 1989 disintegration of the socialist bloc, the United States has held almost unopposed power in the world. In our efforts to understand what went wrong, those of us involved in movements for social change have had to look inside those movements as well as out. Our very identities have been challenged.

For those for whom peace and justice have been lifelong struggles, this continues to be a time of profound loss. We have lost battles and comrades, cohesion and hope. I grieve again for Haydeé Santamaría, heroine of the Cuban revolution who, dispirited, took her own life in 1980. And for José Benito Escobar, martyred Sandinista leader whose working-class consciousness would surely have been wounded by later leaders' corruption.

We continue to work in our communities and globally. An anti-war movement is growing more rapidly than it did during the Vietnam War years; its response more creative, its vision more global and its links more international than previous movements. But the forces lined up against us are also stronger, more brutal and unabashed in how they wield their weaponry of destruction, more shameless and at the same time a great deal more sophisticated. Without a broad understanding of power—as wielded by governments, corporations, and also within our own ranks—I fear we don't stand a chance.

This grossly unequal balance of power, impossible to ignore, has led some of us to reevaluate power itself, to consider it a political category and one that must be thoroughly explored if we are to envision new and more enduring strategies for social change. Many of our own most painful losses can be directly attributed to a failure to challenge power inequalities within our own movements. I think now of Salvadoran revolutionary and poet Roque Dalton, tortured to death in May of 1975 by a renegade faction of his own movement. I think of Comandante Ana María, second in command of that country's revolutionary forces, stabbed to death in 1983 on orders from her superior. These are personal memories, as painful and vivid today as all those many years ago. Looking to the immediate future, I believe that until we rid ourselves of our patriarchal conditioning and take a realistic look at today's alignment of forces, nothing will change.

A reevaluation of power in our own ranks would mean, first of all, a solid commitment to embrace and empower every group. We don't need organizations fighting for workers' rights but without a gender perspective, groups struggling for a particular race or ethnicity but unable to consider the needs of other races or ethnicities, women's groups that have no use for lesbians, movements whose goal is to strengthen the family that do not respect all types of families, and so forth and so on—we can all fill in the blanks. For change to be real and endure, every person must feel represented and empowered to speak and act.

It may be a truism to say that the 9/11 attack brought terror home. Still, it bears repeating because so few in this country had any awareness of the massive acts of terror suffered periodically by so many others throughout the world. Sadly, most still don't. U.S. Americans have been educated in isolationism and to believe we are unique, superior, and strangely independent of the rest of the world. In a nation founded on the decimation of its original inhabitants and developed with slave labor, racism remains a useful weapon of control.

In the attacks on New York and Washington, we experienced what so many in other countries have experienced many times over, in assaults too often perpetrated or supported by U.S. foreign policy. Not once since 9/11 has Bush or any other government official mentioned the terrorist attacks upon others: 400 Guatemalan villages razed and 400,000 Guatemalans disappeared during the 1970s and '80s; Chile's 1973 coup that left approximately 20,000 dead; U.S.-supported massacres in Indonesia, Congo, El Salvador, Palestine—the list includes dozens of countries on almost every continent.

Major players in today's struggles are the various brands of religious fundamentalism that have taken power in a variety of countries: most prominently Muslim and Christian but also

Jewish, Hindu and others. Fundamentalism permeates and leads these times. In the United States, a mentality born out of Christian fundamentalist dogma continues to rally the ignorant and silence the thoughtful. The standoff between Bush and Islamic terrorists is in fact a standoff between two fundamentalisms.

The evils of religion in general, and patriarchal religion in particular, threaten us from all sides: in the sexual abuse cases and their respective cover-ups that have surfaced within the Catholic Church; in rigid doctrines that place the United States alongside the Vatican and a few of the more retrograde Muslim nations in their attempts to sabotage every international conference or forum searching for solutions to the world's critical problems; and in the fundamentalist ideology that threatens public education, health care, individual privacy, women's reproductive rights, scientific inquiry, the movement for a dignified death, and the lives of millions of women and gay people here at home.

"Fundamentalism for All Seasons," one of the longer essays in this collection, reflects my concern with and rage at the encroachment of this dogma, how it drives public policy, and the increasing impact it is having on our traditional separation of Church and State.[7] Many of these pieces speak of the hypocrisy that pervades our society. Several examine the deliberate cooptation of language as a necessary precursor to the cooptation of lives.

A gender analysis informs all these pieces, and I want to say how important it has been to have been part of the late twentieth century and early twenty-first century community of feminists in the United States and throughout the world. I owe a special debt of gratitude to Brazilian Moema Viezzer, Nicaraguan Sofía Montenegro, Mexican Marcia Legarde, internationalist María Suárez, and U.S. Americans Elizabeth

Kennedy and Gerda Lerner, among others.

These women have had the opportunity of testing their ideas in conflict. Life and death situations show us how the demand that gender be factored into every analysis can add depth and staying power to struggle and, conversely, how giving in to patriarchal privilege holds us all back. We continue to listen to one another, work off each other's ideas, and push those ideas further. Of all the philosophical leaps I have been privileged to witness or been part of, feminism is undoubtedly the most important: the movement in thought and activism that has enabled me to see most clearly that an unjust distribution of power lies behind all other injustice.

Since my last collection of essays, I have moved from a position that factored feminism into a pretty traditional Marxist world view (class as the primary contradiction) to one that refuses to privilege class over gender, nationalism over internationalism, sameness over diverse cultural identities; even the human species over those many other species with whom we share planet earth. I have found myself opening to ecological and environmental concerns, ever more aware of the ways in which all forms of abuse and domination interact, and increasingly convinced that if we continue to destroy our nest, social change may become irrelevant.

I had begun to move from viewing oppression as primarily economic to understanding it as a much more complex phenomenon—economic yes, but also patriarchal, racial, and cultural—back in the mid 1980s, when I began to remember a personal experience of incest. I had long been plagued by a pervasive phobia, a horror of mushrooms, and upon my return from Latin America, was able to avail myself of the feminist psychotherapy just then beginning to help so many unearth repressed memory. This therapy was crucial, not only to my own process of healing but to a more inclusive understanding of how power abuse works.

By that time I had experienced first hand the domination of less powerful peoples by superpowers acting in defense of their own interests. So it wasn't that much of a leap for me to understand that the invasion of a woman's or child's body by an adult (usually male), with power over her life, mirrors the abuse of power that takes place when a small country is attacked by a larger more powerful one. Back in the early 1970s, when the second wave of U.S. feminism was gaining momentum, we used to say the personal is political. The connections I was making in the mid to late '80s deepened my understanding of this idea, and showed me how global and domestic violence are related aspects of the same problem. Both have their roots in patriarchy.

Place has also been important in my recent political development. In 1984 I came home from 23 years in Latin America. For a variety of reasons—some of them political, some family-centered, some springing from youthful rage or a natural sense of adventure—I had experienced the life of an expatriate, the loneliness of being an outsider, distance from the language of my roots, the great gifts of other cultures, and the deep pain of separation from home.

Returning to my early landscape—the deserts and mountains of New Mexico—an increasingly intimate relationship with earth, air, space, water, rock, and the creatures that inhabit this place, helped me begin to understand and more deeply value the relationships. It also gave me a renewed sense of the importance of place to one's identity. David Orr has written: "... the way in which indigenous peoples certified adulthood was rooted in place. A child became an adult in a place. We don't do that ... Education ought to allow for bonding to the natural world."[8] Becoming more aware of the environment has also led me to think about technology: over-saturation of information, noise pollution, and other areas in which inventions that aid us in some ways hurt or disarticulate us in others.

Language translates our stories from one generation to the next. And language carries our energies and dreams from one community or individual to another. Language is in continual flux. It changes to reflect new ideas and new ways of expressing those ideas. As I find myself more and more fascinated with the corruption and abuse of language, I am also more conscious of our need to take language back from those who distort and use it against us. As a writer, I am interested in developing a language that tells our real stories, resists cooptation, says what we mean.

During my years of coming into maturity, many different social groups have explored how to say more clearly what they mean, and to demand from others a linguistic clarity based on respect. These groups have looked at conventional language usage and found it necessary to reclaim certain words while discarding others. We have come to understand how important it is that we defy the imposed silences and refuse to allow our language to continue to be usurped by those who would destroy us.

Women have struggled for a language that does not favor men or simply assume women are included when male forms of speech are used. This struggle has its English-language history, now twenty to thirty years old. In Spanish the history is younger, but in some ways also more complex; the fact that Spanish is a gendered language has made it necessary for Spanish-speaking feminists to develop complex yet viable ways of dealing with pronouns, articles, and verbs. Female and male word endings, typically expressed by an "o" (male) or an "a" (female) now often employ the @ sign to represent a less gendered written form. The spoken language is harder to manage. But these feminists have introduced *el o ella, ellos y ellas* (him or her, a male and female them) and this usage is beginning to be adopted even in the academy and by conscious politicians.

A number of other factors and conditions are clearly foundational to the ideas expressed in these essays. One is age. I have arrived at a time in my life when I am aging fast yet comfortable in my skin, accepting of my limitations, and at the height of my ability to make connections. Another, undoubtedly linked to the first, is a narrowing of my arena of struggle. I no longer believe I must do it all, participate in every protest or demonstration, personally engage in every effort with which I fervently agree. Perhaps age is also partially responsible for this narrowing. At first the shift reflected simple exhaustion. Now it involves choice. I choose to put my energies into listening, reading, pondering, exchanging ideas with others, and using my writer's tools to go more deeply into an issue than I might have when doing it all meant a much more superficial engagement.

There is also a flip side to this deepened awareness and connection. Age, for me, has brought with it a loss of rapid-fire expression. I forget words, often for long periods of time. I am haunted by images of my father's death from Alzheimer's. I have learned to speak from notes rather than extemporaneously, to leave a blank when writing—to which I may return when the lost word surfaces. In ways I am still exploring, these difficulties are giving me something rather than only taking something away. I speak of all this in the essay "Forgetting Remembered."

Important to my growth is a really solid primary relationship. Barbara and I have been together seventeen years. For the first time in my experience, I love and am loved by someone who is unwaveringly committed to my growth, as I am to hers. When we've talked about our good fortune at finding one another, or wondered out loud about the glue that holds us together (two women of such different ages, backgrounds, experiences), this absolute commitment to helping the other grow is always up there at the top of the list. No unspoken competition.

No discomfort or jealousy. No resentments. Absolute trust.

Barbara's support ranges from encouraging me to believe I deserve the time it takes to do my work to contributing economically and emotionally to that time, from reading and critiquing my pages to delighting in their publication. The absence of all those old energy-consuming complications provides the peace and space that have made it possible for me to come this far. Its simple fullness is something for which I am grateful every day.

I don't believe women alone recognize patriarchal social forms, or that lesbians have an advantage when it comes to rejecting violence or abuses of power. Many lesbians and heterosexual women buy into our consumerist culture, engage in power games and reproduce an unequal distribution of power as lovers, parents, in families or work places. Still, a conscious relationship between two women can be a powerful basis from which to move forward. Perhaps my emphasis should be on the conscious rather than on the sexual identity.

I have found continuity in the lives of my children, and their children. My son and three daughters each have families of their own. In Montevideo, Mexico City, and New York, they and their partners do work they love. All of it is socially useful, and it gives me great joy that each has wanted to give something back to his or her community. At this writing, there are nine grandchildren. Coming to terms with what each of my children has chosen to pass on to his or her children has taught me a great deal about my own choices, affirmations and errors. My father died in 1994; my mother is now 93. As they take leave and the young ones come into their own, I feel ever more consciously positioned on that bridge that sways equidistant between us. This two-way vision also profoundly informs my current perceptions.

Despite their range of subject matter, all these essays are

about power: who holds or withholds it and from whom, what it means, how it is distributed, used and abused. Together, they are intended as a plea to reexamine power as a political category. The division between those who have it and those who do not is the single most important sociopolitical contradiction. Money alone does not adequately define power differences; these are defined as well by class, gender, race, sexuality, age, culture, tradition, education, health, geography and so much more.

I intend this collection to be a point of departure for ongoing discussion. I rarely see my work as finished in any definitive way. Life moves too fast, especially now. One can go back to something written three or four years before, find the general premise still interesting, add or delete a paragraph or make other sorts of changes, and decide it is ready to go out into the world once again. But always, in my mind, it is another point of departure. An important lesson of these years has been that statements we once believed beyond argument were at best half-truths, misunderstandings, even lies. Process is as important—sometimes more important—as product.

And I think we who are on the far side of sixty must be willing to share our process, to pass it on with heads held high. In our various struggles to bring about a better world, we made many mistakes. Some came from a failure to honor imagination as we honored reason, accept our self-proclaimed leaders' points of view rather than hone our own powers of analysis, embrace political dogma as if it were religious scripture. Some resulted from being unable or unwilling to extend our class or race analyses to other social groups. Most, I believe, can be traced to not looking first and foremost at power.

We must fight hard these days against the tendency to despair, to become bitter or lose hope. We must hold on to the knowledge that even when some of our assumptions or methods were wrong, what we struggled for is possible and must remain a goal. And it is a worthy goal, an important goal, a goal that today—more than ever—is the only one that may enable us to survive. We and our fellow creatures. We and our earth, the air we breathe, the water we drink and food we eat. We and our future, and our children's future.

CHAPTER ONE

Is It Really
a Global Village?[1]

I

Why do they hate us has to be the most frequently asked question of the new century. I have a different question: why is that even a question?

Halfway down Highway One, The People's Republic of North Vietnam, fall 1974. A river. My young guide and I stand on the deck of the makeshift ferry that will carry us across. The bridge was bombed out by my own country, rebuilt by the Vietnamese, bombed and rebuilt again, and would continue its dance of destruction and resurrection until six months after my visit—when the Vietnamese would permanently eject U.S. troops from their beautiful land and build a bridge to last.

I know about the bombing, of course, and when the war is done will learn that my country dropped more bomb tonnage on Vietnam than was dropped by both sides in World War II. I do not yet know their victory will come so soon. In North American as in Vietnamese minds, this war has been forever.

Now, swaying with the motion of the moving platform, I notice the inquisitive expression of a young peasant woman standing nearby. Her question goes to my guide. I have become attuned to the answer—"My"—and know I have been identified: U.S. American.

For a moment so brief I barely catch it flickering in the questioner's eyes, I observe the deepest, purest hatred I have ever seen. Then, quickly, the woman recomposes herself behind a lovely smile:

"Welcome to Vietnam," my guide translates.

***

Spring, 1962. I am buying fruit at a large Mexico City market. It's been a year now since my arrival from New York, and my Spanish is improving, although even in this new language my friends sometimes note my Jewish Brooklynese with thinly disguised amusement.

The woman who arranges her piles of oranges in elegant pyramids notices my accent as well. "Italian?" she asks. I don't even hesitate before I nod. Young and barely beginning my long political education, I somehow understand that I do not want to be perceived as an Ugly American.

These days I sometimes think of that long-ago encounter. Did the fruit vendor's inquiry reflect ignorance or kindness? And what did my lie say about my own self-image at that point in my life? I know I already felt ashamed back then of an American Way of Greed I was just beginning to intuit. A few years later, and with a better understanding of what the history of U.S. relations with Mexico has meant to Mexicans, I might have revealed my national origin—if for no other reason than to demonstrate that not all U.S. Americans are alike.

***

In subsequent years, living first in Cuba and then in Sandinista Nicaragua, I am often privy to earnest explanations by those whose nations a succession of my country's governments have blackmailed, blockaded, invaded, occupied, plundered, sometimes all but destroyed. "We do not hate the American people," someone in an elegant living room or meager hut will insist, "We love the American people. Good American people. It is your government we hate. We know how to distinguish between the two."

Often this assertion is made by children ten or 12 years of age, *children I encounter in the streets as I walk or photograph. I remember a graveyard, Managua, winter of 1979. These children are curious, peer intently at my face, touch my clothing. "We do not hate the American people," the children say. My eyes wander from theirs to the recent gravestones. I exhale, slowly.*

I think of the decades of shameless support a succession of U.S. administrations gave to Somoza, the dictator finally overthrown by the Sandinistas just months before. President Teddy Roosevelt had called the first Somoza "a son of a bitch, but … our son of a bitch." While enjoying U.S. support, the Somoza family killed and imprisoned thousands, while keeping the great majority of his country's people in misery.

These children are making a distinction many adults in our country cannot make, and to which grown men in our government pay lip service at best. No one should take seriously the humanitarian claims of officials who speak of the loss of civilian life as collateral damage, or alternate the dropping of bombs of mass destruction with the dropping of fast-food propaganda on hungry people.

Moments. Memories. Threads woven into the experience that informs my world view.

II

Are we really a country of good people, people not to be confused with our government's criminal policies? Can we continue to say, as ordinary Germans did during World War II, that we do not know? Should we be paying closer attention to the Refusniks in Israel's army, more than 500 at this writing, who years from now will be able to tell their own children and grandchildren that they risked derision and scorn, and suffered prison, to do what they knew was right?[2]

If, as is so often suggested, we inhabit a Global Village, we

must acknowledge the technology that almost instantly com-
municates one part of the village with another. No longer can
we feign ignorance of what is suffered and who imposes the suffering. Being as in touch as we now are with even the most
remote parts of the world, the question "why do they hate us"
seems rhetorical at best. And yet, because of our political isolation and the fact that the news carried by our corporate media
is so inadequate, many continue to ask that question in good
faith.

We might begin to answer the question of why we are
hated by listening to people around the world, who have been
telling us why for decades. These people are not terrorists, not
the fringe element extremists of a religion or nation. These are
ordinary peace-loving men and women who have made it more
than clear that our foreign policy is killing them.

If despite our technological ability to do so we do not listen, we are no better than absentee landowners, reaping the
benefits of other people's lives. It's time to ask ourselves how we
inhabit this village and who inhabits it with us? How do we
treat our neighbors—the village idiot as well as the playground
bully, the battered and the batterer, the woman who tells the
stories and the children who sit in rapt attention, their eyes
round moons, pools absorbing history?

September 11th, 2001, with all its grief and fear, should
have opened our eyes to what others have suffered, what they
continue to suffer, and how we too often have been a part of the
problem rather than of the solution.

Are we to forever remain irrationally stratified along
national, class, race, gender, ethnic, sexual and other lines? Or
will we one day learn to respect one another's differences and
distribute power in ways that assure a more harmonious coexis-
tence? The idea of a village evokes images of sharing, caring,
mutual aid, and difference as a purveyor of cultural richness,

rather than a justification for hierarchy and oppression.

The average U.S. citizen is compassionate, generous with his or her charitable contributions, emergency aid, prayers, even personal time and energies. A tragedy, natural or manmade, almost anywhere in the world brings immediate and overwhelming response. We adopt impoverished or endangered children, collect so many tons of food and clothing they are often difficult or impossible to distribute to the needy for whom they are intended, and some of us—including many young people—contribute years of our lives to work among and for peoples less fortunate than ourselves.

What is this tradition of giving? Where does it come from? And why do most U.S. Americans, although generous in the one-on-one situation (or the situation painted with a human rather than a political brush), blithely endorse a foreign policy that supports (sometimes even creates) the very situations of inequality so many are willing to help ameliorate?

Why this distance between a people individually so compassionate and collectively so out of touch with reality?

The answer is political ignorance.

U.S. Americans inherit a tradition of neighborliness. The first inhabitants of this continent lived in harmony with nature and one another, and Native Americans today continue to honor kinship patterns that are broadly inclusive. Despite its encroachment upon the lives of those Native peoples, our European pioneering history of extending frontier across a vast and rugged land also gave us an appreciation of human solidarity, hard work and the bounty it can generate.

African slaves and successive waves of "free" immigration all had to rely on solidarity for survival. Our varied roots, then, would seem to combine to form a solid foundation for values of mutual aid and caring. Our schools, our churches, our civic organizations, even our political leaders encourage us in selfless work and generous giving. So we do all right when told, simply, that an earthquake has ravaged such and such a country or a prolonged drought has brought famine to millions somewhere else.

But we have also been taught superiority: we are the richest, the most powerful, the best and—until that fateful day in September—the most secure. We therefore feel an obligation to give to others, and often do so from this position of self-righteousness, a way of assuaging guilt or racking up points against the possibility of future calamity.

What we have not been taught, and turn away from knowing, is how U.S. foreign policy has been directly responsible for the suffering of so many of the world's peoples, those Others who with us inhabit this place we (sometimes glibly) call a Global Village. Whether we look at old programs like the Alliance for Progress (through which the U.S. is said to have taken four dollars out of a given economy for every dollar it invested),[3] or the current structural adjustment programs bleeding so many developing nations dry, U.S. foreign policy has always and continues to aim at turning corporate profit rather than encouraging local self-sufficiency or sustainability.[4]

Our Neo-Liberal exigencies provide a few more crumbs for these countries' owner classes while more intensely impoverishing their poor. The debt interest we have imposed upon them is draining them dry. Our support for cruel dictatorships, some of which we helped bring to power, is humiliating. Our disrespect for their sick and dying, which we call protecting the interests of our drug companies, is anything but humanitarian. Our blatant interference with their internal political processes is disrespectful. Our invasion of their territories and kidnapping of their highest elected officials is obscene.

U.S. Americans learn about the world from history books still grossly biased towards the conqueror, media sound bytes engineered to highlight events of national interest then leaving them dangling like unattached participles, and the rhetoric of public officials whose own knowledge may be limited and who surely favor staying in office over an in-depth examination of any of the problems we or others face. We learn about the world from a media establishment that rates news as entertainment.

In the United States, denial is a national characteristic. We nurture it in our interpersonal relationships, where glossing over embarrassing problems and "putting a good face forward" keeps us from having to deal with uncomfortable or painful issues—and allows us to present ourselves in line with the media image we are constantly called upon to imitate. We do the same thing socially, in our dealings with co-workers, bosses, friends and institutions, right on up to the way we relate to world events, our elected officials and the things they do in our name. Unwilling to take responsibility, we don't have to ponder the hard questions, concern ourselves with issues over which we believe we have no control, or let our spirits sag. And this denial is encouraged by the system in which we live. A numbed and cheerful member of the national community is, after all, a citizen who will continue to follow the leader, shop to keep the economy going, and leave the weightier questions to the "experts."

III

Why do they hate us? We hear this question on the street, in schools and workplaces, from friends. Why do they hate us so? What could have provoked a group of deeply religious (fanatically religious) men to give their own lives in their effort to destroy ours? Many have called the perpetrators cowards. But coward is not the word that comes to my mind when a man sacrifices his own life in an act of this sort.

Fanaticism is certainly part of the equation. Fundamentalists—whether Muslim, Christian, Jewish, Hindu, or of whatever other religious belief—are fanatics. And fanatics see narrowly, understand in accordance with a fervor that excludes rather than embraces. Fundamentalism, by its nature, is a literal reading. Rigid. Outside history, and incapable of understanding events, past or present, through a historical lens. To the Muslim fundamentalist, this supreme sacrifice assures eternal glory.

But why do these particular Islamic fundamentalists hate us, U.S. Americans?

George W. Bush has frequently responded to this question by saying they hate our freedom. Politically naïve citizens parrot this explanation. They hate our freedom and our democracy. They hate our respect for difference, the fact that our women can show their faces (and their bodies), that personal freedoms are cherished here, and well-advertised opportunities for success are available to all.

And yes, the United States does embody a degree of democratic freedom unknown in much of the world. Ordinary American people have worked long and hard and sacrificed a great deal for these freedoms. Women show our faces, have access to education, and have fought for and won important control over our lives. But I would suggest that we are neither as democratic, educated, gender-equal or free as this easy answer implies.

In recent years especially our electoral offices have gone to the highest bidder; the wealthier a person is the more likely he or she is to be elected. Even campaigns for state offices cost millions these days. Democracy, as practiced in the United States, has lost much of its meaning. We seem willing to relinquish our most precious freedoms, gender-equity is currently losing ground, and our ignorance is only too evident in our inability to distinguish between a Sikh and a Muslim, between any dark-skinned person and a potential terrorist.[5] People of Middle Eastern origin continue to be marginalized and harassed, even though the first terrorist attacks in this country's recent history were all carried out by white men: the Unibomber; the FBI at Waco, Texas; Timothy McVeigh in Oklahoma City; two young boys in Littleton, Colorado.

As a nation, we are waging violence in an effort to quell violence—perhaps the most palpable evidence that our integrity is on the decline.

We live in the most loudly touted democracy in history. Yet here we are, with an administration that took office through a coup and is now wreaking havoc on national and international law as it launches a pull-no-punches dragnet against a man suspected, but not proven, to have committed a horrendous crime.

How is it possible that in this unilateral rampage of revenge so thinly disguised as a coalition we have murdered more civilians than those victimized by the September 11th attacks?[6] How is it possible that our government is getting away with vastly reducing civil liberties here at home—all in the name of some vague concept of national security? And how it is possible that our government has been able to develop a rhetoric—repeated by civic leaders and the media—so convincing that the American public still shows overwhelming support for measures that go against every concept of freedom, democracy and human dignity we hold dear?

The answer to the first question has been well-documented, though few news media have published the results of that documentation. Marc Herold, of the University of New Hampshire, writes: "The thousands of Afghan civilians who perished under U.S. bombs did so because U.S. military and political elites carry out a bombing campaign using extremely powerful weapons having high margins of error and with huge killing and blasting radiuses in largely civilian-rich areas."[7]

Since 9/11, rules of law and traditions of fairness have been turned on their heads—more blatantly than ever before. Our Secretary of Defense appears on national television and says yes, of course he would rather see the one we have proclaimed guilty dead than brought to trial. No legal niceties for him.[8] Following the introduction of Marines into the current conflict, a U.S. general goes on record as saying: "Now we own a piece of Afghanistan."[9] And to our national shame no one challenges such statements.

Could this also be why they hate us?

IV

It was such a perfect day, people in Manhattan remember, as they begin to tell their stories of 9/11. Then the perfect day was shattered. And along with it, our innocence.

By this, those who repeat the statement generally mean that our innocence about safety and invulnerability has been shattered. We no longer feel safe here in this powerful country, which up to now protected us from harm. It's not as if the 9/11 attacks were the first crimes of mass destruction on this land. Oklahoma City is a part of our memory, but that crime turned out to be perpetrated by one of our own, a young white Christian veteran. Although the personal sorrow runs as deep, the sense of invasion is less.

I see this loss of innocence differently. I see it as meaning that once we could be the Good Americans, unaware of what our government was doing across the globe. Once, like so many Germans during World War II, we could say we didn't know. Once I could smile back at the Mexican fruit vendor, the peasant woman on the Vietnamese ferry or the children in the streets of Central America, relieved I was still a Good American in their eyes, somehow separate from and thus not responsible for my government's crimes.

In my lifetime, mostly covert actions have become overt, defiant, acceptable. Decades of conditioning and a powerful shift of ethics have brought a people to believe we have the right to impose our will, our might, our force. Not much has changed since the era of Manifest Destiny—only now the masks have come off.[10]

And so innocence is lost.

Checks and balances, so important to the functioning of democracy, are out the window. Government and people become an indistinguishable mass, with the government leading and the people blindly following.

This seems to me to be the real meaning of the phrase "nothing will be the same": no longer is there a place we can hide.

V

The horrendous September 11, 2001 attack on American life left us with a sudden chaotic confusion, a confusion people here had never before experienced. People in Iraq have long known such chaos; the Palestinians have known it. People in Guatemala and Northern Ireland and Haiti and Bosnia and Rwanda as well. But for us the experience is new. Pearl Harbor is sometimes mentioned, but Japan's surprise attack on our ships of war was experienced most dramatically by the sailors on those ships, not by ordinary citizens on mainland USA. We have no recent point of reference for such enormous loss, such an acute sense of vulnerability, such fear these attacks will revisit us, such expanding circles of job loss and loss of security, such rage for which we seek an appropriate channel of release.

We were taken by surprise, torn from our usually comfortable moorings. We began to strike out, blindly, led by a president whose immediate inclination was that of the cornered bully, unable to think and eager to strut his power. Following his lead—not his scripted words—our targets have often been men and women who bear a physical or cultural resemblance to the Islamic fundamentalists who used such low-tech methods to wreak a terrible destruction.

Our ignorance, as a nation, about the beliefs and ways of others, quickly surfaced. Our socially conditioned and government-protected racism continues to engender a violence that daily produces more victims.

And suddenly something called patriotism has become the panacea for every heart-shattering loss.[11] In our grief and fear and rage we look for places to calm the pain. In a hundred different ways our leaders—political, civic, religious, educational—tell us that flying the national emblem is a sign of unity; sitting before the television screen, riveted by every story of heroic human interest, the best way of identifying with those who have lost the most; supporting our president the only possible course of action in a time of war. And spending money we don't have is the way to regenerate an economy shattered by the likes of Kenneth Lay.[12]

No matter that this war is illegally conceived and executed—no national consensus sought, no airing of opposing views permitted. At a time when thinkers are desperately needed, when dozens of alternatives to violence might have been attempted, our president charged ahead with vacuous phrases that obscure more than they explain: "Make no mistake about it...We will seek them out and bring them to justice...It will be a long war, but we will prevail."

For those of us old enough to remember Vietnam, and especially for those of us who have lately bothered to read the doubts, fears and frightening confessions of those responsible for U.S. policy back then, such a tone and the content of such phrases are horrifyingly familiar.

There are alternatives. Feminists have long been good at envisioning alternative choices. It is way past time for us to do so again. We know the difference between power and empowerment. We have experience with listening and mediation rather than this knee-jerk "my dad can beat your dad" brand of violence. We know there are legitimate differences between cultures, and that it's important to explore those differences and be open to their gifts instead of making pronouncements about "axes of evil" and generalizing about those who are different from ourselves. The fact that in the context of the current crisis U.S. law enforcement agencies discovered they had few if any speakers of Farsi, Pashto, Dari, Urdu or the many versions of Arabic, doesn't come as a surprise to us.

Just a few of the more obvious alternatives to unilaterally waging war against a series of nations might have been: 1. recognizing that global hegemony requires moral leadership, not unilateral might, 2. launching a national teach-in on U.S. foreign policy during the last one hundred years, a discussion that truly includes a broad range of views, 3. working to reorganize and improve our own security organizations while sharing intelligence with other nations committed to routing terrorism, 4. using the United Nations as the arena it is meant to be, one in which we may debate the ways and means of fighting terrorism, and 5. recognizing existent international courts or establishing new ones in which to try those ultimately found to have perpetrated what must surely be considered a crime against humanity.

None of these alternatives has currency with our current administration. Instead, an atmosphere has been created in which neither questions nor differences of opinion can thrive. Discussion is too often dismissed or truncated by a single rabid proclamation: "We'll find 'em where they are, and they won't know what hit 'em," "We gotta keep America safe," or "We're gonna bomb Afghanistan back to the Stone Age." These are direct quotes from men to whom we are expected to look for guidance and leadership.

In the terrible days immediately following 9/11, among the 100 members of the U.S. House of Representatives only one voted against giving Bush unlimited war powers. Barbara Lee, Democrat from the San Francisco Bay Area of California, was startled to find herself so alone. Since making her courageous stand, Lee has been forced to employ bodyguards. None of her Democratic colleagues has raised so much as a whisper against this swiftly orchestrated war.

VI

It is our ignorance, racism, and xenophobia that so deftly fills that space between the goodness of U.S. Americans and the crimes committed in our name. It is this ignorance, this racism and xenophobia that make it possible for the same person who yells, "Go get 'em?" at his television screen to donate food or write a check to the hungry of Afghanistan. Our leaders are supposed to be our models. Could anything be more obscene than President Bush urging every American school child to send him a dollar to be forwarded to the children of the country we are bombing so mercilessly?

Perhaps the distance has become too wide. Perhaps the bridges are down. But perhaps it is time for us to reconsider the claim that some have made, that our government has indeed committed awful crimes but we, the good people of this country, have nothing to do with those crimes.

Or perhaps it's too late for such musings. Before our eyes and with our apparent complicity, we have allowed a ruling clique to abscond with our hard-won democracy. Before our eyes and with our apparent complicity, informed discussion has been replaced with the catchy phrase, the titillating sound byte, and misinformation packaged as entertainment.

This war cannot be a reflection of American will because the American people don't have enough information to be able to make an informed decision about its rightness or viability. This war has nothing to do with finding Osama bin Laden and bringing him to justice. It has everything to do with internal U.S. politics, consolidating a corporate hold on power, bolstering a sick economy and bringing domestic policy more solidly in line with a profoundly conservative agenda.

It is also an excuse for the United States to go where it hasn't dared for a while—into countries like Somalia, Colombia, Iraq, Cuba, Venezuela, the Philippines—and "mop them up" before such ventures may be challenged by too many embarrassing questions. Fighting terrorism a la George W. Bush is suddenly the justification Israel uses to explain its continued and ever more brazen attacks against the Palestinians. It is why Putin is no longer challenged for his war in Chechnya.

The September 11th attacks provided the perfect context for a government many would say was not elected and which certainly doesn't have anything like a mandate, to secure dramatic changes with a minimum of effort. From one moment to the next, the rallying call was clear: support the president in a time of crisis, support our men and women on the front lines, don't protest because it isn't patriotic, authorize the spending of billions to keep Americans safe while the funds intended to really keep Americans safe—by providing us with jobs, education, healthcare, and security in our old age—are down-spent out of existence.

What is this war against Afghanistan really about? It would seem to be the first of many battles in a much longer war against all countries dubbed rogue states (read: those that defy U.S. preeminence). Ravaging a country like Afghanistan is leveling a land already reduced to indescribable misery. No rain of bright yellow food packages will restore life to a people already clinging to its most tenuous edges.

The United States and Great Britain will have expended billions on bombing and strafing a country long bombed and strafed by others. Cities and towns will be cleared of one tribal culture so another may take its place. Women, covered from head to foot and stoned to death by the Taliban may now go back to being vilified and raped by Northern Alliance warlords.

America's friends today will be its enemies tomorrow, just as yesterday's friends have now become its enemies. Enemies of the moment even now disperse into a landscape immune to modern warfare—and our highly publicized siege, using the most modern technology of death, will become a long drawn-out guerrilla war. The Afghan people will continue to be its primary victims.

But for the U. S. administration this war has other meanings. It is a rallying call in a time of chaos and confusion. It is a boon to our nose-diving economy. It is a statement of political might (and a personal statement by a president given to showing strength through force). The war provides a reason to continue the production of sophisticated war materiel and apportion money for a Star Wars-type defense shield. President Bush, so recently an insular, inarticulate, slightly laughable figure, has become an overnight success: revered for his forceful handling of a national crisis, leader in a context in which so many feel threatened, and enjoying consistently high favor among the citizenry.

Some speculate that control of Afghanistan—if such a thing is possible—means the go-ahead in a long-planned oil pipeline to the Middle East. Others show that this doesn't really make much sense.[13] In retrospect, perhaps it will be seen that Bush's invasion of Afghanistan really was about getting bin Laden: one schoolyard bully going after another. If so, he is much more dangerous than we imagine.

But whether or not our pundits call it World War III, the invasion of Afghanistan means the final fall into unending war. Afghanistan is conquest for the sake of conquest, justified by a shifting chorus of half-truths and lies. And Afghanistan will give way to Iraq will give way to North Korea will give way to whatever nation must be made to support what the administration in power decides are the national interests of the United States of America.

Consider this. The United States government never took note of Afghanistan's longtime repression and torture of women, never showed concern that they were being denied education and work, or kept inside their homes under the jealous eyes of men. No protest voices around that topic ever came from the ranks of our leadership. U.S. government officials only started speaking out about the plight of Afghan women when we went to war against the Taliban.

Does our government really care about the Afghan poppy fields supplying so much of the world's opium and heroin? This major business is modeled, after all, on the one United States interests have been running out of Southeast Asia for decades. Four months before the attacks of 9/11, the U.S. sent $43 million in aid to the Taliban. The money was supposed to have been earmarked for crop conversion, but who knows. The U.S. supported the Taliban for years, just as it once armed Al Qaeda.

According to the United Nations Drug Control Program, Afghanistan's poppy production fell 96% from a world-record peak of more than a million pounds in 1999. With the defeat of the Taliban on the horizon, farmers are once again cultivating their main cash crop. Can we blame them? The poppies bring one hundred times the meager profit to be made on fruits and vegetables. With spring, families will harvest their poppy crops once more. Children will slit the flowers' fat bulbs and scrape their nectar into sacks. These sacks will bring $100 or more per pound. Thousands of pounds will be hauled by trucks, taxis, and mules over the mountains into Pakistan, where refiners will turn the precious cargo into hundreds of thousands of pounds of heroin worth billions of dollars to millions of addicts throughout our Global Village.

Afghanistan, as a nation, is many things, few of them understood by most U.S. Americans. Tribal men, whose lives have been spent as warriors, fight foreign invaders and neighboring tribes. Women struggle for autonomy, like women everywhere. The country's configuration itself is suspect: common cultures inhabit regions split by a border with Pakistan to the south and borders with Turkmenistan, Uzbekistan, and Tajikistan to the north. These borders, like so many, were arbitrarily drawn, responding more to the geopolitical interests of foreign powers than to the lives and needs of local peoples. No Global Village here. Only global expediency and greed.

What, then, are we left with?

Since 1989 one nation, the United States of America, that has become a hegemonic power, seemingly impossible to resist and capable of bending other nations to its will. Another nation, Afghanistan—poor, war-weary, reduced to a role of pawn in the game of international geopolitics. A fundamentalist network—Al Qaeda—that has one of its bases in the treacherous mountain regions of this second country. Men who have decided their resentment of U.S. arrogance and domination is such that they have declared a Holy War against us. And other men, claiming to wear the mantel of Western civilization, who have declared a Holy War right back.

In this picture we are asked to align ourselves, to take

sides.

But what if we believe there are other choices?

VII

September 11th was a surprise attack. It shouldn't have been. If our law enforcement agencies had been anywhere as capable as we believed they were, it would not have been. Almost every week we hear new reports of unanalyzed intelligence information, FBI field reports that were ignored, and other examples of ineptitude, overwork, or a territorial attitude about sharing information. Suspicious activity by several of the hijackers was noted by the Immigration and Naturalization Service (INS), but they remained free to continue with their deadly plans.

September 11th was like previous terrorist attacks, but larger in scale, more successful from the terrorists' point of view. And it has unleashed a ripple effect upon our society of which we have barely seen the beginning.

We are devastated and understandably want to fight back. But rather than use time-proven weapons such as thoughtful analysis, education, an exchange of intelligence information, patience, careful undercover work, international forums and courts, and a real coalition (built on respect instead of fear), the U.S. government immediately assumed its role as bully. We will fight violence with violence. And since we possess the superior weaponry, we will be successful.

Again, who remembers Vietnam?

We U.S. Americans aren't given a say in this decision. Either we support our president and his speedy enactment of wartime measures or we are considered traitors to our country, lacking in patriotism, ungrateful for our rapidly eroding freedoms. No room for debate, no effort to understand why we are hated by so many around the world and why a tiny minority of these people resort to terrorism in their effort to stop us once and for all.

The bully stance is eminently male. Women, especially, must lead in searching out better ways. Feminists, able to deconstruct power, have the potential for developing new grids in a battle that now assumes life and death proportions.

Women, who struggled for decades within male-centered political structures, know our efforts rarely resulted in an equitable distribution of power. Promises of equality and agency were made, but the nature of the struggles themselves did not allow room for women's input, women's decision-making, women's leadership. Neither have those few battles won truly sought or produced societies in which women or other oppressed groups enjoy full equality.

Afghanistan is as good a mirror of this phenomenon as any. Before 9/11 no one in our government cared about Afghan lawlessness or the plight of Afghan women. Neither foreign aid nor trade agreements took into account the fact that under the Taliban Afghan women were being forced out of schools, denied work, stoned for suspected infidelity or kept hidden beneath clumsy floor-length tents called burqas.

We women know that burqas and veils have been excellent screens behind which those who wear them have felt safe and acts of resistance have flourished. Before Afghanistan there was Algeria and before Algeria a thousand Catholic convents. It is not up to us to decide how Afghan women may wish to dress. But it must be our demand that all women, all men, all people of color and children and old people, of every racial or sexual or cultural identity, be able to live in freedom. Without this freedom, where is the Global Village?

Neither does today's Global Village break down along the borders established by warring powers. In which neighborhood of our village does Mullah Omar's infant granddaughter live? What part of town is home to the Muslim housewife whose husband perished along with so many others in the World Trade Center attack? Where was our pain for the illegal alien workers who perished on 9/11, whose families could not even ask for help? What about the gay and lesbian victims? Why have they not been featured among the New York Times portraits of those whose lives were lost? Why are their loved ones still struggling for the financial aid given as a matter of course to the survivors of heterosexual marriages?[14]

And what about the aging veteran at my gym, who shortly after the fateful attack proclaimed in a voice no one could ignore: "You think I lost one night's sleep over the women and children I gunned down in Vietnam? You can bet your life I didn't!" This from a jovial man whose jokes charmed many during our shared morning exercise sessions. Even if they were shocked by his pronouncement, I think few would judge him brutal or disgusting (adjectives I must use). In the political climate established by the Bush administration, this sort of attitude is legitimized. Those who might once have been more leery of spewing hate now feel encouraged to do so.

If it is a challenge to think of our world as a Global Village, it is much more of a challenge to consider its diverse inhabitants as members of that village. And it is a most difficult challenge to change ourselves and our responses, so that we may begin to act as if we care about our habitat and want it to survive.

If we do want it to survive, we are going to have to reevaluate the ways we act and react. We are going to have to listen to other people in other parts of the world, hear why they hate us and change our behavior so decent people everywhere will feel as compelled as we do to route out violence of every kind. Only a village in which we respect one another—as well as our

earth and the creatures that inhabit it with us—will be capable
of creating a lasting peace, a true security.

VIII

I have a friend who doesn't like the word resistance. To
her it implies a reactive stance, pushing against the same old
power structure that continues to use and abuse us. She wants
another grid, another methodology if you will, where violence
will not continue to beget violence, where the strong will no
longer win and their victims inevitably tire and acquiesce—or
die. I think I understand her desire. I certainly share her hope.
But I feel drawn to honor our history of resistance, even as I join
with her and others to create new pathways of struggle.

I have another friend who talks about a literature of resistance, then quickly assures me she isn't equating the written
word with acts. Action is always worth more, she says. I disagree. I believe we must stop privileging one form above another, and understand that each of us must use our particular talents to struggle in whatever way we can. That all struggle is necessary to humanity's survival.

Among those of us who believe that different values must
prevail, the thinkers will think, the healers heal, the teachers
teach, the painters paint, the writers write, the musicians make
music, the scientists explore our life and time with wisdom and
compassion, the organizers bring us together, and the warriors
lay down their arms and listen.

IX

A reexamination of power is key.

Bush's policy is to fight terrorism with terrorism. If putting
an end to the bloodshed and destruction is his aim, it won't
work. War only breeds war. Violence breeds violence. Those

who support the administration's policies are also responsible for this tragic mistake. Just as we wonder, today, how ordinary Germans could have remained unaware of the stench of human flesh billowing from the ovens at Auschwitz, people twenty, thirty and one hundred years from now will guess we could not have ignored what this administration is perpetrating in our name.[15]

If the only solutions Bush and company can come up with depend upon wiping out the terrorists with a force that kills many civilians, we will spiral into an unending cycle of death and destruction. We will engender terrorism, not quell it. Despite scant attention from the press, there is a broad spectrum of people who oppose using war to prevent war.

Take the administration's efforts to get us on board in its plan to launch an all-out war against Iraq, including permission for a preemptive strike—its primary concern as I write. A growing anti-war movement, millions strong, is not alone in its protest. The United Nations Security Council had been the scene of an unusually protracted and heated debate, with particularly vocal opposition from many of our allies.

The Nobel Committee, in awarding its 2002 Peace Prize to ex president Jimmy Carter, broke with sedate tradition by declaring that the prize should be understood as being given in opposition to Bush's warmongering policies.[16] And in early October, 2002, the CIA itself sent a letter to Congress in which it expressed the opinion that an attack against Iraq would be particularly dangerous in that it would most likely increase terrorist attacks against the United States, not prevent them.

These opinions come from very different sectors, with very different agendas. For different reasons they argue against the administration's terrorist plans. What they have in common is the understanding that terror cannot be stopped by terror. In other words, abuses of power don't work against abuses of power.

We must remember that tragedies of the magnitude both of 9/11 and of the U.S. invasion of Afghanistan continue to claim victims years after their initial impact. More Vietnam veterans have now died from committing suicide than died in the war.[17]

A successful war on terror would require, first of all, an assessment of what terror does, and a commitment to putting a stop to its ever expanding circles of misery, human and material loss, destruction and fear. We must learn to care as much about an Afghan life as about the life of an executive at Solomon, Smith, Barney. We need to assimilate the fact that 3,500 civilians have so far been murdered in Afghanistan; "collateral damage" the administration claims, but a number that already exceeds our own human losses on 9/11.

Most importantly, we need to understand that the effective war against terror will be the one that is waged by those who have the moral courage to break with an eye for an eye and a tooth for a tooth. We need to learn from history, divest ourselves of our sense of superiority and mindless entitlement, open to the most valuable aspects of other cultures, and listen to those whose stories may be difficult for us to hear. We need to be willing to design a different sort of world, one in which political power is redistributed and wealth and abundance used to make life better for more of us.

This change is possible. So is warring ourselves and all of humankind into oblivion. The choice is ours.

—Spring, 2002

CHAPTER TWO

Fundamentalists for All Seasons

(B)elief tends to become fundamentalist when it hardens into an expectation of guaranteed outcome. When the present becomes too strictly fixed as that bridge between past and future, the rigidity of ancient injunction takes over as the only true path [...] This fixedness of destiny, this sense of of being fated, is in general tension with aspects of freedom.

—Patricia Williams[1]

I

*N*ineteen-eighty-one, Managua, Nicaragua. Two years before, a handful of ragged young guerrillas had ousted one of Latin America's most brutal and solidly entrenched dictators, Anastasio Somoza. Not so many years before that, this particular war was almost unknown in the U.S. press: the bearded rebels regarded at best as hopeless dreamers. Now they governed a country, a small country to be sure but the largest among those making up the Central American isthmus. And they were experimenting with such dangerous ideas as land for those who worked it, jobs, education, a monthly basic needs basket for every family, healthcare—what so many here in the United States still consider utopian or threatening.

Central America itself wasn't that familiar to the average U.S. citizen. Now these guerrillas, with their indomitable dreams, were forcing their nation into our line of vision. I had come to Nicaragua at the invitation of Father Ernesto Cardenal: Catholic priest, one of Latin America's most vibrant poets, and the revolution's new

Minister of Culture.

Cardenal had spent part of the war in an archipelago of small islands on the Great Lake of Nicaragua. In the community of Solentiname he had preached Liberation Theology[2] to poor peasants, initiated poetry workshops and distributed the paints and brushes with which people who had never imagined anything beyond survival had begun to produce magical paintings that would one day be shown in museums throughout the world. Now Cardenal's dream was to populate the whole country with poetry workshops, painting studios, theater, music, dance.

I had come to Nicaragua to research a book on the country's women. The Sandinista movement included large numbers of women and girls, some of whom had become military commanders or political leaders during the long years of anti-Somoza war. Mothers and grandmothers had supported their children's struggle noticeably more than fathers and grandfathers. Young women swelled the ranks of the rebel army, until they made up roughly a third of its total combatants.

When I'd finished my book about the women, I didn't want to leave. Which was why, in the spring of 1981, I was working at the Ministry of Culture.

The foregoing is brief background for the story I want to tell.

One balmy afternoon, in the Ministry gardens—the elegant house and its surroundings had been home to Somoza's mistress, off-limits to the public in pre-revolutionary times—a few of us stood around listening to Cardenal talk about the trip from which he had just returned. He'd been in Lebanon, among other Middle Eastern countries, in the war-torn city of Beirut. A giant Ceiba shaded the area where we were gathered; the parrot in the cage that hung from a gnarled old branch began to mimic the lilt of the Poet's speech. I expected Cardenal to tell us about the war, about the difficulties he'd encountered moving from place to place, maybe something about Lebanese culture.

But he had another subject on his mind: religious fundamental-

ism. A philosophical concept or ideology to which I hadn't paid much attention before this particular afternoon. Oh, I had some sense of Christian fundamentalists in the country of my birth, particularly the sect-like congregations such as Assembly of God, Holy Rollers, and the Pentecostals who'd set up their roving tents in the southwestern city of my youth. But these were caricatures in my mind, not to be taken seriously. I considered them, if at all, as I did Survivalists or other right-wing extremists who might surface from time to time in minor news items involving an isolated community or sudden stand-off with the law, usually in some out of the way rural area.

Fundamentalists believe every word of their Scripture to have been divinely inspired. Christian fundamentalists believe every word of the Bible to be true. People who decide that a collection of books by many different people written at different times is the word of God, seem misled at best, profoundly lacking in an awareness of history and intellectual curiosity.

I knew these people often home schooled their children, to keep them from a world they both scorned and feared. I knew they considered women subservient to men. If asked back then, I might also have mentioned the Southern Baptists, a much larger and more conventionally recognized group. But the Baptists I knew in Managua seemed eminently sane and deeply committed to social change. I wasn't sure they were really fundamentalists.

It was Ernesto Cardenal, that afternoon beneath the Ceiba, who talked about religious fundamentalism as a world-wide phenomenon, and whose warning about its dangers sounded a first blip on my mental radar screen—the mechanism most of us share and that warns us to pay attention, this may turn out to be important.

Cardenal likened the struggles of working-class priests and lay people with the most dogmatic or fundamentalist tendency in each of the world's major religions to the class struggle in secular society. He said fundamentalists, like all ruling classes or castes (or those who aspire to that status) hoard righteousness with a terrible jealousy.

Absolute truth is theirs, or so they claim. The right way to think, pray, love, dress, and relate to other humans. Indeed, the only way. Any group outside the approved norm—women who will not submit, homosexuals, artists and other free thinkers, progressives, and sometimes even whole ethnicities or races—are to be converted.

Or destroyed.

Each of these fundamentalist groups—Hindu, Moslem, Christian, Buddhist, Mormon, Jewish, among others—believes it possesses the truth, the law, the way. Stories have come down, ancient stories of events said to have occurred centuries before in another time, another culture, even perhaps another place. And fundamentalist men (for they are almost always men) interpret and sharpen these stories until they become terrible weapons of control. "The Bible teaches us." "It says in the Koran." "The Scriptures instruct us." "The Torah says." The fundamentalists in each of these religious cultures use these weapons, deadlier than the most sophisticated war materiel, to exercise power through fear, especially over those in their communities who are seen to be weaker or more vulnerable: women, children, the old, whoever is different from and easily dominated by these mostly male leaders in their insatiable lust for power.

Fundamentalism. The Law. By definition, a literal reading. No consideration of the passage of time or changing cultures. No margin for interpretation. No transposition to contemporary time or place. No room for modernization, change, discussion, choice. Minds stop. Creativity withers. Finally obedience alone is relevant.

In Beirut, Cardenal had witnessed the ravages of Islamic fundamentalism as well as the living culture of Islam which like all great religions preaches community, peace, understanding, depth of thought, the passing on of a flexible wisdom, compassion, and justice. It had become clear to him that the struggle within Islam between rigid fundamentalists and saner inheritors of the faith was not so different from the struggle within Catholicism.

Perhaps Cardenal recognized this struggle because he was just then beginning to suffer its effects. As a priest, he was being pressured by his superiors to distance himself from the Sandinista revolution, something he refused to do. Within a couple of years the Pope himself would publicly humiliate him. Not that many later, the Vatican would prohibit him from officiating as a priest.

At that moment I began to understand the antagonism that exists in all social bodies—political as well as religious—between those for whom power is the single goal and those they must defeat in order to remain on top. These latter are always those for whom knowing diversity and sharing experience are more comfortable options, whose potential and contributions are thwarted by the usurpers of their power.

As a woman, as an artist, I knew where I stood. As a socialist and a feminist, power itself was a category to which I had given some thought. Although deeply spiritual, I wasn't attracted by any of the organized religions. Still, on that spring afternoon in Managua, I had no idea that only two decades into the future the Poet's words would come back to haunt me. I could not have imagined I would live to see a Holy War fought by Islamic fundamentalists for whom U.S. society represents a culture of infidels and a small man from Texas, a Christian fundamentalist who some months before had conned his way into the presidency of the United States.

II

Even the date seems eerily significant, like one of those signs fundamentalist minds are so fond of pointing out. To me, nine-eleven or nine-one-one evokes an image of some enormous finger dialing for help—but with no one on the other end of the line who urges its owner to stay on the phone or assures the caller help is on the way. The image behind my eyes veers towards the supernatural. It might easily belong to the realm of the religious.

Analogy aside, after 9/11 this is the question I'm left with. What does "on the way" mean to U.S. Americans these days? Where are we, as a nation, headed? Is our road to remain lined with American flags, easy symbol of a people that follows its president wherever he may lead (that blind obedience so important a feature of fundamentalism)? Or will we stand up, in the true American tradition, to demand information, ask questions, make time to consider the ways in which what we do today will impact the future of humanity?

The surprise attacks that rent that pristine September morning in New York and Washington affected a shift in our society more quickly than any in recent memory. The easiest, the most immediate reflection of that shift can be seen in those millions of waving flags. And they wave not just proudly but defiantly, as if to berate or castigate those who will not display the symbol of a government whose policies we find so troubling. Another reflection can be heard in the crude mimicry of our government's empty rhetoric. Words like evil hide a multitude of complexities. Phrases like axis of evil point in a fanatical direction. They are more appropriate to a football cheer or a war cry than to encouraging serious deliberation. But they are not meant to encourage deliberation. They are meant as a call to arms.

Following the attack, the Reverend Franklin Graham said, "the God of Islam is a different God, and I believe it is a very evil and wicked religion." Echoes of President Reagan's evil empire. Both pronouncements are fundamentalist in nature, obscuring so much more than they reveal about the subject of our concern. The question is whether reversion to this sort of fundamentalist language will remain a permanent fixture in the political or civic sphere, or if we will be able to move the pendulum back to a place of reason.

Criminal attack set the stage for criminal response. But few seem concerned, at least out loud. Only a very small minority today believes that the hijackers martyred themselves for what they perceive as a holy cause, and that U.S. government retaliation is but another chapter in a long history of imperialist arrogance. A vast majority of our population—judging from media reports, polls and the like—believe the hijackers were simply abominable criminals, removed from any context we might try to understand, and that immediate and violent retaliation by the U.S. government is therefore justified.[3]

An administration that took office in circumstances charitably described as confused, wasted no time in using the tragedy to push its conservative agenda upon a nation convinced that war equals patriotism. And that a fundamentalist vision—featuring policies such as the so-called faith-based initiatives, school vouchers, government control of women's bodies, school prayer, religious limits on scientific research, government access to the private lives of its citizens, racial profiling, secret trials, the doctrine of a preemptive military strike, and now this all-out crusade against nations judged by the administration to be rogue states—must be prominent on that conservative agenda.

Before the attacks, the Republicans had just lost control of an almost evenly divided Senate. Republican Senator Jeffords from Vermont, troubled by policy directions in his own party, declared himself an Independent. Bush's direction was clear, but it was becoming apparent that he was going to have to fight a lot harder and maneuver with greater sophistication in order to get his agenda through.

After the attacks, everything changed. Quickly, very quickly, a whole new play was on stage.

In the days immediately following 9/11 words such as idiots and cowards flew back and forth. In truth, neither adjective applies to the Islamic fundamentalist perpetrators of the

attacks nor to the government officials who lost no time in
turning the situation to their advantage. Each side very carefully, very intelligently, set out to achieve its goals. Goals that
respond to the fundamentalist characteristics of over-general-
ization, rigid hierarchy, hidden agendas, and male-centered mil-
itarism.

The Al Quaeda terrorists were well-prepared, rigorous in
their planning, capable of low-tech solutions to high-tech problems, and managed a maximum of damage with a minimum of
financial outlay. Having entered this country (most of them
legally), they melted easily into the cultural mix, acquired the
rudiments of piloting large jets at commercial flight schools, and
with bank accounts that were meager by international criminal
standards silently prepared for their big day. They were precise
in their coordination and blind in their fundamentalist obedience. Finally, armed only with their own lives and those of their
victims, they improved upon earlier attempts to bring forth previously unimaginable destruction. And they succeeded.

Could these men or their mentors have known that cross-
country flights carry the greatest tonnage of jet fuel, and that
the intense heat generated by that fuel when it explodes on
impact with very large buildings would be capable of bringing
those buildings down? Quite possibly, although for these men
this may well have been an unexpected plus.[4]

And could the perpetrators, or those who gave them their
orders, have foreseen the ways in which the U.S. government
would embellish what they began? Could they have known it
would use an illegal declaration of war to justify illegal measures, put out continuous warnings of "imprecise but credible"
threats, and announce the possibility of additional attacks as a
way of getting people to continue to show their support—while
at the same time urging us to live our lives, go about our business, and shop to save the economy? Could those men from

such a different culture have imagined how the scenes of death and destruction played and replayed on television screens throughout this country would make us more willing to accept "safety measures" that far from protecting us erode the very way of life our officials claim to be safeguarding?

Because power is the goal, mixed messages have always been a central feature of fundamentalist doctrine.

Did these men have any idea of the enormous ripple effect their action would set in motion: the broken families, tens of thousands of lost incomes, charity corruption and bottlenecks, businesses ruined, a badly damaged economy, general panic and ever widening circles of anxiety and insecurity? Could they have envisioned the ways in which our public officials would fall over themselves in their attempts to look as if they are in command, seem responsible, appear to care? Could they have predicted the morass of power politics and conflict of interests?

Perhaps they did foresee all this. If so, they are geniuses. Geniuses of evil, as our president likes to say. If they did not possess such far-reaching vision, those still alive who are involved in the plot must be celebrating beyond their wildest dreams.

In contrast to the hijackers' detailed preparations, the United States, isolated by its own arrogance and by the way it has set itself above and apart from the rest of humanity, was unprepared for 9/11. There had been several large-scale dress rehearsals. We had more than a few warnings. But U.S. government agencies either didn't pay attention or proved incapable of processing the intelligence it did manage to acquire. These agencies can now be observed in all their bumbling, inter-organizationally competitive and top-heavy ineptitude.

The U.S. Immigration Service—so swift and heavy-handed when it comes to deporting illegal aliens or refusing them entrance into the United States—allowed entire cells of plotters to slip through their grasp. Some of these cells had previously caught the attention of agency operatives, whose supervisors ignored the information. Six months after 9/11, two U.S. flight schools received visa approvals for El Qaeda operatives who had died in the attacks. The CIA, FBI and other law enforcement entities charged with spotting and controlling criminal behavior, had no idea what was being planned, nor the capability to prevent it. And as for National Security, those charged with preserving it were too busy harassing an innocent Chinese-American scientist at Los Alamos to be able to pay attention to groups of men calmly moving towards this ground zero of national tragedy.[5]

Nowhere is this official incapacity more obvious than in the rhetoric uttered since 9/11 by those in the country's highest offices. For most of the first day, President Bush was shepherded around the country, making occasional stops at "secure" places so he could begin to put forth his string of "make no mistakes" and "we will prevails". Donald Rumsfeld and John Ashcroft, soon to be joined by Tom Ridge, were given the task of making periodic pronouncements meant to show leadership and control. They ended up contradicting themselves and each other as they issued one muddled statement after another.

Secretary of State Colin Powell sometimes sounded a faint voice of reason. Some dared to hope **he** might prevail, but it soon became clear he is a loyal member of the administration. Perhaps the only voice of real intelligence, telling an articulate though none-the-less bellicose story, belongs to Vice President Dick Cheney. During the first few weeks following the attacks, what we most knew about him was that he was safe in an unnamed location. Some wondered why he, rather than Bush, was the one being kept out of harm's way. The man has a bad heart and chillingly conservative politics, but acute intelligence: clearly one of the few in the administration so endowed.

Fundamentalism is key to understanding the terrorist

actions, on both sides. Fundamentalism, by its very nature, translates as rigid, narrow, literal, and lacking in nuance. The first thing I believe we need to understand about 9/11 and the U.S. government response, is that both reflect fundamentalist thinking, both are carried out by fundamentalists, albeit of different cultures and religious traditions.

The United States, which surely considers itself among the most modern and sophisticated of nations, is waging Holy War against a Holy War.

III

Although few in this country are familiar with the sort of Islamic fundamentalism that produces an Osama bin Laden or a Mullah Omar, we are learning something about the development of their brand of religious extremism and how it plays out politically. Limiting our analysis to Afghanistan, and going back in time just a couple of decades, we must look at the Soviet invasion of that country: crude secularism thrust upon a people for whom religious practice had been a centuries-old way of life.

In the context of their bitter struggle against the Russians, the Tajik and Uzbek warriors we have come to know as the Northern Alliance raped, plundered, and murdered with abandon. The over-zealous religious extremism of the mostly Pashtun Taliban—which includes keeping women completely covered and inside the home, preventing them from studying or working, punishing loud female laughter with flogging and alleged female infidelity with death—developed in opposition to the Northern Alliance's brutal treatment of women, and its general lawlessness.

As with fundamentalism everywhere, control of women is clothed in a guise of protection, the idea being that women like children are happier if kept safe from the vices of secular society. An analogy can be made to a phenomenon among Christian fundamentalists here in the United States. The Promise Keepers' vow to be faithful to their wives responds to the rampant sexual infidelity in contemporary U.S. society. Fundamentalist Mormon sects, that engage in polygamy despite their Church's disapproval, hold the practice up against what they see as a wanton degeneracy in current U.S. morals. In these cases—Christian as well as Islamic—unbending power recoils from the possibility of an exploration in which the victims as well as the victimizers may take part.

Religious fundamentalism might more accurately be called patriarchal fundamentalism: its philosophical backbone is so completely rooted in male control. Male heads of families do not merely hold power in descendant or horizontal directions, dominating daughters and wives. They also control the lives of their mothers and grandmothers when the fathers or husbands of these are no longer around to do so. Where there is no effective separation of church and state, this control is reflected as well in the political sphere. When Benazir Bhutto was president of Pakistan and her duties called for international travel, she could travel abroad only with her husband's permission. Before western women scoff at such control, let us acknowledge that whether or not the law is so formally established, patriarchal fundamentalism is operative in our countries as well.

By none of this do I mean to condone the horrors of the Northern Alliance or the Taliban, or privilege one form of misogyny over another. But it is important to understand that we aren't dealing here with transparent examples of good and evil. The United States government funded, trained and supported the Mullahs as a local fighting force in its long war against international Communism. Osama bin Laden and his colleagues, it can be argued, are products of U.S. nurture—just like so many other erstwhile friends in its anti-Communist campaigns around the world. The U.S. uses these people while it can, discards them when they are no longer useful, and denounces them when they turn against its shift in political allegiance.

Or they discard and denounce us. In the person of Osama bin Laden we have an example of a Saudi national born into extraordinary wealth, upon whom the United States depended on more than one occasion. But when the U.S. invaded Iraq, using Iraq's claim upon Kuwait as an excuse, Saudi Arabia allowed the U.S. to use its territory for rearguard bases. And when the Gulf War settled into its ongoing and less publicized mode, U.S. military hardware remained in Saudi Arabia.

This angered bin Laden, who like many practitioners of Islam regards Saudi Arabia as his religion's Holy Land. Bin Laden also began to resent the United States' long support of Israel against the Palestinians. From there, it was a rapid descent into flagrant anti-Americanism. The U.S., in its unfailing history of abuse of peoples the world over, has a well-earned reputation for arrogance. Throughout the developing world it would be difficult to find a country where we are not resented or, worse, despised. Because of our consistent support of Israel in its attacks upon the Palestinians, this is particularly true in the Arab world.

When bin Laden stopped responding to the requirements of the CIA, he found his niche among Islamic fundamentalists who see the United States not only for what it does to other countries but also in terms of our popular culture, which in their eyes denigrates their faith, prostitutes women, and encourages vice.

None of this is meant to justify the criminal attacks of 9/11, only to place them in a context we can understand. Violence, from whatever quarter, is horrific, senseless, and ultimately self-defeating. Violence only begets further violence and destruction—whether we are talking about a man beating his wife or child, a Mullah stoning a woman he finds offensive, a State murdering someone convicted of having murdered someone else, a surprise attack against thousands of innocent people, or an all-out military invasion launched against a country suspected of harboring those who may have planned and engineered that attack.

When such violence is carried out in the name of religious values, assumptions of truth or some narrow interpretation of Scripture, it is all the more heinous. Fundamentalism attempts to clothe violence in a directive from God. Let us not forget: most of the world's major religious scriptures contain glorifications of and exhortations to violence. And all the great religions, today, have leaders who preach violence as well as those who preach peace.[6]

IV

Dar Salamay, The Gambia, Africa. Little Mary is four years old. She and other girls—nine, 10, 11 years of age—have just been circumcised. Surrounded by animal sacrifice, dancing and other traditional festivity, they have been forcibly held down, fully conscious, while respected members of their community cut away their clitoris and labia. Marked them for lifetimes of submission and pain. Robbed them of the sexual pleasure regarded by most of us as a natural human right, and leaving them vulnerable to HIV and other life-threatening conditions.

Fundamentalist tradition is behind the barbaric practice of Female Genital Mutilation (FGM), which is perpetrated upon hundreds of thousands of young girls and women throughout parts of Africa and in African communities elsewhere in the world.[7]

***

The respected deacon of a Christian fundamentalist sect tells his wife and children to hurry up, they'll be late. In an hour and a half they will gather, with other families, at the sect's camp in a remote wooded area. After hot dogs and potato salad, the women will chat with one another, busy themselves with cleaning up. The children will play the usual games.

But the men have a different agenda. A black man, who hours before was locked in the town's drunk tank—one of the hunters is also the town's sheriff—is unchained and released into the woods. The men follow, their rifles fitted with telescopic sites. The children hear the shots.

Some will never forget what they witnessed that day. They were not meant to know, but their bodies remember. The knowledge will translate into post-traumatic stress disorder, affecting every area of their lives. It will keep them sick. Some few may be fortunate enough to get help. Some few of these may heal—but only partially. The scars are always permanent. Those who have them are overwhelmingly women whose childhoods were ravaged by extreme Christian fundamentalist experience.[8]

***

Ramallah, Palestine. A middle-aged couple sits before a photo poster of their oldest son. He was 19. Two days before, he strapped a backpack with high-powered explosives to his body, boarded a bus, handed the driver a large bill and refused the change. Then he blew himself up. Into death with him he took a young Israeli mother and her breast-feeding baby, seven other Israelis and six Palestinians—all on their way to work—and two tourists who happened to be in the wrong place at the wrong time.

The suicide bomber's parents look up at the image of their son, smiling from the wall. They say they are proud of him. In their fun-

damentalist sense of law and justice, he is sitting at the celestial ban-
quet table, enjoying eternal glory for his act. The parents say they
would gladly sacrifice their other son, who is playing with a toy
grenade at their feet.[9]

***

Mesa, Arizona. Upon hearing that her mother has breast can-
cer, a woman estranged from her parents has traveled to see them. It
is a difficult visit. Throughout her childhood, the woman's father was
a pastor at their Free Will Baptist Church, a respected member of the
community in which she was raised. He also, consistently and secre-
tively, abused her from the age of six until she stared him down and
walked away at 16.

One kind of man outside the home, another in its secret night-
time rooms. Since this woman was able to stand up to her father, she
only rarely maintains contact. And only because she loves her moth-
er.

Staying away, of course, didn't eliminate the damage this self-
defined Christian man inflicted upon his daughter. She has battled its
residue for years, moved in and out of depression, worked hard in
therapy, and has only recently come to a place of semi-resolution.
Although she will continue to be shaped by her father's abuse, she has
won enough of herself back. Enough to be able to function, inhabit
her creativity, design her own life, identify the shame, the fear, the
rage and their origins. Enough to have been able to make this trip, to
be sitting with her parents now—so much older, broken.

They do not bring up the past. The woman is grateful for this.
She doesn't want to go there. There is no justification, forgiveness or
refusal to forgive. There is only her life now. It includes being there
for her mother, being able to sit in the same room with her father,
knowing she has moved beyond his power. Before the woman says
goodbye, the man who was her father wants to tell her about a reli-
gious experience he's recently had. "I know what God wants of me,"

he begins, "He doesn't want me to be happy, only to do His Will."

The man who was once this woman's father continues to talk. The woman who was once his daughter understands she no longer has to listen.

***

Again, Mesa, Arizona. Within a week of 9/11, and despite official rhetoric urging citizens not to let their rage make them criminals, a man spouting epithets at "all those lousy Muslims" shoots the Sikh owner of a local gas station. The victim is wearing the white turban typical of his religion; the shooter makes a crazed connection with the images of the turbaned Osama bin Laden displayed with a gunsite's crosshairs superimposed upon his face in every tabloid, tract, news story or television screen across the country. Here, as hundreds of times over the next few weeks and months, ignorance and the intentional over-saturation of a misleading image explode into hate, and hate becomes murder.

President Bush publicly laments such crimes. But not enough to advocate for hate crime legislation or gun control. He and his colleagues seem unable to understand that people model their behavior more easily on what their leaders do than on what they say.

Or, they understand and do not care.

***

Twenty men, all members of Al Quaeda's far-reaching terrorist network, awake on the morning of September 11, 2001 in different parts of the United States. They have prepared several years for this day. Perhaps the only thing we will ever know about each is that as he arrives at an airport and boards a passenger jet he believes he is where he is because he is faithful to his God, to the supreme being he calls Allah. We do not know if all of these men know they will die with their thousands of victims. We do know that one of them doesn't make his flight; he will later be found and indicted: someone the government can punish for them all.

After the tragedy—in which close to 3,000 fathers, mothers, husbands, sons, daughters, grandparents and friends lose their lives—evidence is sought and found: mug shots, flight school records, neighbors, rental cars, a will, a pair of highly-polished shoes. As befits this country's news reporting, these items are given endless play. What is not discussed, at least not in any complexity, is the religious fundamentalism that spawns these men and their criminal acts.

On both sides of the divide.

***

September 11th, 2001, Lower Manhattan, New York City. People remember how beautiful the morning was, how blue the sky. Suddenly a Boeing 767 is flying too low over city streets. As horrified witnesses watch, the large jet flies directly into one of the World Trade Center towers, more than a hundred stories tall and just beginning to open its doors to the thousands who labor there each day. Less than an hour later, another jet flies into the other tower.

In Washington, D.C., a similar scene unfolds against one of the thick walls of the Pentagon, that building which is as much a symbol of military might as the New York towers were of economic power. Over a field in rural Pennsylvania a fourth plane goes down. Its intended target can only be guessed.

Terrorism on a scale almost too immense to have been imagined. Terrorism justified, in the minds of its perpetrators, by generations of political resentment and by fundamentalist conviction. Peace-loving members of a global Islamic community must now struggle to distance themselves from those who so grotesquely distort their faith.

***

September 11th, 2001, Washington, D.C. and Ft. Lauderdale, Florida. Government and military officials in the first city and the president who is visiting a school in the second, are told of the attacks. Initial reports are confusing. News flashes pulse with false accounts. The president's job is to appear to be in control of the situation, to display an appropriate degree of rage against those presumed to have carried out the attacks, to offer his condolences to the victims and their families, and to design the nation's response.

In that order.

He is handled more than he handles, but by the end of day one some semblance of a chain of command seems to be in place.

This is when our political and military leaders have a choice. They can seek consensus from the legislative and judicial branches of government, and from experts on Islamic history, religion and culture. They can involve the United Nations, the one international body set up to deal with such a crime against humanity. Or, they can act like playground bullies with much too much power and announce all-out war against those they presume responsible.

Tragically, they make the latter choice.

This opens the door to several unexpected returns. By launching all-out war, coercing other countries to support them in what they glibly term a coalition, and literally daring U.S. citizens to rally behind the plan or face being called traitors, George W. Bush and his administration suddenly secure a place of glory for themselves. It is a place they couldn't have imagined on September 10th.

No need to worry now about education, healthcare, social security or any other of the domestic issues so irrelevant to the Bush agenda. Huge military expenditure, the demolition of any obstacle in the way of a Star Wars defense shield, men and women becoming patriots by going off to kill those who have been declared their enemies, and a performance rating higher than he could have dreamed: all are suddenly there for the taking. Not only will the small, bumbling and inept but crafty man from Texas enjoy a popular first term, he is all but assured of a second.

Less than a week after 9/11, Jerry Falwell and Pat

Robertson—two influential figures in this country's Christian fundamentalist community—join in a statement blaming lesbians, gay men, abortion providers, the ACLU and others for the tragedy. We have brought such moral devastation to this country, they say, that God removed his shield and let this happen.

Albeit half-heartedly, Bush and company distance themselves from the statement. In their effort at preserving a measure of credibility, Fallwell and Robertson also later retract. But those of us who care to file the history away remember the deep links between the Republican political machine and its Christian fundamentalist supporters.

One of those links who now enjoys an immediate power surge is Attorney General John Ashcroft, Bush's Homeland General in the war against the American people. Ashcroft's conservative philosophy was never a secret. Now he has free reign to act upon his fundamentalist beliefs. For just as the U.S. has bombed and shelled its way into Afghanistan and is preparing to do the same in a series of other countries, the Bush administration is waging a war against our rights and security here at home.

Nine Eleven provided a perfect excuse for the administration to roll back dozens of our hard-earned civil rights, even going so far as to undermine some of the most important safeguards of the Constitution. Without any palpable objections on the part of legislators in either major political party, the Justice Department has announced it will engage in widespread racial profiling and blanket attacks upon peoples of Arabic and Middle Eastern origin, imprison uncharged suspects indefinitely, and deny them customary lawyer-client confidentiality. Based purely on the dictates of this administration, broad new wiretapping and other surveillance practices have been put into effect. And, despite some outrage articulated by a few courageous people in both parties, secret military trials will replace the criminal trials which have for so long been a part of the American way.

V

I go back to Ernesto Cardenal, so many years ago, sharing his observations about religious fundamentalism and class struggle.

The events of 9/11 remind us that power is most highly prized by those who have no identity without it. In order to hold onto illegal power, states as well as individuals must destroy those who get in their way.

Religious fundamentalism promotes an almost always male power, presumably validated by God and exercised against those within the powerful's sphere of influence. This sphere of influence may be a couple, a family, an organization, a community, a nation or—with today's hegemony—a world.

Respect for difference may be the only thing capable of cracking the armor that protects this sort of power. Presumed sameness supports those who would hold onto ill-gained power at any cost. This is why racism, classism, sexism, homophobia, and other forms of prejudice are always the tools of choice of the powerful.

Since Christian fundamentalism preaches Armageddon—the end of the world—there is no need to protect our environment or precious natural resources. Ronald Reagan's Secretary of the Interior, James Watt, believed we might as well use all the resources at our disposal since we wouldn't be needing them for long.

If we can empathize with the Afghanistan woman beneath her burqa, *the girlchild in The Gambia victimized by female genital mutilation, the multiple wives of Mormon fundamentalists, or the vast majority of U.S. women who must deal with the effects of incest, battery, rape and everyday sexual harassment, we will begin to understand that within the world's diverse philosophical and political systems our struggles link all who strain against patriarchy even as they separate us from those who misuse their power against us.*

Although millions of the world's men suffer because of their class, race, or other identifications, it is not an accident that so many of the stories I tell concern women or girls; or that almost every terrorist, mullah, pastor, priest, president, general, or fundamentalist spokesperson is male. Throughout history misogyny has been a weapon of the powerful. Our feminist time has come, allowing us to see all power imbalances more clearly.

It is time to ask ourselves if we can identify more easily with the Afghanistan woman, children and men, oppressed—in different ways—by the Northern Alliance, the Taliban, and U.S. bombs, than we can with our own country's political administration, so eager to wage State terrorism in our name.

It is time to make a stand against fundamentalism of whatever brand—for justice, for life.

—Albuquerque, Winter, 2001

CHAPTER THREE

Who Lies Here?

I

Frontline is one of those television shows that propose to take a subject and give us an in-depth look from a balanced confluence of angles. Television, as a medium, and depth as its descriptive adjective, have today become increasingly antithetical: almost an oxymoron. Still, in contrast with what we are subjected to on the commercial networks, we want to expect more from Public Broadcasting. Frontline is a Public Television show. Many still tend to believe its message.[1]

December 19th, 1995. Frontline visits beggars. Men and women, several of them homeless, are paraded before the camera. Through a skillful weave of stories and commentary, we are encouraged to come to conclusions, make judgments. And indeed this piece is filled with moments that touch the viewers' emotions, even, perhaps, open some small window on what it is like to be without the comfort and security of a home.

One of these is the segment in which we watch an elderly white woman and a younger black woman who is part of her street family as they spend one night in a hotel. The older woman has gathered enough in coins and bills to be able to buy this room for a few short hours. And she takes care of her own. Both women luxuriate in baths. We hear them talking about how precious and precarious this parenthesis of warmth and cleanliness is, the safety of being indoors, a piece of furniture to set their things on, beds.

Yes, this is documentary television at its best. And also at its most seductive in terms of creating a context in which we

believe not only what we see with our eyes but what the program's politics present as truth.

Deborah Amos of National Public Radio is the reporter.
Her interviews are edited with running commentary on the
nature of life for our most disadvantaged citizens. And she
returns again and again to questions designed to elicit facts, the
facts that combine to create the stories of these lives.

The stories are important. The voices with which we
choose to speak—the words, images, gestures, texts—establish
who we are in the world. By our stories others know us. By their
reflections in the eyes of others we learn to know ourselves.

In the words of the ancient Psalms, we live our lives as a
tale told. And "This is what fools people," Jean-Paul Sartre
warns, "a man(sic) is always a teller of tales, he lives surrounded by his stories and the stories of others, he sees everything
that happens to him through them, and he tries to live his own
life as if he were telling a story."[2]

But never in a vacuum.

In Some Notes on Lying, Adrienne Rich has written that
"Lying is done with words, and also with silence." And she goes
on to explain that "In the struggle for survival we tell lies. To
bosses, to prison guards, the police, men who have power over
us, who legally own us and our children, lovers who need us as
proof of their manhood."[3]

In the telling of our lives, therefore, truth is constructed by
need and by current circumstance, as well as by a perception of
what is real. By a language of expediency as well as by what
memory holds. And memory is present even when we have
been well trained in its denial. Central to each person's truth is
the degree to which she or he retains control over its use.

Told stories also require the seal of proof: He himself said
it, and so (baring recognized delusion, dementia or some other
condition that challenges popular assumption of one's ability to

express oneself rationally) it must be true. Or, conversely: It was only her story. It has not been verified (by a reliable source, some expert whose opinion we may accept without question) and therefore we doubt its veracity. Told by someone we have been taught to regard as incompetent, or even simply as Other, the story remains suspect.

Now this Frontline story presents us with an elderly man. Wrapped in tattered woolens, he is wheelchair-bound, pushing himself along with one good leg while the other sticks out in front of him like a child's. Hand-printed on a small cardboard sign is a capsulated version of his story: the Vietnam veteran without a job, the man begging for help. The television camera zooms in on a Purple Heart, pinned to the subject's worn lapel.

But wait. In an aside, the reporter tells us that this man's name could not be found in the Vietnam War records consulted by the program's researchers. There is no proof, then, of his Purple Heart. He **did** fight in Korea, she concedes, as she reinterprets his story, imposing her version of its truth. Perhaps he believes that the more recent and better-known war will tug at a greater number of heartstrings, inspire more abundant giving. She goes so far as to ask him if this is the case. He admits that it may be.

In a quest for sympathy, this man has changed his story. He has lied.

In yet another segment, the same reporter interviews a young girl, perhaps fourteen or fifteen years old. She stands in a dilapidated doorway, calling out to passersby: "Can you help me? Can you help me? Sir, my mother is on dialysis...". Again, the woman mediating between our conditioned disbelief and the subjects of this story tells us the girl is lying. No record exists of her mother as a patient at New York Hospital.

But this time Frontline goes further. It confronts the mother with her daughter's story. "Do you know that your daughter says you are on dialysis?" the reporter asks. The mother's identity is shielded by a technique meant to imply fairness, avoid humiliation; one of those digital patterns of blinking rectangles hides the woman's features from our sight. But words condemn, and even this inadvertent failure to look us in the eye suggests as well a departure from truth. "We can find no record that you are or ever have been a patient at New York Hospital," the interviewer insists. "Why do you think your daughter says you are?"

"My daughter is telling the truth as she understands it." The mother's voice is firm. Her daughter's suffering is enough, without subjecting her to further suspicion or humiliation.

Frontline has fulfilled its mandate of careful research and impartiality.

Proof and truth are safe.

Who lies here? Who is silent? Who refuses or refrains from speaking? What silences fill the air of these times? How do we interpret them? And the lie: we are accustomed to asking what it tells us about the person who speaks. But what does it tell us about the forces that conspire to create its necessity.

We inhabit a society in which lies are ever more routinely used by those in power to direct and control the lives of those they relegate to positions of powerlessness. Still raised with the myth of honesty, that old protestant staple The Golden Rule, and hard work as a sure route to success, we founder in an ever-thickening soup of lies passed off as truth. Worse, these lies are uttered by authorities we are told are experts in their fields. Acceptable "proof" is provided.

Indeed, we are bombarded by lies posing as truth: in the advertising that sells us everything from automobiles to beauty aids; in the rhetoric of pharmaceutical companies that use the testimony of fictitious experts and fictitious users to sell us products whose proven worth is evident only in their ability to make money for those companies, and whose dangerous side-effects are flashed on the TV screen too fast and in letters too small to be read; in the campaign promises that unravel as soon as a politician is safely in office; in the studies commissioned to convince us that this or that public policy will benefit us in some way; and in the distortion of language used in all of the above.

The rhetoric of popular morality tells us truth is essential, proof necessary. Yet our every interaction is based upon the acceptability—and advisability—of lying. A belief in lies of every magnitude has become the public story of our time, the backdrop against which more personal lies are fabricated.

The beggars interviewed on Frontline are caught in the act of necessary lying. Relativity is not considered. Like the mother on welfare, who must say she is not married in order to receive her meager stipend, like Adrienne Rich's powerless who survive by learning to lie to those wielding power over them, these are people encouraged by the way in which society is organized to develop a talent for deceit. Discarded by a system that does not adequately protect them, they are forced to invent the stories that may bring relief.

Without specifically articulating it, and in the long-honored tradition of "impartiality," the TV reporter reveals her stereotypical prejudices. Perhaps people who cannot tell the truth about their lives do not deserve better ones. The viewers' own frustrations also contribute to his or her willingness to believe that the subject is lying; why should this beggar, too lazy to work and not honest enough to tell the truth, be the recipient of government handouts—provided, after all, with my tax money? All the various ways in which our society distorts power conspire to tell us the story we are conditioned to hear.

Focusing on the Frontline feature may be unfair. Deceitful reporting is everywhere. Our media provides us with a constant barrage of official and unchallenged lies. The politician's rhetoric. The soap opera's storyline. The glamour of violence. The happy ending. A Rush Limbaugh, with his battery of insults and untruths. And, nightly and daily, through and between each show, making their ever more insistent demands upon our attention, the outrageous claims of commerce.

Television commercials constantly tell us that such and such a medicine for gas is twice as effective as another, that "more experts recommend ..." and that "eighty-five percent of doctors have prescribed ..." Not too many years ago we watched an elegantly suited line of tobacco CEOs tell us that cigarettes are neither addictive nor harmful to human health. As they lied, they raised their right hands—swearing to tell the truth, the whole truth and nothing but the truth. Minimal common sense should have told us that those statements and the ones we hear today are claims whose "proof" resides in greed: the seductive image, an authentic-sounding verbiage, the highly evolved science with which today's advertiser sells his product. In other words, in the lies that sophisticated PR and expensive lawyers fabricate. News reports, TV drama, and commercials are all classified as entertainment when it comes to the ratings that determine whether or not they will be shown, and at what time of day or night.

More recently, we have learned that corporate America employs other means of selling its products and services. Well-known public personalities—film stars, athletes, even artists and scientists—have admitted to mentioning these products and services by name in interviews or other public venues. Some have even admitted to being paid for this advertising.

Second-rate actors and actresses now roam our city streets, pretending to be ordinary men and women playing with a new gadget. Passersby notice, stop to talk, and look at the product in question, never realizing that they have been hooked by people paid to elicit their curiosity.

These are stories designed to sell products. Or ideas. Or misplaced belief. That they are mostly lies is irrelevant. Or, not irrelevant but in fact enormously relevant to the task at hand, which is not the service of truth or the well being of the consumer but the making of profit.

Sophisticated studies show that if such claims are voiced by authority figures—the white male doctor in a well-appointed office setting, the white male professor, the film star or athlete with image recognition, the very beautiful young woman—belief is almost instantly obtained. If statistics are presented in such a way as to imply success—financial, romantic, a cure—belief is there for the asking. Proof of the type our society reveres resides in the power to convince.

So, why are we given these product stories without the warning or aside that assures "impartiality?" Why must the stories of the poor, contrived to evoke the sympathy they so desperately need, be "balanced" by revelations of investigations that question their authenticity, while the stories big businesses tell are left to stand on their own? Why are the former presented as lies, while the latter remain unchallenged, unexposed? Capable investigative teams surely have the ability to research both.

Money, of course. Corporations buy reliability. Homeless men and women have nothing but their need, and the guile they learn on unforgiving streets.

II

A couple of days later, in the same week of the Frontline piece, I go to see the film Nixon. Rhetorical critics warn, as they have about earlier Oliver Stone creations, that this is not an accurate portrayal of history. Artistic license has been taken, events changed or even added to build dramatic tension; details often respond more to the director's **vision** of history than to its prosaic order and approved documentation (and the word "vision" is always oh so suspect!) In other words, lies are being told. I remember reading that Nixon's daughters do not like the way Stone has rendered their father's life.

The film absorbs and compels me. Given my particular experience, Oliver Stone's truth is one that makes sense to me. The story of the Nixon presidency put forth on the large screen—and this is rare in the Hollywood venue—digs beneath the surface of a man's life. It moves out into his presidency's revelations of paranoia, disregard for basic ethics, bombast and perverse anticommunism, to give us as close to an authentic story of the times as we are likely to get from entertainment.

Nixon-the-film gives us a man twisted by a dysfunctional childhood, uncomfortable in his own persona to the point of a forever insatiable need for love, and so intent upon fabricating the life story he wishes history to preserve that he sets up an elaborate system to record it. The tapes are destined to reveal his every blasphemy and blunder. Among much else, it is Stone's attention to Nixon's mania for perpetrating this story of his life—by rigorously preserving it on tape—that stays with me when I leave the theater.

It reminds me of a more recent politician's need to record his every word, his simplest daily act. Senator Robert Packwood also produced play-by-play evidence of the sort that conspires to show a person for what he is, or bring a wrongdoer down. Packwood, too, was done in by the megalomaniac's need to leave a document. In his case it was a diary, in which he wrote of each unwanted assault upon the women in his employ, each vain combing of his hair, each criminal misappropriation of funds.

Nixon's tapes, and the eighteen and a half minutes crudely cut from their sequence, led to the impeachment proceedings against him. Packwood's diary, at first withheld and then offered up with almost childlike glee, put an end to his tenure in the Senate. In both cases, official stories were effectively shredded when bits and pieces of the real ones leaked through the protection afforded by power, those carefully constructed safeguards of a patriarchal system.

Indeed, many of the men who helped put an end to these two careers themselves live lives that are rife with similar ugliness. Perhaps they believe that by permitting the scapegoating of one of their own, they gain some measure of immunity. Judging from history, perhaps they do.

Nixon and Packwood's obsessions with the importance of their every word and deed boomerang to precipitate their falls from power. Almost imperceptibly, these men are ripped from omnipotence and made objects of public embarrassment. And because our society moves towards an ever more liberal way of dealing with men who wrest power from other powerful men, we will undoubtedly see more of this sort of exposure. John F. Kennedy had his extra-marital affairs while the press, then respectful of men in high office, looked the other way. Bill Clinton had his and paid the price.

It seems to me that some powerful men refusing to allow other powerful men to get away with the lies that protect their images, is not really the point. When a better truth is told about those who don't hold power as well as those who do, we will know we are making changes that will help us all live healthier lives.

III

The private versus the public view. How difficult it is to bring these two disparate realities into a single focus. I know this intimately, from my own experience. Several years back, I began to retrieve memories of my maternal grandfather having raped me when I was an infant. And later, memories of my grandmother looking on. Gradually, through the work of feminist therapy, whole pieces of my early life began to surface. More importantly, I could finally begin to make sense of a pervasive phobia, grapple with inabilities never before understood, confront head-on a reality with which I continue to struggle.

I wrote a book about my experience.[4] I named names, and reproduced photographic images of this grandfather who had been a Christian Science practitioner and was referred to in our family as a saint. Who appeared so above suspicion, so harmless in his expensive suit, gold-rimmed glasses and professional manicure. People still write to tell me my story has helped them understand their own. Yet most members of my family either actively fought against my decision to publish, hid or ignored the book because it embarrassed them, demanded "proof," or very belatedly (in some cases after coming to understand that they too had been abused) expected me to sympathize with them.

I did.

Those who feel threatened by their revelations most vehemently sustain official stories, and they put enormous energy into condemning those who dare to produce an alternative script. Uncomfortable revelations of truth call forth the loudest denial from those who may somehow be implicated by such telling.

Accusations of self-indulgence, craziness or other dismissals are like insurance policies; they attempt to preserve credibility where the perpetrator hopes it will remain. Those implicated also fear that if the truth is known, their own digressions may come to light. Patriarchal systems such as ours are clearly set up to make such cover-ups easier, and more believable.

This is equally true in the once private arenas of father/daughter abuse or spousal battery and in the more public political or social spheres. In both places our inclinations and responses are conditioned to facilitate belief in and acceptance of the official text, suspicion and trivialization of life as it was experienced.

IV

The feminist anthropologist Ruth Behar has pondered the dilemma of personal and public truth in ways I find particularly useful. Born in Cuba, of parents who took her into exile when the 1959 revolution came to power, Behar straddles antagonistic cultural and political worlds. She is also a woman in male-dominated academia and a superb oral historian in a field where rich white men have forged the rules of ethnography.

In *Translated Woman, Crossing the Border with Esperanza's Story*,[5] Behar records the life of a poor woman of the Mexican countryside. Esperanza is not her real name, but one the narrator chooses for herself; in Spanish it means hope. Such respect, symbolized by the anthropologist asking her subject to choose her own name, permeates this book.

But Behar also grapples with the issues inherent in the larger sociopolitical context. She dares to cross a number of borders, consciously and with no small degree of risk. That border drawn by U.S. expansionism into Mexican territory symbolizes these all too starkly.

There is the border determined by colonialist positioning, situating Esperanza on one side as the colonized and Behar, even when she is an immigrant and a woman of color, on the other as the colonizer. There is the border between the "ignorance" of no education and the academic seal of approval implicit in the life of a full professor at a major university.

There is NAFTA. There is a chasm.

From the beginning, Behar is concerned with "[t]he question of whether feminism translates across borders" and admits that it "has lately begun to preoccupy feminist ethnographers who want to learn how to listen and respond to the words of women from other cultural, racial, and class backgrounds."[6] Behar addresses this difficult question courageously as well as brilliantly. She balances her interpretation of Esperanza's story with her own: a woman who is the product of a family located in two worlds—uprooted, displaced, in perpetual cultural, political and educational conflict.

Ruth Behar's parents are simultaneously shamed by the disobedient daughter who went public with family secrets, and proud of the successful daughter who published a book. Her mother rents a hall to throw a lavish book party, but privately berates her for making her father feel bad. Her father buys copies of the book for his business associates, then rants about incidents revealed which he at first denies and later obliquely admits. "Writing about the shame seems only to compound the shame of the shame," Behar says.[7]

But *Translated Woman* proves problematic beyond the intimate confines of Behar's family of origin. The New York Times, in a review titled "The Academic and the Witch," celebrates her ethnography while castigating her venture into autobiography: "The lesson is clear, the lives of anthropologists are rarely as rich and fascinating as those of their subjects."[8] Behar has dared to challenge the traditional colonialist/colonized telling of a story. She has crossed a line. And academia as well as the larger social construct will be formidable opponents. One can only wonder what prejudices led this particular reviewer to find the life of a Mexican peasant woman so much richer and more fascinating than that of a transplanted Cuban woman from a working-class background who becomes an anthropologist at a prestigious university and an ethnographer who is courageous enough to look not only at her subject but herself.

In the complex reality we inhabit, The New York Times sells books—despite its failure to grasp this feminist anthropologist's important break with patriarchal stricture (scripture?). Within a month after the review appears, the first edition of Translated Woman sells out. Negative or vapid publicity, especially in the right place, is worth more than no publicity at all. Our stories are so often shaped and set through the bludgeoning power of mass commercialization. What does this tell us about lies?

V

To bring forth the real story requires pain and courage. Happily, we live in a time when feminist theory has shaped new questions within a broad range of disciplines; and rebellious community provides the safety necessary to an authentic revisioning of our lives. Many women and increasing numbers of men are finding new ways to approach memory, to reclaim hidden stories of powerlessness that can help them retrieve authentic power.

And this leap can be felt in the global arena as well as in the most intimate. The disintegration of the socialist world provoked a general reexamination of stories we once accepted at face value, whatever our positions in the fray. In many of the Eastern European countries, failures to transition to capitalism followed by reelection of many of the old Communist leaders, continues to challenge popular perception.

Through the ongoing muck of inequality, a telling of real stories is being achieved in the space carved out by women and men of conscience: Julius and Ethel Rosenberg, Malcolm X, Adrienne Rich, Daniel Ellsberg, Rigoberta Menchú, Anita Hill,

Alice Walker, Martina Navratilova, Nelson Mandela, Barbara Kingsolver, Gloria Anzaldua, Aung San Suu Kyi, among others. Each in her or his way insists, against extraordinary odds, on telling the story long buried by opposing interests.

Needless to say, patriarchy will not go gently into that good night of its own demise. Too many stories, too much non-fictionalized history, threaten the pillars upon which the system stands.

This juxtaposition of fiction and truth may reveal itself in unexpected circumstances. Recently I had the occasion to visit the home of one of our country's most infamous statesmen. The man himself was long gone; his widow graciously allowed us entrance to their mansion because it had been the house in which my mother grew up. My brother, sister and I were bringing her back to revisit childhood memories.

William Casey headed the Central Intelligence Agency through one of its darkest eras. In room after room, his library still occupied shelves that rose from floor to ceiling. There were hundreds of history books, all written by great white men. There were sections on biography, intelligence, counterintelligence, war. My brother—who is a lover of books—and I came away with a unanimous observation: we hadn't seen a single volume of poetry in this house. No books by women or people of color. And most interestingly, no fiction. Not even the occasional bedside table paperback.

The powerful seek their truth in stories scripted by the powerful, and their preferred genre is patriarchal history. Fiction and poetry perpetuate the ordinary man or woman's truths, memories, capacities for innovation and creativity. The energy of the erotic made verb. Dissent and its imagination. Stories that upset the status quo. Stories more real than The Truth.

In the global or public sphere, the rhetoric of free world democracy (its current incarnation: neo-liberalism's version of globalization) perpetuates stories of charity to the starving hordes, self-improvement and advancement for those who embrace the International Monetary Fund's development model, and the crumbs of trickle-down reward for those who eagerly mirror the customs and longings the United States holds out in bribe.

There is more of a connection than many of us would like to believe exists between such stories and those that would deny the Holocaust took place, ignore the way our histories have been shaped by the kidnapping and enslavement of Africans, or bury the real history of our country's first inhabitants.

VI

To keep the more hidden, private, relationships in line, we have male-centered Judeo-Christian dogma, the thunderous authority of a partially-read Freud, the profit-motive of western medicine and other "helping" professions. We have laws and a scale of values that perpetuate the subservience of women, people of color, the sexually different, and the poor. And we have a whole backlog of theory that can be brought to bear when needed.

One such "theory" is the recently showcased False Memory Syndrome, authored by those who have most to lose from women's collective retrieval of what was perpetrated against so many of us. No sooner did a modest number of women begin to remember our abuse, to publish real names, place responsibility where it belongs and even achieve some small measure of success in the courts, than the old boys proceeded with their deliberate campaigns of defamation. Telling our stories is clearly dangerous to those who benefit from our powerlessness.

Memory, they claim—and against all evidence to the contrary—cannot be retrieved from childhood, infancy, or before. Children are not to be believed in any case. Proof is needed. And of course it must be proof of the sort their experts are willing to accept.

No matter that the False Memory Syndrome Foundation was started by a man whose daughter had accused him of incest. No matter that the same foundation is headed by men with uneasy links to the pornography industry and other institutionalized child and woman abuse. No matter that the retrieved stories make perfect sense, and that acknowledging them allows us to understand patterns of behavior in the abused as well as in the abusers. The (overwhelmingly female) stories must be discredited. We must be made to believe that early childhood memory is questionable at best, suggested by feminist therapists who have an ax to grind, and fabricated to keep us all divided.

But who is this "all"? The (mis)use of unity-versus-division has long been a weapon in the hands of those in control. Throughout its sordid history, officialdom has frequently planted seeds of division to keep the powerless down. We are told that women's desire for freedom is responsible for male dissatisfaction, children without fathers, poverty and crime. Some of us have been told that pandering to the needs of specific social groups causes disunity and dilutes struggle. Politicians often claim that an influx of minorities brings down property values or weakens our system of education, that immigrants take our jobs, that drug use by the most disenfranchised (rather than its sale by profiteering governments and mafias) is to blame for the violence in our communities. All in order to keep us firmly in line.

No sooner does the telling of our stories become a movement, no sooner do we point to those truly responsible for our inability to know who we are, than all the big guns swivel in our direction—in a well-orchestrated battle for maintenance of the status quo. The so-called False Memory Syndrome is one of these guns; it has big money, guilt and fear behind it.

It is interesting how quickly the media, which at first reacted sympathetically (or at least "impartially") to stories of memory retrieval, snapped to near regimental attention in its backing of this new official line. Everyone seemed relieved. No more need to look at all that dirty laundry being dragged before our discomforted senses. Judges and juries are being swayed. Many women, who had begun to speak loudly their language of truth, have retreated once again into silence.

And all returns to a comfortable balance once more.

Or does it?

Not for long. Memory has an obstinate way of rearing its empowering head. False memory is indeed a contradiction in terms, an oxymoron of patriarchy's last gasp late twentieth century attempt to keep us in check.

In order to be able to speak with our own voices, to claim the space of our real histories, all those who are routinely cubbyholed by an exploitative system must learn to trust our memories, feelings, and experience. Our lives often career between the self-knowledge that persists in surfacing and those well honed devices used to keep us dancing to the master's tune.

These are the devices that weave the lie to which we are taught we must aspire. When we tell a different story, an uncomfortable one, or one that threatens the positions of those who control our lives, we forfeit the right to be heard, to be taken seriously, to be dignified by belief.

We will always be asked for proof. And our proof will never be good enough.

Who lies here?

Those who profit at our expense are right to fear the stories we tell.

CHAPTER FOUR

Forgetting Remembered

The dilemma of my journey is that
my destination is not a point on the
map but an elusive territory with shifting boundaries.
—Sylvia de Swaan[1]

What is memory? Origin, identity, survival instinct or necessary conduit to our past, physiological attribute or mental exercise, proof or mystery? Is it always, as World War II concentration camp survivor and novelist Agate Nesaule warns us, "unreliable [as] it works by selecting, disguising, distorting"? Does routine always limit its brilliance, age burden it with loss? The late Soviet psychologist A. R. Luria was a pioneer, and remains a singular figure in the study of this elusive subject. In his classic *The Mind of a Mnemonist*, he presents us with S., a man who literally could remember everything he had ever seen, heard, or experienced.[2]

When faced with someone like S., we naturally wonder if we all have a similar potential to remember and have developed but a tiny fraction of it, something like what most home computer users feel about the tiny part of their computer's capabilities to which they have access.[3] If so, have our vast reserves of memory been damaged, or not sufficiently developed? And if underdeveloped, might it be possible for us to learn to develop them further?

Would such development be desirable or undesirable? One often imagines increased memory as nothing short of wonderful, but reading about people like S. it is clear that this is not always the case; indiscrete bombardment of any of the senses presents as many problems as possibilities—sometimes more.

Today we are much more likely to confront the loss of memory than its overabundance. A generalized concern about memory loss permeates our collective consciousness. Television talk shows have made it a focus of popular attention. The evening news features periodic health segments in which possible cures are discussed.[4] Many more people than at any previous time seem to suffer from some degree of memory impairment. Can it be that, as a people, we are losing the memory of who we are? That our frantic and seemingly limitless technological advance is taking us ever further from the healthy habitat and equity of resources which once helped define us as human?

Gloria Steinem, at 61, is reported to have said that she had reached the age when to remember something is better than an orgasm.[5] Such publicly expressed concern with memory loss, aside from reflecting a shared reality, undoubtedly has much to do with the baby boomer generation coming of age. So many of us are now in our sixties or older: women on the far side of menopause, men moving beyond the proverbial midlife crisis. We may be taking care of aging parents and beginning to worry about our own later years. The increase in commercials that push adult panty liners and diapers, dietary supplements for the "silver" years, and denture adhesive, all attest to this. Our collective concern about memory loss is one more part of this picture.

Certainly there are other components of this historically rooted memory loss that seems to affect such large numbers of us now. Advanced capitalism, while making life easier for the few brings increased exploitation and oppression to the many. As economic crises deepen, hard times also become more "acceptable," that is to say a difficulty we expect to endure and do not question. As we struggle to survive, we forget who we once were or how much easier it may have been to live the way we did. Technological innovations tend to take the place of self-reliance or some of the more community-oriented solutions.

Within the capitalist mode, male supremacy and misogyny affect women's collective memory—urging us to forget many
of the most important ways in which we are women—just as
racism erodes memory of cultural identity for African
Americans, Hispanics, Native Americans and others.
Heterosexism and homophobia lead lesbians and gay men to
forget who we may never even have learned we are. Current
identity politics goes a long way towards restoring memory, and
fortunately we inhabit a time rich in its affirming power. Still,
the erasure of self is a complex process and what it may do to
other aspects of our memory is only very partially understood.

In popular terms, what do we mean by memory?
Physiologically speaking, the idea that memory resides in a center of some sort, for example a single area of the brain, is highly disputed today. Contemporary theories suggest that memory
may be distributed not only in the cortex but throughout the
entire body; that every cell holds its own version of memory,
and that this memory, rendered dormant by trauma or other
conditioning, can be awakened or made functional again
through a variety of psychotherapeutic techniques.

Hypnotism is one of these, Rapid Eye Movement another.
Reichian work of various types, often referred to as body work
and involving stimulating parts of the body where memory is
stored, has proliferated with the development of a number of
different therapies.[6] Many women today enjoy powerfully
changed lives as a result of these techniques.

Body work, particularly in the context of the feminist
community, has proved useful to many women and some men,
for whom remembering childhood abuse brings release from the
torture of displaced memory, memory temporarily obscured by
the horror of the act itself, or by the perpetrator's effective
silencing techniques. Many of us have managed to retrieve con-

sciousness of events not previously remembered, the hidden presence of which produced all manner of problems in our lives.

Such memory retrieval, when linked to the adult's ability to sort out innocence, blame, guilt (who really was responsible for what), has been shown to radically alter a person's perception of self—and therefore her or his ability to function. Domestic abuse has been likened to the trauma of war, in that the residual damage of the former, like the shock of the latter, can produce what we now recognize as Post Traumatic Stress Disorder.

The above described memory work threatens patriarchal domination in ways that are as far-reaching as they are profound. Those who control us, whether individually or as a society, cannot afford discovery. That is to say, a freely functioning memory. There is no question but that such discovery would radically alter current power relations, still overwhelmingly unfair to women and other vulnerable sectors of society. It is not surprising, then, that as soon as a few women successfully sued their perpetrators, based upon their retrieval of childhood memories, the perpetrators themselves came up with "proof" that this sort of memory work is invalid.[7]

The retrieved memory/false memory dispute aside, the real experience of thousands of women offers substantial evidence that memory does, in fact, reside throughout the body. And that it can be rekindled. It also soundly supports the idea that we must look at mind and body as parts of a whole, not fragmented in the manner of most western medical and psychiatric practices.

II

For the purpose of this essay, I will define memory as the ability to hold, retrieve, articulate and refer back to an experience in whatever part of our being; to recognize that experience continuously, from one moment to the next, or following a time of not remembering. To hold the recognition and to be able to use it. Or to be confronted with it, perhaps even against one's will. Memory preserves and brings history to life. Our stories, both sacred and profane, allow us to know ourselves.

The significance or meaning of articulation can be tricky of course. Is it articulation from the perspective of the person remembering, or must it assume a form that is recognizable to others? In this essay I wish to use the term memory in its broadest definition, that is however an individual is able to express such reference to experience.

The Yugoslavian feminist writer Slavenka Drakulic wrote: "Once the concept of 'otherness' takes root, the unimaginable becomes possible."[8] She was referring to twentieth century holocausts, then repeating themselves in her part of the world. Scapegoating, torture, and genocide are always easier perpetrated against those who have been made Other. For what is so obscenely possible to become unimaginable once more, the concept of otherness must be uprooted. Unfortunately, not an easy task.

I have always associated colors with letters and words. M is dark red. Anger is dull brown, sometimes a pale metallic green. Safety is blue or creamy white. My tendency to imbue language with color is an active part of my memory. Recently I learned that this condition is not unique; it is called synesthesia. It seems we are just beginning to discover and study the interplay between memory and other senses.

Many believe that it is our capacity for complex language that sets humans above the so-called lower species. The ability to communicate—successfully developed in cetaceans, some apes, even certain canines—has made them, in our eyes, more human these people claim. This vision, again, results from our obsession with viewing ourselves as the highest form of life, and thus justified in attempting to dominate all others.

Such anthropocentrism ignores the variety of communication systems employed by thousands of other species. The complex mating dance that allows one albatross to find its lifelong partner, even when all look (and some scientists believe smell) the same. The whale song heard halfway round the world, before industrialization's noise pollution drastically shortened the distance of its clarion sound.

Feminist women, who have lived for so long and so uncomfortably with androcentricity, are finding it easier than most men to conceive of relationships that are less caught up in a belief in our superiority, less vertical or hierarchical. But female or male, and despite our best intentions, when it comes to automatic or unexamined responses most of us are still mired in the repetitive swamp of patriarchal and species-centered conditioning.

We have also been slow to recognize other communicative cultures, in humans as well as in animals. It has taken us centuries, for example, to understand that the deaf inhabit a communicative culture—three-dimensional language and its many byways—and at least in some milieus no longer force them to rely solely a superficial transliteration of heard speech.

Oliver Sacks, in one of his insightful essays on the deaf person's spatial mode of communication, points to a "language of an entirely different sort...that serve[s] not only the powers of thought (and indeed allow[s] thought and perception of a kind not wholly imaginable by the hearing), but serve[s] as the medium of a rich community and culture ..."[9]

The common exercise of memory does seem to me to be a prime prerequisite to all types of language. Which undoubtedly is why those who are prelingually deaf and thus unable to grow naturally into oral speech are so often mistakenly presumed of inferior intelligence: "deaf and dumb." Unable to remember not only how that sound is made or what that gesture looks like but also what it means, it is difficult to conceive of communication. Yet language of every sort is enriched by all manner of non-verbal communication: stance, gaze, energy, skin upon skin, even tone, taste and smell. All take up residence on memory's landscape.

Society overwhelmingly defines us by how we communicate. Can we say what we mean? Convey what we feel? Talk our way into or out of a situation? Even make appropriate small talk? Are we convincing? Able to relate appropriately to others? Can we stand up to be counted? Yet we must ask and ask again: are we at fault when we cannot fulfill all requirements of such social expectation? Or is it the society we have created that is deficient because it's recognition of alternative forms of communication remains so limited—and limiting?

Particularly interesting when considering language, memory, and the roles each play in our identity, are those overlays of individual and shared memory we call stories. Collective memory is quite literally our history: where we come from, how we got here, what possibilities exist for our future lives and for those who will come after. The cultures of different groups are preserved and kept alive through each group's collective memory: tradition, values, shared experience, custom, symbol, sense of honor, humor, manner of play, excitement, mode of agreement or disagreement, and art, among much else. Memory is root, arrival, word, image, subliminal influence, recognized feeling, barrage, common practice, life breath and death gasp.

Without memory, in its deepest and broadest definition, we cannot move upon this earth. Nor can we envision, create, or change the statements of our lives. For the individual within the group, memory narrows into specificity, identity, the possibility for a healthy sense of self, and meaningful relationships with others. For the individual and the group, our lives are a struggle to preserve and pass on the stories remembered and reclaimed.

The Laguna writer Leslie Marmon Silko put it succinctly: "I will tell you something about stories /...They aren't just entertainment. / Don't be fooled. / They are all we have, you see, / all we have to fight off / illness and death."[10]

I approach definition here by talking around it, by posing questions, responding to them, and finding that they in turn suggest others. But we always come back to the beginning. What is memory, really? How can we break it open, look at its components, define its texture and significance? And if we succeed in taking memory apart so that we can study each of its parts, would this not be a reductionist exercise, as misleading as so much of our so-called scientific process?

Surely memory is more than a complex system of electrical impulses, as in the physical brain swirls and twists freed or destroyed by decay or medical malpractice. Is it not also a spiritual essence, as in "the spirit within"? Might it not include a stretch beyond that which is currently acceptable to the minds of pragmatists, as in the ability of some to remember past lives? Is it not the sum of all our stories, those handed easily from generation to generation and those ignored or erased by hate or fear? I am more and more convinced that memory is not limited to that part of the body called the brain, but is stored in every cell, and clearly in ways we do not yet fully understand.

I have spoken about memories that reside in different parts of the body. When these are blocked, for whatever reason, they inevitably do us harm. If in the chest, they impede easy respiration. If in the stomach or gut, they disrupt digestion. If in the neck or shoulders or lower back or knees, they may keep us tensed, often to the point of chronic pain. A number of contemporary wellness practices work with these manifestations.

Successful body work therapy produces a marked improvement in physical health as well as empowerment through a
reconnection with that which was done to us, often as children,
and then was blocked by fear. Perhaps we do not yet understand
the many ways in which mind and body are one, but we cannot
ignore that they are.

A range of different healing disciplines work with this
knowledge: yoga, rolfing, acupuncture, polarity, Tai-Chi and a
variety of other martial arts. Therapeutic touch is beginning to
be employed with patients in major U.S. hospitals; the initial
evidence suggests it improves their chances of coming through
surgery well and of healing more quickly and permanently.
Therapeutic massage often evokes memory flashes, images that
may bring a sudden chill or flood of tears, or provide a missing
link to some aspect of self-knowledge. A good chiropractor
knows that muscles remember skeletal assemblage, and works to
enable them to retrieve that memory. More and more, good chi-
ropractic is not about "cracking bones," but adjusting muscle
and tissue so they will remember to hold them properly.

Just as we recognize the ways in which our bodies remember experience and store such memories for future use (or hide
them in fear), we come to understand that the earth—that great
body—does the same. Toni Morrison has written: "You know,
they straightened out the Mississippi in places, to make room for
houses and livable acreage. Occasionally, the river floods these
places. 'Floods' is the word they use, but in fact it is not flooding;
it is remembering. Remembering where it used to be. All water
has a perfect memory and it is forever trying to get back to where
it was. Writers are like that: remembering where we were, what
valley ran through, what the banks were like, the light that was
there and the route back to our original place. It is emotional
memory—what the nerves and skin remember as well as how it
appeared. And a rush of imagination is our 'flooding.'"[11]

III

As my father gradually moved into the terrain of Alzheimer's memory loss, he became quite adept at developing the compensatory practices that allowed his family the denial we nurtured for so long. In restaurants, he would reach into his pants pocket for a little slip of paper. He had written a list of what he wanted to eat; and we made small talk at the table, pretending not to notice as he read his order off. At least he can still read, we thought, the letters still speak to him.

My father confessed he'd forgotten how to subtract, then how to add; and asked us to re-teach him these skills. Faced with the inevitability of declaring it futile, of telling him he had lost that function and most likely would not be able to regain it, we tried as one would with a child to explain the processes by steps. But of course he could not remember those steps. That part of his memory function was gone.

It is clear to me that we pay too much attention to the defects of those suffering from conditions we find frightening or do not understand. To use the language of Oliver Sacks again, "we [are] far too concerned with 'defectology', and far too little with 'narratology', the neglected and needed science of the concrete."[12] In my father's case this may have meant worrying so much about what he could no longer do that we failed to appreciate the ingenuity in what he did do, the map it might have helped us trace.

My friend, and her husband who experienced a similar age-related memory loss, did a much better job than my family and I did with Dad. They grappled forthrightly with the situation, hoping to avoid the pitfalls of denial. When he became disoriented, she acknowledged the loss and prodded him to use as much of what remained as he was able. Intellectual stimulation clearly delays mental breakdown. It also presents us with moments we must be prepared to embrace. Following one such insistent exchange, this man looked at his wife and asked: "What happens if I forget that I love you?"

When it came to memory, I inherited a series of rather traditional assumptions. I tried, during my father's illness and its consequent alteration in our relational capacity, to experiment with other ways of looking at memory's role. But I guessed wrong more often than right, and don't believe I made things any easier for him. Ultimately, I too felt alone, isolated in my attempts.

My father could not tell me what he felt. My mother, in her discomfort, mostly agreed to explore my alternative routes and then could not or did not want to do so. The nursing home caretakers were trained in standard western medical practice: make such patients "comfortable" while treating them like children and reaping the considerable profit—which of course does not accrue to them but to the companies for which they work.

I accompanied my father on his journey through Alzheimer's misunderstood downward spiral. I remember, visiting him at the nursing home, how frequently he would ask me what he had. "Alzheimer's," I would tell him and, at least early on, explain the condition as well as I was able. "Uh, do you have to say..." and his voice would stumble. Then, again, "Do you have to say...disease? Alzheimer's Disease?"

I wanted to nudge our conversations towards what to me seemed more meaningful, before it was too late. He wondered about nomenclature. At the time I was puzzled by this insistence on the correct name. In retrospect, I believe it was part of his quite desperate attempt to situate himself, to hold on to some sense of identity in what must have seemed a vortex of confusion. Then too, disease may have signified illness to him, which would have meant remaining in the nursing home. Perhaps without the added word, he saw the possibility of going home.

My father did not appear to fully lose what we understand as memory until days before his death. Even when he began to refuse food and drink, he continued to give those of us who loved him the feeling that he identified us and was aware of our presence. Then painfully sought and much more painfully uttered sentences gave way to a word or two. Speech disappeared behind the faintest of smiles or the squeeze of a hand.

Up until his last few days of peaceful stillness there was a linkage of energy, something rare and not easily described. When he was finally gone, I was left with a haunting ambivalence. On the one hand I wished we had talked more, been able to put into a language that I understood the many facets of our love. On the other, I wanted to believe we had managed all that he found necessary to express.

Our family physician wanted a brain autopsy performed on my father, so as to be able to make a scientific diagnosis of his condition. It was for us, his children, she said; it would be useful for us to know if indeed he had suffered from Alzheimer's. In fairness I should say that she was looking to a future in which a cure or some preventative protocol might be developed. Without the time to think this through and under the duress of our loss, we agreed. The autopsy was performed, its findings not surprising. Dad's final neuropathological diagnosis was: 1. Alzheimer's Disease, 2. Parkinson's Disease, and 3. Atherosclerosis of the Circle of Willis.

Of what real use was this knowledge to adult offspring who may or may not inherit our father's tendency towards these ills? To date there is no cure for Alzheimer's, and no undisputed preventative prophylaxis. There is nothing my sister, brother, or I can do with the facts thus confirmed, except to anguish at each of our own misplaced words. We can fear the onset of illness when, in fact, the reason for midlife memory loss may as easily be traced to the economy, pollution, stress, a speedup of life rhythms, or any combination of these.

Much more realistic, it seems to me, in explaining the apparent upsurge in Alzheimer's, may be the fact that technology has pushed U.S. Americans to live so much longer than they ever had. Two observations made by a practitioner of alternative medicine also seem interesting to me. One, she says, is the fact that we breathe thirty percent less oxygen than one hundred years ago, particularly in the industrialized world; thus less oxygen to the brain. The other is that a century ago midwives delivered babies and immediately placed them on their backs. When doctors took over obstetrics, they began placing newborns face down, their heads turned to one side. The practice has been noted in cases of crib death, but this healer also believes that the early twisting of the brain stem pinches off a considerable percentage of initial oxygen flow, causing Alzheimer's in later life. No authorized studies have been done, of course, and there is no scientific proof of this. But she says that many doctors are now rethinking the procedure, and suggests her clients sleep on their backs with a rolled up towel beneath their necks. She contends that people who do so will notice a measurable increase in memory.

I also factor pollution into the equation. I mean pollution of the air we breathe and the water and food we ingest, but also the noise pollution that confuses our senses, deadening our natural ability to listen. And the inability to listen as we once did, necessarily affects memory. I mean the pollution created by the economic crisis tearing at our sense of security. The stress of not knowing whether we will have health care when we need it, or even if we'll continue to have a job. To say nothing of our government's insistence on launching one war after another, so that the fear of an imploding world outweighs all other fears. All this, and more, plays havoc with our memory's health. We might call it stress pollution.

There is also the unique twenty-first century pollution created by an over abundance of information itself. Compare what one needs to know to be able to use an old manual typewriter with what one needs to know to use a home computer. The computer vastly multiplies our options, it is true, but we must fill our minds with banks of information in order to be able to exercise those options. How much can the human mind absorb without filtering out what is not immediately relevant?

When we dial a telephone number and are confronted with an electronic menu rather than a human voice, or any other computerized system replaces human interaction, our ability to center, to gather ourselves in and function from a place of safety, may become polluted beyond recognition. Technology itself, so rich in promises of human betterment, seems to me to be the ultimate in polluting forces.

A friend recently suggested that our dramatically changed nutrition may be one reason for the increased incidence of depression we see in this country today: the enormous consumption of fast food, white bread, saturated fats, artificial colorants, preservatives, pesticides, animal hormones, antibiotics, sulfites, nitrates, sulfides, nitrites, and genetic engineering. It is proven that contemporary eating habits are behind the rise in diabetes, obesity and other serious conditions. Might they not also contribute to memory loss?

IV

I had been grappling with noticeable alterations in my own memory since much before my father's diagnosis, certainly long before the visible changes in his functionality. I found these alterations extremely difficult to confront, and even more difficult to explain to others. When I mentioned them, or tried describing their characteristics, some well-meaning friend or family member would inevitably respond by making light of the affliction.

"Don't worry," he or she was always quick to say, "I forget things all the time." Or "That's nothing, it happens to everyone." People seemed more interested in trying to make me feel better than in listening or making room for an honest consideration of what I was experiencing. Faced with this sort of consolation, I felt trivialized, sure no one understood what I was going through.

By the time I returned to the United States, in 1984, I had lived in Latin America for 23 years, the last four in Nicaragua. There I had shared the rigors of impending war with friends and colleagues forced into a rapidly worsening situation of uncertainty, fear, and constant stress. The decision to come home had not been easy; my body yearned for familiarity of landscape, family, language, culture. But I was leaving behind my comrades and the dangers they continued to face. My homecoming was complex. The war didn't fade, it simply assumed a different shape.

Today the signs of Post Traumatic Stress Disorder are more widely recognized than they were then. A fraction of the challenges I confronted might have been enough to produce a diagnosis of this qualitatively different stress, and there were those who recognized its presence and warned against my continuing on with business as usual. Others only smiled and assured me everything would be all right.

Women especially may be slow to acknowledge this sort of alteration in ourselves. I knew there was danger, but was conditioned to try to walk around or climb over rather than stop and explore it, or try to understand and consider its potential damage. Certainly, at that point, I did not think of trying to examine the changes I was experiencing for what that might offer in a positive sense. All I wanted was to escape their claim on me, and the fear it engendered.

My first indication that I was experiencing an unfamiliar state was what began to happen when I spoke in public. I might be giving a poetry reading or a lecture. The audience might consist of thirty people or a thousand. I might be exhausted at the end of a tour or fresh at its beginning. Suddenly, and then quite predictably, I began to suffer what I could only describe as white spots. In the middle of a phrase or even a word, an irregular white shape would appear, obstructing my mind's view of what came next. I had no idea how to proceed.

The whiteness was viscous yet brilliant, almost back-lit and of an irregular, rubbery shape. An entity. It was as if my open eyes were being invaded by a physical intruder, sometimes a succession of intruders, an army of intruders: blotting out thought, the ability to formulate words, the possibility of communication itself. I experienced the onset of approaching confusion, but this was a specific event, a contained presence. Would I be able to walk around it and find relief on the other side?

The first several times I experienced the white spots I believed I had fallen noticeably silent. As calmly as possible, I waited for them to recede before continuing my presentation. Later when I mentioned the problem to friends in the audience, they assured me they'd observed no hesitation on my part, nothing that interfered with the natural flow of language. And so I came to understand that the shape and duration of the phenomenon was non-linear, impossible to measure in ordinary terms. How then to treat it?

The fact that as far as my audience was concerned I seemed able to compensate and continue uninterrupted relieved me of excess worry. But it didn't resolve anything. I knew my communicative processes were affected, that they weren't working in a way that was familiar or felt comfortable.

Whether or not the occurrence was visible in my public persona, surely it was a sign that my memory had suffered a change of pace. And what if the condition worsened?

The human body and will are both amazingly resilient. Perhaps good fortune also played a part in how I was able to find my way on unfamiliar terrain. This time around, it proved possible to continue working, pay attention to the stress factor, obtain helpful tools from a therapist I was seeing at the time and support from my considerable network of friends. I made it through. I learned to use notes, sometimes even read a public talk instead of maintaining my pride in extemporaneous presentation. Eventually the white spots appeared less frequently. For a while they disappeared.

The most valuable lesson I learned from this experience was the importance of acknowledging what was happening to me, not denying or wishing it away. It was enormously important that I had a partner with whom I could speak easily about my fears, in the certainty that she would listen and not assure me she knew exactly what I was going through. Although I do not wish to compare my transitory state with the problems faced by those diagnosed with some type of senility, for those for whom there is no return, I believe we need to look for new ways to acknowledge and address the social reality of shifting memory.

Trying to understand, even share, responsibility for the sufferer's situation, although important cannot be our only goal. If, as in the case of menopause and other natural changes, we are open to the revelations of uncharted experience as well as grieving what has been lost, we may find that we are able to learn from the former while more appropriately sympathize with the latter.

As a poet, I see all sorts of possibilities in memory's changing structure: rhythms and cadences never before explored, new breath lines, time that becomes form, senses that manifest themselves as palpable objects. Of late, I have tried allowing myself the daring and freedom of such exploration instead of doggedly attempting to escape what is as yet unknown. One might be able to trace new maps, I reason, if one were able to relax and acknowledge these challenges rather than hide from and fight their assault.

I am not advocating sitting back and awaiting the onset of physical or mental disintegration. I am all for fighting environmental death, for preserving what is left of our land and air and oceans. I am for eating as intelligently as one is able and integrating regular physical exercise into one's routine. I know how important it is to remain vitally, passionately, interested and involved in whatever keeps one engaged—with others and with oneself. Continued intellectual stimulation is the surest way to a more connected, aware, and alert aging.

But when age or genes or illness or post traumatic stress alter—temporarily or permanently—the brain's capacity to recall and convey, how much easier and more productive it would be if we could accept the altered state and feel supported, validated in our exploration of its possibilities. My thinking about this was unexpectedly reflected in a New York Times obituary I happened to read as I began these notes. My old friend Larry Eigner had died at the age of 68.

Larry and I never met and hadn't communicated for years. But I vividly remember his strange-looking letters (strange by conventional standards of neat typing or orderly paragraphs), and their exquisite sensitivity. For Eigner was a fine American poet who suffered from cerebral palsy. Writing, like speech, must have been excruciatingly difficult for him. But he used his affliction. His obituary was right to say that "[h]is disability had a profound influence on his poetry, which often captured, in emotional bursts of language, fleeting impressions received through the window of a house, an airplane or a car...'It seems I feel the world as a neighborhood, or two dozen miles of it, anyway,' Eigner once told an interviewer. 'My eyes are still big for my head; most things were always tantalizingly beyond or almost beyond sight and hearing, out of reach.'"[13]

For more than a courageous few to turn disability into creative possibility, social attitudes would have to change. It would have to be all right to walk upon this unknown territory, purposefully and without shame. Patience would be called to new highs. What needs to be expressed would not remain unsaid. Communication might open like a flower, finding new ways to acknowledge abilities lost and images or sensations newly encountered.

Today my white spots a decade behind me and my father's death from Alzheimer's beginning to recede, life has not "gone back to normal." When I am tired, I still frequently lose words or the ends of sentences. I must wait for their return or be all right with the fact that they may not return.

V

This is the way it is now. Someone asks me something. Is it only when someone asks? No, but the anguish is greater then because I must struggle through their awful wait for an answer. Perhaps the person does wait. The expression on her or his face becomes an accusation: something is wrong. This may happen as well when I am the one who has initiated the exchange. But the other's impatience is less present then. And I may feel that my struggle is too generous, or not generous enough.

In either situation I step right up to the threshold of the word I seek, then discover it isn't there. I cry out, but no sound interrupts the awkward silence. And I think: I am at the very door to this word's house; how is it that I cannot enter?

But this attempt at description doesn't fully convey the time that strains against my will. An impression, a cloudiness or glitter is what I see. Enough to taunt me with its loss. Much like the vague outline of a human being, in rapidly dissolving sparkles of light, as it disappears when a Star Trek character is molecularly transported from one place to another. Or the small white cloud my father's ashes formed as they lifted and dispersed on the breeze, caught on the surface of the photo taken as I tossed his remains in our beloved foothills. In such sketchy image, some semblance of the lost word taunts me even as it refuses to lock into focus.

When I began to experience this repeatedly, I actively fought against the word's refusal to give herself up. I literally felt my body reaching for the unremembered, stretching to grab the illusive, to trap it and bring it triumphantly within my grasp. See, then speak. A translation from the visual to the verbal.

Now I try a different strategy. I stop and wait. I remind myself to remain calm as I search for the illusive image. And I have noticed that in this waiting, in this apparently empty space where what is sought has so far refused to appear, a great deal is going on. Perhaps if I pay attention to this newly discovered busyness, I may learn to decipher the puzzle. I have come to understand that the strategy is geared as much towards allowing myself to explore an entirely new place as it is to searching for the lost word.

Microwave. Yes, microwave is the word I so desperately sought. I wanted to tell my partner that I'd put her breakfast coffee in the microwave. But I couldn't say microwave. I'd said "Your coffee is in the ..." and stopped. Did a failure of memory blot out the letters, the components of the word? Allowing for questions, other possibilities around the mechanics of word loss, leads me to inhabit a place other than that stifling maddening one in which I used to struggle. And it is this new place—quiet,

peaceful, unexpectedly removed from the stress of my days—
that gives up the word. It also tells me why I forget.

Here it is now: microwave. Not brittle-edged or crackling.
No more static. The visual edges of the picture are soft, easy.
Microwave. Image rather than sound. A dance beyond dancers.
I know that a full minute or more has elapsed in silence. Barbara
looks at me, waiting. I see the picture now. Softly the word
appears. And softly I speak it: microwave.

This space seemed empty but isn't. What is going on
eludes me until I purposefully move away from what I so desperately want to see and pay attention instead to what's there.
The sandy floor of a dry arroyo bed cuts between boulders and
juniper as it moves up through rocky foothills. Desert lichen—
pale creams and greens and burnt oranges—dust the surface of
millennia. I have left myself behind, far below. Above, a deer or
longhorn sheep may surprise me. I watch for footprints in the
softer sand. The word I sought comes unexpectedly now, but not
necessarily in its own clothes. It may smile shyly, pretending to
be something it isn't. Soon, though, it gives up artifice, stops
taunting me, stands still. I can hold it, and all that surrounds it,
perfectly.

VI

Given the above, we can move in two directions.
Certainly we must struggle against the destruction of life as we
cherish it. Simultaneously, we may also opt to explore where we
live on this map we have created.

As a society, we have developed neither the ideology nor
the tools to deal with the human side of what we rather glibly
call progress. Nor have we been able to explore memory loss as
a natural or unnatural part of the aging process. Whatever its
cause, and it is clear that there are many, we seem all too will-

ing to consider such loss as devastation, finding it difficult or impossible to contemplate it as transformation—or transformative.

When we lose the quick turn of phrase, the rapid rejoinder, the capacity for instant recall, we are immediately punished by condescension or dismissal. And we respond in kind: "Oh, I'm so sorry...How stupid of me." Our dominant culture, with its allegiance to built-in obsolescence, its adulation of youth and perfection, sees aging only as deterioration. And that which is no longer functional or new is disdained, discarded for a newer model. A few may give lip service to an honoring of the wisdom that may come with age. But such wisdom is rarely recognized or rewarded in the larger society.

I believe that women understand an insistence on what is socially acceptable much better than men, for we experience its assaults all our lives. Social response to but a few of our significant transitions amply illustrates my point. When we menstruate for the first time we are told that we are sick, weak, over-sensitive, irritable, destined to incompetence. And this only builds on earlier messages. So much of who we are presumed to be depends upon our ability to fulfill a socially conditioned paradigm of beauty and service.

As we age, we must deal with other expectations. And with the stress that often overtakes us in those places where social expectations are criss-crossed by real need and creativity. We are bombarded with products guaranteed to keep our skin wrinkle-free, our hair gleaming, our natural odors camouflaged, our size and shape as they were before we bore children, our bladders controlled (or at least prepared for accident). And when we reach menopause—the magical change that can signal the onset of a special knowledge and tap into our deepest memory—we are made to feel old, feeble, stupid, spent, useless, unwanted, no longer capable of reproduction, which is, after all, our most socially acknowledged role.

Patriarchy has made a science of cutting women off from the real memory of our lives. At what moment in our history did we capitulate, stop inhabiting a female wisdom and creativity? When and how did the process of our subservience begin? If we remember, if we reconnect with who we were, an ages-old system of domination and control would crumble. No wonder those of us who begin to remember, or who advocate paying attention, are so despised.

To those who profit from our subjugation, our forgetting is the very foundation of our usefulness. Resistance moves against the social grain. To embrace may be more fruitful than to constantly have to defend. I remember the great midwestern writer Meridel LeSueur, in her eighties at the time, describing old age quite literally as decay. She spoke of an amazing chemical change, an effervescence that exuded a qualitatively different sort of energy. And her writing of those years clearly reflects this energy.[14]

Men are also subject to social norms, but these are much looser, less stringently enforced. And there is more room for flexibility. The young man who doesn't fit the norm is seen as merely quirky, while his female counterpart is judged wanting. The man whose physical shape or size do not conform to current fashion may be big, heavy, strong, powerful—all adjectives that denote interest rather than inadequacy. Such women are fat, ugly, gross. Unmarried men are bachelors, unmarried women spinsters or old maids. Men who know what they want are assertive, women with a similar knowledge strident. Men are taunted when they are small, timid, or weak, all qualities presumed to be feminine. I could extend this list of comparisons but they have been discussed at length and in many other places.

This is beginning to change. Because of our conditioning,

and surely as a result of the upsurge in feminist consciousness which has dared to reexamine and challenge that conditioning, women have come to question the many ways in which society would rather pronounce us irrelevant than explore our reclaimed identities.

And there is something else that accounts for our greater cognizance of change. We have always been the caretakers. We are the ones who are around to notice that our aging sisters and brothers lack much of what they once possessed, but acquire as well alternative attributes. And that these attributes have substance, beauty, use.[15]

VII

Now I notice changes in other aspects of my memory function. A familiar face may never elicit a name. A whole piece of my past may be remembered one-dimensionally, by virtue of having spoken so often about it, but have faded experientially. Or I may suddenly remember, from many years before, a scene and all its implications, with a vividness and clarity that almost knock me over. Still, I tend to place myself less often in positions from which I know I will be required to produce a rapid-fire response.

Other alterations have surfaced. More than once I have looked at a car and called it a flower, seen red and verbalized blue, heard myself fail to express an idea as I still believe I can express it. I work hard to avoid covering for these events, to pretend they are not happening. By acknowledging them, to myself and others, I feel I am taking the first steps in the direction of open-ended discovery, and perhaps modeling for others one alternative approach to memory loss.

The quality of my dreaming has also changed, but—perhaps more significantly—the movement from dream to wakened consciousness. This movement appears more seamless. Images and ideas that come to me in dreams are more likely to reappear in wakeful thought. Connections are more readily accessible. I might even say that I remember my dreams more vividly, certainly more usefully. Process seems to be taking the place of product, event, object, end result. Is it possible that memory of process expands as memories of specific people, places and moments become less accessible?

This recalls a much earlier period in my life, when I used dreams to work out issues encountered when awake. In my twenties and thirties, even into my early forties, I often went to sleep consciously determined to dream the solution to a problem. This might range from a philosophical question to something much more mundane, such as how to set a shirt sleeve into a shoulder seam or how many minutes to develop a roll of film I had pushed in the camera. Morning almost always brought the answer, as I expected it would. This was an ability I had come to miss, and one I am delighted to have regained.

Still, there is the constant question: are the blips stress-related breakdowns in an otherwise healthy system? Or are they the warning signs of something more definitive?

Memory takes on renewed importance today, as those of us who have given years of our lives to struggles for more just social arrangements have watched those arrangements founder or fail. Some of us who once eagerly, even blindly, followed the dictums of political, religious, or other organizations, are questioning many of their tenets. We are engaged in a reassessment that moves us to a deeper valorization of human creativity. I am sure there is a connection between the complex and seemingly more prevalent memory problems which we as a society are experiencing and the great number of memoirs being written today. Are we fighting to hold onto the stories of our lives which we see being erased by technology and official discourse?

We have witnessed the failure of patriarchal family structures, and continue to experiment with more humane relationships. We have witnessed the failures of socialism as it was designed by men, and must work together to salvage what is useful from a variety of attempts. If we are to continue working towards the creation of truly inclusive societies, I believe we must reconsider memory. Its long ignored, misunderstood, or hidden role is critical to such work.

Without claiming to fully understand it, either in its generality or as it relates to me specifically, I have tried looking at my own experience of altered memory. I have wanted to substitute fear with playfulness and a certain sense of abandon. I have treated the broken or substituted words not as fear-filled pits but as signs from a deep unconscious, as points of departure for mind travel and free flowing association.

At the same time, I find that I want to balance this sense of the earth shifting beneath my feet. I search for and experiment with practices I feel may center me, may nourish and anchor my memory. Experiences as diverse as letting myself drift in the silence of a Sunday morning hike, casting a feminist Tarot, making time for a particular exchange of ideas, or engaging in a daily physical workout have all, in different ways, helped resituate my memory.

When I have been able to allow myself to wander on such terrain, the rewards have been spectacular. I have experienced loss of body tension, a feeling of lightness, a more centered perspective, an ease of being and notable improvement in my ability to re-member (re-member: reconnect as well as simply recall). This promotes a decline in anxiety, a vastly reduced need to "sweat the small things" and an ability to pay more attention to that which I may have the power to change.

I cannot tell you that forgetting makes me happy or does not threaten me with bleaker days to come. I want to remember my life, its every texture and crevice. I want to recall and offer my living—in poems, essays, relationships, activism, and in a memoir deep enough to hold its adventures and amazing grace. I want to remember, as well, so that I may model for my grand-children and great-grandchildren my generation's struggle, achievements and mistakes.

Retreat may begin at any time in a person's life. The essen-tial difference between entrance and exit is that during most of the long slow leaving we may be able to teach ourselves and others to be conscious of new knowledge, actively seeking new modes for its expression. If we open ourselves to its magic, mem-ory reduction might well become memory refinement.

Now I am aware of a new dimension to my living: the act of forgetting remembered. The stories approach full circle. And there is a larger freedom to explore language, sound, image, taste, smell, and whatever else may surface—in any combina-tion. I honor memory failure as well as memory. Just as in birth we feel our way into the life cycle—eyes closed or unfocussed, movements tentative and awkwardly reaching, a consciousness being formed on the move—so may we retreat from the heights of analytic thought by feeling our way back out.

—Winter 1996-Summer 2002

CHAPTER FIVE

Lesbian Mother

Lesbian mother. In earlier times the characterization itself would have seemed an oxymoron. Lesbianism being the essence of deviance and motherhood the sublime and sacred reason for every woman's existence. An aberration not because there weren't innumerable lesbians who were mothers—coming out before, during or after their primary birthing years, or unable ever to come out because publicly assuming a lesbian identity wasn't something women could do, whether or not they had children.

To those for whom difference itself is threatening, particularly those zealots of the religious right, the lesbian mother represents the most frightening of Others: a woman who does not need a man to make her feel complete, and who disregards convention to the extent that she would bring a child into such an abnormal family configuration.

Lesbian mother: rebel or devil incarnate. Perhaps no other identity so visibly rejects the male-controlling-female equation through which patriarchy holds onto power.

It is still difficult for many in our society to understand that lesbians with children are simply one of many different sorts of families: extended intergenerational groups of one design or another; single mothers (straight or gay); gay male couples with kids; children with transexual or transgendered parents; variations on the so-called nuclear arrangement, therapeutic foster parents[1] (that most heroic group of all); adoptive parents of whatever gender, race or culture, lovingly raising previously parentless children; communes; collectives; and more.

Lesbian parents may themselves vary greatly, from a mother who comes out in later life to the aware young lesbian who decides to mother and carefully chooses between adoption, insemination, or sex with a friend. And lesbian adoption today may mean anything from rescuing an unwanted Chinese baby girl or mal-nourished Rumanian orphan to taking a local child of another race or mothering a child of whatever origin who is disabled in some way—among many possibilities. With insemination there are options too: should the sperm come from a friend or anonymous donor; will the father be involved?[2]

A lesbian who is a mother, or a mother who identifies as lesbian, is today a commonly expressed duality, at least where I live. In the United States, especially in the larger urban areas, several generations of struggle for gay rights, for visibility, acknowledgment and justice, have made it easier to identify as a lesbian with children. To demand comprehension and support for the child with two mothers. To seek communities of similar families. But it hasn't always been so. In many places it still isn't.

In some of the European countries the battles have been parallel; in Latin America, Africa and Asia more difficult. And yet there are few places in the world today where lesbians with children are not at least marginally visible. Perhaps only in those countries where extreme religious fundamentalism rules (Muslim, Jewish, Christian, or other). In such places, too, there are lesbian mothers. But they are unable to name themselves, inhabiting in painful isolation extremely vulnerable lives.

Until I was in my late forties, I functioned as a heterosexual woman. By then I had four children: a son on my own and then three daughters with two different men. I've never really known how to respond to the question: were you born a lesbian or did you become one? A product of my time and place, socially conditioned to a particular role, I was drawn to men and grew up imagining I would find one with whom I could make a life.

Had women been acceptable subjects of my attraction, I might well have come out earlier. Because they were not, I cannot honestly know if I was "born" or "made."

Becoming a mother for the first time at 24 and for the last at 32, I never experienced planning motherhood with a female partner, giving birth with her beside me, or negotiating a playground, public school, or lesbian household with kids. The closest I came to the latter was when my youngest daughter was still living at home, at age 17, and I began the relationship with the woman who 17 years later remains my life partner.

Coming out in maturity, I was spared the youthful pressures to be someone who didn't feel like me. I did not have to endure a psychiatrist trying to "cure" me, the shock treatments routinely imposed upon young lesbians in those years, or the religious repression suffered by so many in my generation. By the time I knew I was queer, it was relatively easy for me to claim the condition. I knew society's homophobia and heterosexism, knew I would be shunned in some circles, but then I had always been shunned in those circles—for a variety of conditions, attitudes or activities. One more "deviance" wouldn't make that much difference.

When I told my elderly parents—I was in my forties, they in their late seventies—I expected them to be supportive and they were. They and I both knew that if they were not, the result would be a distancing none of us wanted. But there was also a genuine caring, an ability to put essence before appearance. One of my parents' qualities I have most appreciated has been their ability to grow and change with their times.

Years before, when I became pregnant with my son, I had startled my mother and father by informing them that I was having a child on my own. No, my pregnancy had not been an accident, I said, I wanted and planned for this child. It was 1960. In my class and culture, single motherhood was probably every bit as shocking then as lesbian motherhood is today. Perhaps more, because there was no community to embrace the choice. My father especially was upset. Yet Gregory won him over in a matter of days, and for years afterwards he periodically apologized for having once displayed anything less than a full welcome to that first grandson he adored.

Three decades later, when I told my parents I was a lesbian, the revelation wasn't so shocking. It must have been uncomfortable for them, but I think they had come to view my choices as opportunities rather than shames to be endured. Then too, I had already given them four grandchildren. Heterosexual society's inability to conceive of lesbian motherhood, and the desire of parents to see themselves perpetuated in their grandchildren, are certainly among the reasons many pray their daughters adhere to a more conventional lifestyle.

Because my father was already ill, I told my mother first, choosing for our conversation lunch at a cafeteria she liked. When I said "Mom, I have something to tell you," I saw the anxiety in her eyes. Her knuckles went white against the table's edge. "I'm a lesbian," I continued, and she relaxed. "Oh," she said, "I thought you were going to tell me something bad."

My mother made several interesting comments in the course of that first conversation. One was that she and my father "had always suspected." Another was "You're lucky, you know, that you were born 30 years later than I." I've continued to wonder what she meant by that.

Dad responded to my news with the same loving support that characterized his relationships with all his kids. "I love you," he said, "whatever you are." Above all, he adored my partner Barbara. Until he died, they had a special closeness. She always says she was lucky to have had a loving father for those few years, something she hadn't known in her family of origin. Like many, my parents found it easier to accept difference in the

children they loved than to extrapolate from family to a broader social analysis. We had an aunt who lived with her woman
partner for years. Clearly they were lesbians, but the word was
never used. By the time I came out, my Aunt Janet and her lifetime companion Phyllis were long dead. I sometimes asked my
parents about them; they'd always insist: "But we don't really
know that they were lesbians."

It was the attitude about "some of my best friends are such
and such" or "oh, but I know plenty of whomever." This was
supposed to prove a lack of prejudice. Tolerance is not the same
as asking the real questions, exploring cultures, embracing inti-
mates. Still, it's better than religious- or fear-based shunning.

Telling my children was quite another experience.
Speaking from the older generation (the mother, in a certain
sense the model) to the younger, is necessarily different than
speaking from the younger (the daughter, who has always been
a rebel) to the older (parents who had learned to live with their
daughter's rebellion).

My son Gregory, then in his late twenties, was in Paris at
the time. Having moved to that cosmopolitan center from
much more conservative Havana (conservative insofar as sexual identity was concerned), he had been exposed to a homosexual community and had friends who were homosexuals.

I came out in the middle of my immigration case (the U.S.
government was trying to deport me under the ideological
exclusion clause of the McCarran-Walter Immigration and
Nationality Act). Because "sexual deviance" was another of
McCarran-Walter's 34 clauses, I chose not to be public about
my lesbianism until my case was won, or lost.[3] My son's support
was instantaneous, as it's been in every other arena. I remember
him telling me he knew the closet must be an uncomfortable
place for someone like me, and that as soon as my political situation allowed me to come out, my children would stand

behind me.

It wasn't the first time Gregory had taken it upon himself to speak for his sisters—a habit reflecting both his own deep sense of right and a prerogative beyond his jurisdiction. My lesbianism had to be a jolt to my son, at least on some level. How he dealt with it, I may never know, except that it surely had to do with his love for me and innate sense of fairness. He and his wife stood behind me, and so did their children. They never hesitated before introducing my partner and me to their friends. They took their children to gay pride marches and spoke to them of gay culture. And the children themselves embraced us in ways that made very clear the depth of their family's acceptance.

I remember one warm fall day at the working-class beach community where Gregory and his family had taken us. By this time they had moved to Uruguay, and we were visiting them there. My oldest granddaughter was eight or nine at the time, and as she played with a friend a few feet away I saw the other little girl point to Barbara. "Who's that?" she asked. Without missing a beat, my granddaughter told her "Oh, that's my grandmother's partner."

Several years later, when the grandkids visited us, we took them on a road trip. One night, in the motel room, they lined up on the edge of the bed across from us and began: "Can we ask you some questions? You don't need to answer if you don't want to." We said sure, and they began—more than an hour of conversation about our being a couple. It was their very first question, though, that made the deepest impression on me: "How did you have the **courage** to come out?" I can't even remember which of the three asked it.

My daughter Sarah lives in Mexico. She came to visit and I wasted no time in coming out to her. The half hour ride from the airport home would be our opportunity to talk before I introduced her to my partner. Sarah was silent for several minutes. She stared straight ahead at the road unfolding before us as we approached the mountains. Finally she said something about needing time to adjust. That she **would** adjust didn't seem to be at issue.

During that visit Sarah asked to be taken to places and events where she could experience the gay community. We went to a softball game and a bar. At the latter a very butch young woman in a tux asked her out onto the dance floor, once and then again. I watched her following the woman's lead. She seemed more amused than anything else, but also as if she were having a good time.

Over the years, Sarah has gotten a bit more, but never completely, comfortable with her lesbian mother. A few years after I assumed my lesbian identity she, and a husband who is now her ex, planned their wedding at a time when Barbara and I would be able to attend—then asked us not to be out at the event itself. We agreed, thinking to give her what she needed on her day. It was a mistake I won't repeat. Since then we've all grown older and wiser. I don't believe that particular charade is anything Sarah would ask of me again. Certainly it is not something to which I would agree.

At first my daughter Ximena had the most difficulty with my changed sexual identity. She also lived in Mexico, and a lesbian acquaintance—her best friend's sister—had recently committed suicide in the isolation of that country's particular brand of homophobic oppression. Ximena told me she loved me, supported every part of who I am, but also had some problems with my new identity. She asked if we could go together to see a therapist, and insisted he be Hispanic (Spanish-speaking), male, and heterosexual.

I found such a professional here in Albuquerque, and made an appointment. Ximena brought her list of questions: Where you and my father in love when I was born? Did you ever really love any of the men you were with? Does your new identity change the way you feel about me? Does your being a lesbian mean I will be a lesbian one day? Roberto—this was the therapist's name—listened and responded. But mostly he made it possible for Ximena to express her fears in an environment that felt neutral and safe. Gradually, this daughter was able to share this new fact of her mother's life with her own circle of friends, and found among them those with the lesbian sister or the gay uncle—in other words, an acceptance she didn't expect. My partner is closer to her than to any of my other children. Ximena's husband may be the single family member who is least innately homophobic.

If Ximena initially had the most difficulty in accepting my new sexuality, her younger sister Ana had what seemed to be the least. Ana was living in New York City when I came out. Gayness was an accepted fact of life, and the several circles in which she moved were also particularly sophisticated in this respect. On the other hand, she was still in her teens and still wanted a "normal" mother in ways her siblings no longer did.

There is a scene etched behind my eyes. Ana, living with me at the time, had gone out to California to see a man with whom she was involved. When she came home a few days later it was no longer just the two of us; my life partner had moved in and she had to adjust to sharing me with her. One night I entered the living room to see Ana and Barbara faced off on the couch. Ana was shouting at Barbara, who was looking at her in stunned silence. "I hate you," Ana was screaming, "and I know it has nothing to do with you being a woman. It would be the same if you were a man. I just want my mother back!"

Since that dramatic moment Ana has grown up, she and Barbara have become good friends, and my youngest daughter has given many examples of the depth of her respect for our shared lives. At their wedding, she and her husband made sure we both occupied our legitimate places in the weekend-long celebration. Barbara was asked to design and produce the invitations, and later to fashion the place cards for the wedding dinner. Like my ex-husband and his wife, we each took our place at the head and foot of one of the long dining tables.

I believe my children and their children now live comfortably with the fact that their mother/grandmother is a lesbian. Or as comfortably as is possible in a world still rife with homophobia. As a couple, Barbara and I feel easy in my children's homes. Indeed my mother, brother, sister, children, daughter- and sons-in-law and grandchildren are, for Barbara, the people she considers family. What we leave to this world will be theirs. They will succeed us.

But I have been speaking here as if coming out as a lesbian was the most natural thing in the world. I have talked about my family's responses as if my own transition was utterly unproblematic. As a matter of fact, it did feel pretty smooth. But one cannot live in a homophobic society without internalizing some degree of homophobia, however minimal. It is like racism. To be born white in a racist society inevitably carries with it its dose of racist conditioning. As I write this, it occurs to me that for quite a few years one way I displayed my own unconscious discomfort with being a lesbian was by making sure to mention that I was also a mother.

Shamelessly, I used the fact that I have children to make myself appear more normal in society's eyes! A lesbian, well yes, but a lesbian with children after all—and so perhaps a more acceptable woman. I honestly don't believe I was conscious of this internalized homophobia until I began to think of my life as a lesbian mother in the context of writing these pages.

Little did I imagine that I was using my own condition as a mother to make my lesbianism more acceptable—an embar-

rassing twist to the oxymoron! But writing without self-examination isn't much worth the effort. We learn about the world
from what we are able to learn about ourselves.

Am I a different sort of mother now that I am an out lesbian? Perhaps. I am different in that I am happier, more true to
myself, more fully who I was meant to be. That's always good for
any psyche, and conducive to becoming a better human. I am
more centered, more alive. And that, along with all the other
aspects of the woman into whom I am maturing, must affect
who I am to each of my children and grandchildren.

As awkward as my lesbianism may be for some of my children or grandchildren, I believe that it also enriches their lives.
Knowing the Other—in one's own family—after all, deepens
the human experience.

Paradoxically, I believe that my lesbianism also makes me
easier with men. In our deeply heterosexist society, a woman's
relationship to men and to a particular man is too often sexually charged, the aura of sexual intimacy—conquest and submission—either alluringly present or something to be consciously
avoided. This socially constructed aura has been lifted from my
life. Now I am freer to follow my natural instincts in cherishing
the male friendships I have.

Openly assuming a condition much of society scorns, provides a sort of balance to one's life. The important things
become more important. Trivialities can more easily be discarded. Chance encounters tend to cut to the chase. A lot of the
irrelevant details are set aside. As with other life commitments—to feminism, anti-racism, humanism, peace and social
justice—one more part of who one is falls solidly into place. It's
like finding an important piece of the puzzle and putting it
where it belongs.

And here let me say, for the record, that I am not for indis-
criminate outing. I respect each individual's decision to be out

or not; there are job, family, and political considerations that
can stand in the way (one of which I myself lived through for a
while). But being out carries with it the enormous privilege of
being of an oppressed group. This not only allows one to join a
particular struggle against intolerance and bigotry, but makes it
possible to identify with other oppressed peoples as well. I can
think of no other condition more useful to recognizing the
urgent need to create understanding and shun hatred. Society
needs such recognition, acted upon by every person every day.
The personal as political is no longer a slogan, then, but a way
of life.

We live in a time of hypocrisy. Our president and other
public officials lie and deceive, yet we continue trying to teach
our children to tell the truth. U.S. foreign policy is said to be
based on other countries' respect for human rights, except when
our national greed is fed by looking the other way.[4] Democracy
is advertised as American as apple pie, yet everyone understands
that those who govern us consistently get where they are by
virtue of political connections and the vast sums of money
spent on their campaigns. Young people become desensitized to
violence—indeed they become experts at it—by playing video
games where he who kills the most wins. Yet we are surprised
when these same young people use real killing rampages to
assuage their isolation and despair.[5] In the more personal
sphere, the nuclear family—mother, father, children and dog—
remains the standard, while the vast majority of the country's
families look entirely different.

In this country more than half of heterosexual marriages
end in divorce. Growing numbers of families are headed by a
woman, who earns 67% of what a man with the same job would
earn, and often without that man's security or benefits.
Different sorts of family configurations are everywhere visible
today: single mothers with one or more small children, extend-

ed families in which grandparents and aunts have important responsibilities, and yes, lesbian mothers with or without partners. Yet the media and consumer messages aimed at the family today, continue almost exclusively to address the old mother-father-child variety—in our culture referred to as nuclear.

Whoever and wherever we are, we are surrounded with multiple examples of non-traditional families. (The term non-traditional itself is a gross misnomer. What tradition are we talking about? Do the Iroquois not have a tradition in which uncles join fathers and aunts mothers in taking responsibility for children? Are not all manner of extended families stalwarts of our heritage?) We can keep our distance, pretend that those who conform such families are not who they are, and thereby contribute to their sense of inadequacy and shame. Or we can embrace all the different families held together by love and mutual concern, thereby expanding our acceptance of as many family forms as there are people who love one another.

The human family is vast, with many different faces. Apart from insisting upon our own multiple identities, we can recognize and spend time only with those who look like us, or we can get to know the greater human family in all its diversity. The choice is ours and the latter choice is the one that gives us—and society—more. In any case, each generation pushes the line on what is acceptable. What may have shocked our grandparents will be as natural as breathing to our children's children.

We can resist change, or anticipate it. Those who take the risk are that much further ahead.

I have talked about the lesbian mother as part of one among a variety of families. But what about the lesbian mother herself, uniquely? Of course there are lesbian mothers and lesbian mothers. It matters if we are wealthy or poor. If we raise our children alone or with a partner (whose health insurance we can rarely share, social security and tax filing never). If we are black, Latino or white. If we are an enrolled member of an Indian nation, moving between traditional and white-dominated society. It matters if we struggle with a disability (beyond the fact of our lesbianism, which is generally considered a disability by society). It matters if we are young or old. Still, I would like for a moment to ponder lesbian motherhood in and of itself.

A lesbian who makes the choice to mother brings a child into a family that is free from the most obvious characteristics of patriarchy. This is not to say there are no heterosexual unions in which both woman and man struggle against the male domination in our society. Or that all lesbian partnerships escape problems of control. Or even that a single lesbian mom may not absorb the problems of authoritarianism. We all live here. We all breathe the air.

But the model is different, and that's a start. Children who grow up experiencing love and caring from women, or women who do not reflect the prescribed norm, are also more open to other deviations from that norm. They tend to accept and embrace people of other races, cultures, social or economic classes, ages, abilities. When their children reach school age, teachers and other students are also forced to look at the woman-centered home as a possible option, thus broadening their horizons as well.

Fundamentalist rejection of "the homosexual lifestyle" (as if there were only one!), beyond its roots in a rigid and ahistorical interpretation of something they have decided to call God's Will, also endorses one example over others: the narrowest and most conservative of patriarchy's faces. Man submits to God, women and children submit to man, and the family pets may be kicked around by any of the above. Homosexuals—claim these rigid interpreters of God's law—do not set a good example. And in patriarchy a woman alone, a woman who by the very way she lives her life shows that she is not dependent upon a man, is the greatest aberration there is.

The bumper sticker "Hate is not a Family Value," says it all. In a world in which it has been made legitimate to invade other countries when our government doesn't approve of their internal policies, or close down preventative social programs while increasing the budget for more security, more metal detectors, more cops here at home, we need all the respect for difference we can encourage. Not lip service or empty rhetoric, but diversity in action. A lesbian mother speaks, to the child involved, of difference. Of possibility. Of choice.

I would like to be able to say that the lesbian mother, by virtue of her lesbianism, provides an alternative to patriarchy, that she seeks other models for her children: men who are honorable and gentle, interracial couples of whatever sexual identity, healthy and loving communities. Unfortunately, this isn't always the case. We lesbian feminists tend to expect all lesbians to be feminists: a big mistake. Lesbians can be religious fundamentalists, conservatives, alcoholics, drug users, irresponsible human beings and as dysfunctional as anyone else. But when becoming a mother prods a lesbian to think about values, she may well end up espousing those of openness and honesty. The contradictions she herself experiences may encourage her to think about issues of power, authoritarianism, and injustice.

Our children and grandchildren desperately need to experiment with models beyond that of the nuclear family, which has shown itself to be so inadequate, just as they must experiment with social orders more effective than this thing we call democracy. Every day there is more violence, more horror perpetrated in the name of right, more acceptance of what even a decade or two ago would have been completely unacceptable. Rather than remain hung up on the rules invented by those who hate, isn't it time we look beyond their labels to the lives themselves?

Today's relationship questions should be: Is there mutual support? Is there prohibition of all forms of violence? Is there independent thought and analysis? Is there accountability? Is there a healthy independence? Is there kindness and encouragement for growth? Is there joy and creativity? Is there attention to what births rather than the perpetration of what kills? If these elements are present, the model—be it of a nation, a family, or an individual—is to be gratefully nourished.

CHAPTER SIX

Shame as Political Weapon

The hard sell has lost some of its effectiveness in this country today. The soft sell acquires new and more sophisticated techniques as the science of marketing impacts ever-greater demographics in our society. One among many examples is the pharmaceutical industry. Against a backdrop of seductive images, it exhorts the viewer: "Ask your doctor if such-and-such is right for you?"

The medical problem being targeted frequently goes unmentioned. This is not an oversight. Images of young-looking, happy, successful people are enough to seduce the viewer into asking their doctor to prescribe the product—whatever its purpose may be. (The excellent PBS weekly "Now With Bill Moyers" recently featured an interview with a physician who claims these techniques have ruined his relationships with his patients and his ability to treat them competently.[1])

Viewers are thus shamed into asking their doctors about products they believe will make their lives look like those portrayed on the screen. Who wants to admit to not knowing what the miracle drug is for? It's a sort of consumerist Emperor's New Clothes.

Another technique uses hired actors who attract attention on busy street corners. They prominently display a new cell phone or digital camera, sparking the interest of passersby. People notice, stop, and ask about the product. As they mention its many attributes, the actors let these strangers play around with it, try it out. Those thus entrapped believe this to be a chance encounter. They cannot guess they're talking to actors who are being paid by the product's manufacturer. Most would be surprised to learn the truth. Many would surely be ashamed to admit they'd been tricked.

The latest and perhaps most sinister device in marketing's arsenal is shame. Or maybe it's not so new. Shame has been used forever to manipulate people's emotions, attitudes, and conduct. What seems new is the crudeness with which it is being harnessed today by an interconnected system of commerce, government, media hacks, and societal peer pressure. Shame, deeply embedded in our social psyche and possessing almost limitless coercive possibilities, has become the domestic weapon of choice.

Shame is an easy manipulator in a society like ours, in which racism, sexism, heterosexism, xenophobia, and an idealization of the young and beautiful have such deep and pervasive roots. Where any sort of difference is scorned and homogeneity revered, the implication that a person is Other is often enough to provoke denial.

Oppressed groups are all too familiar with shame. It has been their lifetime companion. Women know about the emotion. We have a history of being blamed for what is done to us, no matter the circumstances.

Young girls in my pre-Sputnik generation[2] were routinely told we weren't good at math or the sciences. If we were inclined towards these disciplines—or worse, excelled at them—there was something innately wrong with us. As girls, in fact, being seen as outstanding in any subject but home economics carried its aura of discomfort. Better to let the boys prepare for careers; they'd get the jobs, and we could always hope a good marriage would mean one of them would take care of us, their devoted and supportive wives.

Girls with the talent or desire to play sports had it just as hard. "Remember to let him win" was the standard advice given the girl who played ball with the boys on the block. But the social conditioning that produced generation after generation of girls taught to subsume our intelligence, skills and ambition to the men in our lives became even more dangerous as we grew into young women.

Now we really had to serve in silence. We'd been trained not to let our boyfriends get "carried away." Men had a hard time controlling their animal instincts, we were told, and if "something happened" it would be our fault for leading them on. The varieties of social shame that burden girls as they go through school, even today, is one of the most insidious shapers of personalities.

And this double morality continued to plague us into adulthood. If we were raped it was because we asked for it, or our skirts were too short. If we married and our husbands hit us, we must have done something to deserve the abuse. For years—lifetimes, in many cases—shame kept women from reporting these crimes.

In the business world we were trained to work hard behind the scenes while letting men take credit for our efforts. They, after all, needed the raises, the job security, and (for their fragile egos) the accolades. Long after statistics showed growing numbers of women as single mothers or heads of households, educational institutions and governmental agencies continued to promote the idea that most working women were simply out there making a bit of extra pocket money.

No one has put it better than Katha Pollitt, in one of her Subject to Debate columns of 1994. It is as applicable today as it was then: "Women have been unfairly blamed for a lot of things over the years—the Fall of Man (sic), their own rapes and beatings, autistic children...But poverty? Women cause **poverty**? That is the emerging bipartisan consensus, subscribed to by players as far apart as Charles Murray and Eleanor Holmes Norton, Dan Quayle and Bill Clinton, *National Review* and *The New York Times*. All agree that unwed mothers, particularly teenagers, are the driving force behind poverty, crime and a host of other ills...To say that unwed mothers cause poverty is like saying hungry people cause famine, or sick people cause disease. Out-of-wedlock births do not explain why...corporations nationwide are laying off thousands of white-collar workers, or why one out of five college graduates are working at jobs that require no college degree. Imagine for a moment that every teenage girl in West Virginia got married before getting pregnant. How would that create jobs or raise wages? Marriage might benefit individuals (or not), but it can't bring back the coal industry. Family values didn't save the family farm, and they won't save the millions of people who have been rendered superfluous by the New World Economic Order."[3]

Feminism waged a long and tenacious process of educating the public to the lie inherent in assumptions such as these. The introduction of public school programs to encourage girls in math and science; Title IX victories[4] and the role models provided by outstanding women athletes; better sex education, rape crisis centers and battered women's shelters that work to highlight and discredit violence against women; and the few women who have managed to enter the all-male clubs and break through the corporate glass ceiling have changed the landscape of all women's lives.

But the old ingrained attitudes die hard. It is still far too common to witness a woman who has accomplished something important, or offered a good idea, retreat in shame; or to hear her say: "Oh, I'm so sorry," after an incident that clearly was not her fault.

Shame, it seems, is here to stay.

Women aren't its only victims. How often do we hear

someone claim that the poor are poor because they're lazy—not because they have had less education or opportunities? And how many who are poor internalize this assumption, resigning themselves to lethargy—giving up—because the assumption that they cannot or will not proves too overwhelming to buck?

Similar traps can be deconstructed—each with its own cultural particularities—for minorities, the aged, children, the differently-abled or any other group outside the mainstream. African Americans (or Native Americans or Latinos) have no ambition. Gay men are flamboyant and frivolous. Lesbians just need a good man. Talking about instead of directly to an elderly person is, sadly, commonplace.

Internalized shame is an insidious byproduct of public ignorance, and discriminatory attitudes and practices.

No wonder, then, that in the current crisis both corporate and governmental America have found ways to put shame to work for them.

Particularly appalling is the way George W. Bush and company have shamed U.S. Americans into supporting every warmongering adventure and every domestic cut-back since 9/11. The tragedy provided him with the perfect context.

The method is actually quite simple. It involves using a real event (in this case, a national tragedy that understandably has taken possession of the nation's consciousness) or a popular assumption (such as the inherent weakness of women or the presumed laziness of the poor, etc.) as an armature upon which coercive manipulation can be constructed. A supposed corrective is put forward, forcefully and with great conviction.

For example, the way to stop international terrorism is to hunt down and bring to justice (read: kill) every terrorist in the world. To this end we must go to war and then go to war again, invading and murdering the millions of innocent people among whom our leaders claim these terrorists are hiding. The immense amount of money needed to carry out these military operations necessarily means cutbacks here at home: we must sacrifice the social programs, public education, healthcare, roads and other infrastructure our country so badly needs. And we must be willing to sacrifice some of our civil liberties as well. The war effort requires sacrifice.

To question these decisions is to display a lack of patriotism in time of war.

But who declared this war? A president who has given himself dictatorial powers. Who decided that invading Afghanistan would bring down Osama bin Laden? Who, in fact, judged Osama bin Laden responsible for the 9/11 tragedy? Certainly no public debate, based on an analysis of facts. Even in Congress fear of being considered unpatriotic and concern over reelection silenced any meaningful dissent.[5]

Facts barely enter into the equation; hard as they are to come by in a system of information quite obviously controlled by official interests. We must trust our leaders, we are told. And we are shamed into doing so.

Immediately following 9/11, my mother faced an interesting dilemma. She resides in a senior citizens' community, in which individual apartments line halls on six floors.

"Everyone has a flag on their door," she told me one day, "I suppose I'll have to get one and put it on mine." Flag-waving doesn't reflect my mother's politics, and I asked her why she felt she had to display a flag just because many of her neighbors did. (I knew not **everyone** in her building had a flag, and had to imagine it only seemed that way to her.)

My mother explained she was ashamed not to display the flag, when not doing so would so clearly place her in the minority. "What do you think your neighbors will do to you?" I asked. "Well, I suppose they won't do anything" was her hesitant response. Yet she remained anxious and unsettled. "This mass flag-waving is coercive," I insisted, "a way of bringing people into line behind policies we don't agree with. Why don't you fly the United Nations flag, or some other symbol of world unity and peace?"

Mom liked the idea, and remembered she had an image of a peace dove on a small banner she'd acquired somewhere. She put it on her door. None of her neighbors said a word. One cannot know if the stand she took induced anyone in her community to think about symbols, much less question their meanings. Still, with a bit of help my mother was able to shed the shame inherent in rejecting this national dictum to fly the flag—clear evidence of support for the president's policies.

This incident reminds me of a passage in Gerda Lerner's beautiful autobiography, *Fireweed*. Lerner, an Austrian Jew, describes life in Vienna during the rise of fascism. "Seeing the swastikas everywhere" she writes, "—in the lapels of pedestrians, in the shop windows, on the flags flying from all the houses—you felt disembodied, emptied of yourself. This was before the obligatory wearing of the Jewish star, but an absence is as strong a sign as a presence. People glanced at you as you passed by and they noticed the **absence**, the swastika that was not there, the sign not carried before you as protection, and they knew. You were not one of them; you were the Other."[6]

I wondered if my mother feared that by not displaying the flag she would be marked in this way. Perhaps she also feared what the outcome of such marking might be. Fortunately, we live in a country where some measure of freedom remains. But concentration camps were once built here, during the years of anti-Communist hysteria, for people who opposed the red-baiting policies of those times. That these camps were not used is not of much comfort. As we know, Japanese and Japanese Americans were forced into camps for several years, for the only crime of having an ancestral connection to a country with which we were at war. (It's interesting, and smacks of the racism in our society, that German Americans weren't put in camps. Japanese Americans suffered the shame of a presumed identification with the enemy, and also because of the color of their skin.)

I don't believe it is alarmist to fear a repeat of such history. Today in the United States a clever administration has managed to shame an entire population into accepting policies that fly in the face of international law and go against our own best interests. By proclaiming an Axis of Evil, Bush has imposed a list of enemies to be eliminated. At this writing, polls (undoubtedly also biased to favor those who support the administration's policies) show a 70% approval rating for the president's handling of the war. Attorney General John Ashcroft has been busy defining categories of enemies here at home.

Ashcroft, a fundamentalist Christian, holds thousands of uncharged Arabs and Arab Americans in a closed prison system, and protest is so far limited to civil rights lawyers and a few others. A spy on your neighbor program, reminiscent of the worst of McCarthyism, has been launched. There is some outcry, but mostly people are willing and eager to participate.[7] Shame—at not being thought patriotic, or not supporting the president in a time of war—seems to be working wonders once again.

The current economic crisis is another arena in which shame has become a powerful motivator.

Corporate America, finally having stressed beyond endurance the seams that have held it together—the special laws, gentleman's agreements and eyes cast in the other direction that have kept it from imploding before now—seems to be coming apart. Is it just a few greedy companies (as corporate America would like us to believe) or a system coming undone? Will corporate capitalism have enough tricks up its sleeve to be able to fix the crisis?

The white-collar criminals have no apparent intention of desisting from their monstrous moneymaking schemes. We watch as one conglomerate after another is forced under by the disgusting (though far from shocking) spectacle of cooked books, CEO dishonesty, elaborate sleight-of-hand schemes, off-shore incorporation to avoid paying taxes, and other legal loop-holes afforded the wealthy and powerful. Tens of thousands of people lose their jobs, their retirement, their health coverage, their children's college funds. Shareholders lose their invest-ments. Overall market losses affect even—or especially—the small investor: the worker who has saved for years in order to augment a meager Social Security check, the parent who is growing his or her child's college fund.

Crooked CEOs aren't going to rehire the hundreds of thousands they've let go, or give back the billions they've stolen from pension funds and investors. Disgraced corporate figures continue to reap the benefits of obscene salaries, bonuses and stock options. They continue to enjoy their city mansions and chalets in Vail.

Who is supposed to fix this? The American people, of course. All the administration need do is shame the public into spending more money. "Increase consumer confidence" has become the mantra. And by showing consumer confidence we show our patriotism as well.

This is, after all, what we've been taught to do. Responsible money-management, it's called. Brokers and finan-cial planners earn three-digit salaries advising their clients to buy, sell, diversify. George W. Bush, when still candidate to the presidency, made his case for taking some of the responsibility for Social Security off the government's shoulders and giving it to the private investor. "It is the people's money," Bush intoned, "we trust them to invest it wisely." Since the corporate crisis, he's stopped talking this line.

Bush, Cheney and other government luminaries have their own histories of participation in the sorts of schemes that have surfaced: devious business practices, elaborate strategies designed to hide losses and show unreal gains, suspicious sales of large quantities of stock just before that stock plummets. The administration assures the public that such practices will not go unpunished. Yet the culprits in power are able to hide behind simple refusals to testify or make their records public. The laws they propose to keep other corporate criminals in line add up to little more than photo ops of a few unlucky scapegoats in handcuffs, and the suggestion that if and when they do serve a bit of prison time they might want to think twice about bringing their golf shoes.

U.S. political rhetoric has the unique ability to be able to humiliate even as it shames.

Even if a few of these white collar crooks do serve time, and given voter outcry it seems likely they will, they will do it in federal prisons that are clean and airy, sleep in dormitories rather than crowded cells, enjoy tennis courts and unlimited communication with the outside world. No gang-rapes for these men. After serving brief sentences, they will most likely return to the world of high finance—with a deeper resolve to cover the paper trails.

Ordinary citizens can (and frequently do) go to prison for stealing the contents of a convenience store cash register or writing a bad check. In numbers two to three times their percentages in the general population, African American, Native American, Hispanic, Latino and other minorities do more time under worse conditions than their white brothers and sisters. Three percent of the total U.S. population is incarcerated now, the highest percentage of any country in the world.[8]

Punishment for those whose crimes fit the corporate model cannot be compared with the punishment suffered by petty criminals—in length of time served, prison conditions, or the impact upon the prisoners' future lives. No matter that this latter group is responsible for tens of thousands of their fellow citizens losing jobs, careers, retirement, hope; while their counterparts in the ordinary criminal population may have burglarized a single home or stolen the contents of a lone cash drawer. Class and culture speak with the master's voice.

And so does shame.

The above is typical of life in our country today. It has become an acceptable feature of our national culture. How far corporate crime is allowed to go, and how many of those guilty will be brought to some sort of justice, remains to be seen. To the extent that segments of the voting public protest the obvious injustice, there is always some impetus for the politicians to push for a few cosmetic changes.

What interests me, in all this, is the use of shame as political weapon, the way in which corporate capitalism has succeeded in getting the average American to believe that this crisis is our fault. Or, conversely, that we have the power to turn things around.[9] Through a clever perversion of language, the media's unwillingness to question government lies and half-truths, and the administration's post 9/11 ability to equate supporting official policy with patriotism in time of war, people are coerced into believing that by increasing their consumer confidence—investing in a failing market, spending more money and buying more goods—they will show faith in the system and fix the economy.

It is up to us, we are told. We must show that we still have confidence in the American Way, regardless of how blatantly the American Way has let us down.

At the very least this is a crude misplacement of responsibility.

"If consumers tighten their purses, a second recession becomes more likely," declared The New York Times in a front-page article headlined "Stagnant Wages Pose Added Risks to

Weak Economy."[10] This is the sort of doublespeak that passes for analysis these days, even in the nation's most respected media. The referenced article explains that "Although the recession has ended, the wages of more than 100 million workers are still stagnant..." What recession? When and by whom was it declared? And when did it end? Yet without ever having officially acknowledged a first recession, we are now being told that if we don't spend more freely, a second is likely.

This is reminiscent of the reasoning put forth when preparing for and launching all those undeclared wars. Not to mention that with diminished or nonexistent wages it's awfully hard to consume.

Still, the exhortation repeats itself across every television screen and many times throughout an evening's viewing. It is up to us to save the day: the ordinary man and woman with neither the power to curb corporate malfeasance nor the clout to punish corporate criminals. We've got to consume, to spend, to show our confidence in these elected (?) officials and blood-letting corporations, or our economy will fall apart.

Bush has introduced a new element into this exhortation to spend, this claim that by showing consumer confidence we will save the economy in this difficult time.

The additional element is patriotism. By spending we can show that we love our country, hate terrorism, and are doing our part to save democracy. No matter that if we have been downsized, robbed of our pensions and children's education funds, and must pay our own health insurance, it's hard to come by either the confidence or the money.

The billions taken from us by corporate criminals and the cash ordinary citizens are expected to cough up are linked in this rhetoric although their real connection has been painted over. Its connection has been erased by power politics, then reestablished by the governmental doublespeak that has become the language of our times. In this way, we are induced to speak of our own lives in ways that bear them no relation.

Save democracy by destroying democracy. Preserve freedom by relinquishing freedoms. Protect the environment by poisoning the environment. Avoid nation building by invading nations. Fight terrorism by becoming the world's most powerful terrorist.

When will U.S. Americans stand up and refuse to be talked to as if we cannot see through the doublespeak? When will we see through the doublespeak? When will we reestablish the connection between the billions robbed and the billions we are being urged so confidently to spend? When will we refuse to shoulder the responsibility for situations that those we have elected to represent us are unwilling to shoulder themselves?

The best way to achieve responsible leadership is to replace the criminals who rule us with men and women who remember what democracy is supposed to mean. A difficult task, given what our electoral process has become. But perhaps not entirely impossible. First, though, we must unmask the psychobabble by which we are being manipulated.

The use of shame as political weapon is at the core of this psychobabble.

Shaming people into believing that the solution to a foundering economy will come through increased consumer confidence, is not unlike the rapist or batterer shaming his victim into believing that she is to blame for what he is doing to her. Or the shame we heap upon the poor and homeless so they will believe their situation is a result of their own inadequacy, laziness or lack of ambition.

Feminists have spent years educating the public to stop blaming the victim. Now we need similar mass education to unmask false patriotism as a stand-in for debate and analysis, false shame as the weapon of choice that encourages us to comply with criminal policies rather than to think and feel for ourselves.

CHAPTER SEVEN

Doublespeak and Doublehear,

Anita Hill in Our lives[1]

From October 12 through 15, 1991, millions of women in the United States were riveted to our television sets or radios. Many men watched too, and some women and men who follow political events more closely were engaged even earlier by what was happening. But from the 12th through the 15th a process unfolded in the U.S. mass media that held particular impact for women. An African American law professor named Anita Hill sat before a panel of fourteen white male senators and defended her accusations of sexual misconduct against a poorly qualified conservative black male who President George Bush had nominated to become an associate justice of the United States Supreme Court.

There was much that was noteworthy in both the events themselves and the process behind them. Presidents Reagan and Bush had been nominating a succession of conservatives to the High Court as part of their overall program of pushing back class, race and gender gains, First Amendment guarantees and worker's rights—all won since the 1960s. As the last of the constitutional justices grew old and retired, these presidents had been successful at stacking the court in favor of their neo-conservative agendas. Sometimes they miscalculated, as in the case of Robert Bork. That people's victory showed the need for minor concessions in order to present an impeccable mask behind which fundamentalist ideology could wait, ready to spring into action.

Clarence Thomas, a black man who was born and raised in Pinpoint, Georgia and had worked his way up the American ladder to graduate from Yale Law School, was ideal. Only 43, his tenure on the Court promised decades of anti-democratic, anti-working class, anti-minority, and anti-woman decisions.

Sometime during Thomas's senate confirmation hearings his opponents got wind of rumors that he had sexually harassed one or more women who'd worked for him at the Department of Education and the Equal Opportunities Commission. The name Anita Hill was mentioned, and senate staffers tracked her down at the University of Oklahoma Law School where she taught. It took a number of phone conversations to convince Professor Hill to come forward with her story. An FBI investigation had been conducted during the all-senate hearings, but the senators obviously hadn't paid much attention to the charges. After all, they'd been made by a black woman. One wonders how this part of the history might have played itself out had it been a white woman charging a black man with sexual misconduct of the type described in detail by Hill.

But some unknown someone—a member of the senate judiciary committee or his staff—leaked the report of Hill's charges to the press. Leaks are common on Capitol Hill. How much was made of this one was undoubtedly due to people from one party being eager to get something on those from the other, with perhaps a bit of real concern thrown in. The threatened scandal put pressure on Congress to hear the accusations. In the midst of the usual ruckus about who leaked the information (government is almost always more concerned about **how** things happen than what happens), the judiciary committee decided to hold special public hearings so they could air Anita Hill's story.

During the public hearings, and especially when Thomas himself was given the opportunity of answering Hill's charges, the administration used race as a political ploy to try to mask or divert the gender issue. The very nomination of a man with such a poor legal background but who was black, had been a political rather than a legal choice. But then Thomas, in a posture as unbefitting a judge as it was possible to assume, refused to hear or address the charges against him. Instead, he relied on the effect of loaded images such as "high-tech lynching" and the discriminatory implications implicit in references to the sexual characteristics of black males. This move was designed to shame and subdue those white men questioning him. As a result, for the purpose of the hearings and in spite of some extraordinarily credible character witnesses, Anita Hill's allegations were defeated as they were uttered. Nothing would now prevent Thomas from sitting on the Court.

Here was a soon-to-be-confirmed Supreme Court justice being afforded the deference that would have been his had he already been confirmed. Had Hill given in to emotion, had she raised her voice or responded angrily to any one of the committee's patronizing taunts, or had she in any other way strayed from her dignified, concise, and underplayed testimony, it would have been over even sooner. She would certainly have been labeled strident, hysterical, even crazy. She handled herself with admirable restraint, yet she was defeated before she began to speak. That is, if one sees winning or losing as exclusively circumscribed to the Thomas nomination.

Important as that nomination was, Hill's testimony goes far beyond it. The reason so many millions of women sat mesmerized before our television sets that weekend in October of 1991, the reason many of us tuned our radios in as we drove back and forth from work and even sat in parking lots—unable to tear ourselves from this woman's story—was that she was speaking for us. Her voice was our voice. Her story is one that belongs to the vast majority of working women in this and most other countries of the world.

And if we look at the larger picture—not only sexual harassment on the job, but sexual abuse in all its forms—we know that Anita Hill's experience and her telling of that experience belong to women everywhere. They belong to all those—female or male—who are rendered vulnerable by virtue of subservient positions within the patriarchy: a system supported and strengthened by a capitalist economy, imperialist expansion, classism, racism, sexism, homophobia, and colonialism outside and within our borders.

An African American woman, a devout Christian and political conservative, well educated, unmarried, with her proud parents standing beside her, a woman who had also been born into poverty, one of 13 sisters and brothers, Hill graduated from the same Yale Law School attended by Thomas. She worked for him at two different government agencies, and then went on to a tenured law professorship at a major university.

Hill had nothing personal to gain and much to lose by breaking 10 years of silence about what she had suffered in Thomas's employ. But she decided to tell the story so many of us have been forced to swallow in silence. We who have lived through our own versions of her experience heard her loud and clear. We who have been sexually harassed, used and abused, and were afraid to speak in order to keep jobs, incomes, children, status or dignity, had no trouble relating to what she said.

Anita Hill spoke for us: we who have spoken and were not believed. We who have not spoken because we **knew** we would not be believed. We who knew that if we told our terrible secret we would gain nothing and lose what little we had.

In the end, Anita Hill was not believed either, at least by the white males with the power to confirm Clarence Thomas's nomination. But her words were not spoken in vain. Unacceptable as was the prospect of Clarence Thomas on the bench, there is a larger picture that has to do with the prevalence of sexual harassment and woman abuse at every level of our national life.

Anita Hill's testimony brought this hidden but ever-present reality into public view. This is why we were mesmerized by her testimony. Through the doublespeak of congressional jargon, through the committee rules and all their officious interpretations, through the indignities suffered by Hill as opposed to the respect afforded the man she accused, the courage of her lonely voice still sounds.

Doublespeak is an interesting phenomenon. George Orwell (1903-50) coined the word to refer to a language that appears to be the opposite of what it is. Mass media relies heavily on this device. Technology provides new ways to ensure that language serves the interests of those in power. It was no accident that Anita Hill's testimony was scheduled during daytime television, when only five millions viewers tune in, and Clarence Thomas's was broadcast at night when it would be seen by 30 million.

But when an experience is shared by a large enough number of people, and when some of them have been courageous enough to break the silence, doublespeak may come up against a kind of doublehear. For it is absolutely clear that those looking and listening during that weekend **heard** two different stories. Those who have experienced and so understand the reality of sexual oppression, heard one. Those who have sufficiently internalized patriarchal values heard another. This is one of the things we mean by the gender gap.

Those who lack the experience and thus the knowledge, who protect themselves when they claim that sexual harassment is infrequent or must be **proved**, were suspicious of Hill's words. Why, a man who would do such things would be in a mental institution, wouldn't he? She must be doing this for personal reasons, probably put up to it by one of those feminist special interest groups. Or maybe she wants to write a book. The "experts" spoke of fantasy, faulty memory, and a woman spurned. A judge wouldn't lie, would he?

But those who have shared the experience heard Hill's words quite differently. We were listening to something we knew to be true. As one of Hill's witnesses, Ellen Wells, so eloquently responded when questioned as to why she thought Hill hadn't documented what Thomas had said to her: You don't have to write it down, Senator. It's etched in your body forever. You only wish you could forget.[2]

We have all been wronged in the person of Anita Hill. Black women, faced with a false choice between race and gender, suffered the most. All women who carry in our bodies a memory of sexual harassment and how it is protected under patriarchy, have been publicly denigrated; once more the power of the male hierarchy has won out. And the American public has what the first Bush administration foisted upon us: a Supreme Court stacked against everyone's best interests.

Nevertheless, Anita Hill's voice is a part of our process now. It sounds with all the voices raised at great personal risk, with courage, in ever widening circles of reclaimed power, by women and men no longer willing to allow the perpetrators to go unchallenged. We tell our single stories and we tell a collective one—of minds and bodies damaged by abuse, un-redressed grievances, travesties no longer willing to be silenced. Increasingly, our story is also about the healing and reclaimed energy unleashed by our ability to speak.

Those few who spoke out before Anita Hill contributed in tangible ways to her ability to go public. She in turn strengthened the resolve of many who have spoken out since. We give

and take courage from one another. In our individual and collective refusal to suffer in silence, we make it easier for those on
down the line to speak out as well.

Together we create a safe space where we may call abuse
by its name, identify our abusers and demand accountability.
When our rage speaks louder than a status quo that would protect the abuser, our lives and our children's lives become healthier, freer and more creative. We are blessed with the dignity of
all our memories retrieved.[3]

CHAPTER EIGHT

Where Do
They Stand?[1]

During the last two months of 2000 the world watched as the Republicans shamelessly stole the presidential election and the Democrats, showing more "sportsmanship" than intelligence, spun the event as democracy at work. The U.S. electorate had fragmented along seemingly irreconcilable lines.

Two to four percent voted for Ralph Nader, unmindful of the damage a Bush win would thrust not just upon the next four years but much farther into our future—or perhaps still convinced that another Bush administration would hasten and/or strengthen the struggle for change. Forty-eight percent voted for Bush, hoping for a legal win but confident that in the event such a win wasn't possible, good ole boy backroom conniving would give them the election—which is precisely what happened. And forty-nine percent voted for Gore, hoping the majority showing would put their man in office and, if it didn't, looking to patience and fairness to preserve their image. Neither patience nor fairness came through for them, but the sad stance still seems to be: show you are an honorable loser and you will be redeemed.

Twelve members of the House of Representative's Black Caucus, reflecting a much larger sense of outrage in the numerous communities that knew we had been snowballed, stood up in Congress to protest an acceptance of this unlawful electoral college vote. Their rage was palpable, their position clear. And for the first time since this whole sorry chapter in American history began, I felt represented—if only for a few brief moments.

Represented by 12 articulate black legislators. I am white. Yet I sat before my television, heart pounding in identification with this gesture and then, immediately, amazed and once again outraged that no one—not a single senator: African American, Latino, Asian American, Caucasian, woman or man—could bring her- or himself to sign onto that protest. One would have been enough; if not to make a tangible difference, at least for my sense of self. One senatorial adhesion, by U.S. congressional rules, would have placed the whole obscene mockery in question.

It didn't happen. Business as usual. Al Gore, in one of his last acts as head of the Senate, took yet another opportunity to show his good sportsmanship by smiling patronizingly and urging the body to order. One wonders if this attitude continues to bring admiration from his colleagues or whether many of them, like much of America, sees him now as the low-key, wishy-washy, middle of the road and vacuous contender he'd been all along.

But my concern is not Al Gore. I am haunted by the fact that not a single senator signed onto the black caucus protest. Does one have to be black to feel outraged by a stolen election? Who stood with those Jewish retirees in Florida's Palm Beach county, who sure as hell didn't vote overwhelmingly for Buchanan? Who stood with the thousands of other Floridians whose votes were annulled? Who stood with the hundreds of thousands of voters throughout our self-proclaimed democracy, whose votes have long been ignored, thrown out, mishandled or wrongly tallied? Who will stand up—now that this electoral debacle has received both the U.S. Supreme Court and Congress' seal of approval—and protest our democracy's democratic failure?

Obviously, no one.

Some columnists and editorialists—even some in the corporate media—exercised their freedom of speech by pointing out the various anomalies of this election. Protesting a point of order or some other detail, rather than the stolen election itself, showed modest concern without risking the bad publicity (or worse) of visible outrage.

Tens of thousands made our voices heard as we protested the inauguration on January 20th. For years to come, scholarly theses and popular books will be written about this most blatant of stolen presidencies. But not a single white senator (there are no black senators) was willing to trade an ounce of Washington clout for a pound of dignity.

I am intrigued by the blatant racism that prevents 100 white senators from siding with their black congressional colleagues. A few days after the sham, in a related incident of far less import but which is nonetheless analogous, I commented to a friend on a local restaurant's refusal to hire gay and lesbian staff. "Let's not eat there then," my friend said, "I wouldn't want you to compromise your principles." "Why are they only my principles," I replied, "shouldn't they also be yours, and those of anyone who rejects homophobia?" Are we still so mired in racism, sexism, homophobia and other forms of social fear, that we cannot automatically—without thinking twice—stand with all victims of injustice?

I understand that conventional social psychology trains us to position ourselves as close as possible to the circles of power. This is how we grasp whatever crumbs of privilege may trickle our way. If we stand with an oppressed group, we are likely to share some measure of its oppression. Rhetoric aside, conformity is the safe place to be. As long as this is the case, nothing will change.

After this shameful show of cowardice in the U.S. Congress, my evening newscast offered a 15-second glimpse of the press conference given outside the hollowed hall. One of the black caucus members, a woman (the newscaster didn't bother to tell us her name), spoke forcefully into the microphone: "We will never, **never** forget this," she said.

I hope some of the rest of us won't either. And that we will find ways to do something about it.

CHAPTER NINE

Those Women Who Row the River

Imagine walls of massive rock, where 250 million years disappear without a trace into something called The Great Unconformity. Think of a river named the Colorado, for the deep brown red of her waters before men built a dam to harness her course. Learn that this section of river now issues from under Glen Canyon Dam, keeping a steady 48 degrees in stark contrast with July's 100-plus heat.

Two hundred eighty-seven miles of river flow between these canyon walls, building in height and drama. Here light moves across shadow, and shadow cuts back through light. Deep in the Inner Gorge, billions of years of polished black schist are infused with stripes of pink granite, and these glisten richly in the midday sun.

Sturdy Tapeats. Muav, Kaibab, Toroweap and Redwall limestones. Coconino sandstone. Bright Angel shale. Uplifts and faults. Sedimentary buildup. Volcanic movement. Erosion by wind, water and time. Dazzling golds, multi-hued reds, enveloping purples and browns. Grand Canyon, where the Colorado parts its series of rock strata, is a geological event that touches the most vulnerable places of the human spirit while resisting the vocabulary we invent to speak its name.

River runners talk about what these waters mean to them. There's this river—they begin—this fury cutting through the southwestern United States. This rush of sometimes green sometimes red-brown water and sediment, calm current and pulsing hydraulics, boils and swirls and sudden crashing waves.

Politicians, developers and engineers have never been able to conquer her—though not for lack of trying. The dam, of course, affects her movement and levels. But the river, with her surprises, survives. The place bends time and space, is ancient and new, and we—if we watch, if we listen—may find ourselves renewed in her arms.

This is a story about the women who row this river in a world of men. Nine women in particular, who rowed in the summer of 1997, for twenty passengers—also women. I am one of the passengers. We have come from different places with varying expectations, some seeking challenge, others quiet retreat.

Many of us are long-time friends, others meet for the first time in Flagstaff, the night before we put onto the river. At trip's end our answers for what this experience brought into our lives will differ. But there will be agreement on at least one point. Beyond individual hopes, divergent needs, first and most importantly the river will have given us ourselves.

And it is these nine boatwomen who will have made this possible: by revealing the river's mysteries, offering them in manageable pieces, explaining—never too little or too much. Empowering rather than engaging in displays of power. From their individual experiences they introduce us to this place they love, and introduce the river, who takes us all in her stride, to our shy or awestruck tracks.

These are the women who will help us not to fear her waves, who will teach us how to lie down on her clean sands, tread lightly and put one foot before another when walking her side canyons; so that we too may discover a few of her secret places. Theirs is the job of gifting: unfailingly attentive, good-naturedly patient, wise.

And we? We are writers, poets, artists, an anthropologist, a math professor, a filmmaker, a steel worker turned book

binder, a special education teacher, nurses, an investment coun-
selor, a builder of houses, a women's radio show facilitator, massage therapists, a midwife, a muralist and graphics designer.

Some of us have been here before, for others it is the first
time. All of us consider ourselves feminists, all in one way or
another are activists for justice and for peace. We come from
Albuquerque, Tucson, San Francisco, Berkeley, Syracuse,
Minneapolis, Tampa, McAllen, Hartford, and London. Mostly
women of cities, we will spend the next two and a half weeks
with the nine of whom I wish to speak. Together we will run the
Colorado through Grand Canyon.

Our trip leader, Jano, is baptizing her own dory on this
trip. It is still hard for women to get certified on this river, that
is to accumulate enough trips so they may become licensed to
carry passengers. Women row baggage rafts for years before they
get to row a passenger raft or dory. Men often show up at one of
the companies and are hired on the spot. Most women down
here work as helpers or cooks before they are hired as "boat-
men"—the gendered title still used by men and women alike.
Women row rafts, some operate motor rigs. Few row dories,
fewer still dories that belong to them.

Jano's boat is one of five sleek, 15-foot wooden beauties
taking us down river. Among those craft that navigate the
Colorado, dories most approximate the first boats known to
have completed the run: the keeled cutwater used by Major
John Wesley Powell, Nathaniel Galloway's flat bottomed
design, Norman Nevills' cataract, and the series of scows that
pioneering boatpeople have been evolving ever since.

Jano built her dory weekend after weekend, driving in to
Flagstaff from her teaching job on the Navajo reservation at
Ganado. In the construction process, this 31-year-old writer and
teacher learned to shape and lay the fiberglass decks, mold gun-
wales of pale ash, attach hardware for the hatch covers and

decipher the math that brought it all together. At long last she was able to choose the rich cranberry color that would balance the white of its hull. Like many dories, Jano's boat is named for a place gone beneath the crippling weight of development. It is the Animas, after the Animas River in Colorado, now devastated by industry and development.

At almost 50, Ote is our oldest woman at the oars. She will be rowing Dark Canyon, in its classic design a sister to the Animas. Ote is tall and lithe, sinewy of body, weathered of face. At a critical point along our way, she will give me an image I will not lose: her determination standing and straining as she manages to bring her dory back upriver and in through a fierce eddy line, just below the worst of Crystal Rapid.

At mile 98-1/2, Crystal is the Colorado's most technically difficult rapid—on the special Grand Canyon scale of one to ten, it is rated a 10+. A huge hole drops just below its glassy tongue, giant waves crash in every direction, and a treacherous rock garden separates its upper and lower sections. In her capacity as trip leader, Jano decides that Crystal is the only one of this river's 47 major rapids we passengers will not be permitted to run.

Our guides will take it on in twos, each woman bailing for her sister and then running back along the shore to repeat the process with a second boat. We will walk across the debris field which borders the rapid. The boatwomen tell us there are two eddies, and they will try to make it into the first, thereby avoiding our having to extend an already rugged hike further down river to the next.

Before attempting this feat though, they tie up their boats and climb a rise of rock to scout what they are about to navigate. One collects dry branches that another tosses into the current, to see which way they move. Then the women are ready. Quick hugs and into the boats. We passengers begin our trek.

One after another, each spot of color approaches the rapid: toy-like images far below us in the thunderous river—now visible, now disappearing beneath huge surges of spray. It is all about entering correctly. As if suspended, each dory floats for a moment on the swelling tongue, then plunges into the current.

Only Ote finds herself in position to try for shore at the first eddy. She knows how important it will be for at least one boat to pick up the more physically challenged among us. In her mind, failure is not an option. And—every leg and arm muscle taut with the effort—she makes it through. No one else comes close.

But I am going too fast. Ote's accomplishment is still far ahead of us, down river. As we put onto the river at Lee's Ferry, this moment and others of equal drama are yet to come. Now the women finish loading their boats. Jano caresses the Animas with pride. Elena, who is a public health nurse off-season, will row the Phantom. The boatwomen's artistic talents are evident on the flat sterns of all but one of the dories (Mary's Mille Crag Bend is pointed on both ends).

It is Mary, the artist and graphics designer, who painted the Ticaboo's daturas and the black Mimbres figures that dance beneath the Phantom's transom. Ote, also an artist, placed the vivid yellow and black butterfly on Dark Canyon, the exuberant bouquet of wildflowers on Animas.

Now Mary laughs as she runs her rough fingers over the cracked gray decks of the Mille Crag Bend. Like Jano's Animas, this boat belongs to her, a long-held dream. Not a week before our trip she'd gotten the phone call from Martin Litton, writer, conservationist, founder of Grand Canyon Dories. And grand old man of the Colorado.

"You want the Mille Crag?" he'd asked her, referring to his old Briggs boat, for the past eight years laying unused up at Hurricane. "Yes I do," Mary managed to sputter, caught totally by surprise. On a number of occasions she had asked her friend to sell her this boat. Now she breathes out: "How much to you want for her?"

"What, you rich or something?" the man's gruff laugh accompanied the question. And so the dory was hers. A gift. Before putting onto the river, Mary barely had time to drive up to Hurricane and retrieve her boat, make sure she was river-worthy. Any major refurbishing or repairs would have to wait until after our trip.

I have also learned that Mary's acquisition of the Mille Crag Bend has a more poignant story behind it. Two weeks before our trip, these women and their river community lost Dugald Bremner, fellow boatman and friend. Dugald died in a crazy kayak accident. It had taken four days to get his body off the northern California waterfall.

A few months before his death, Dugald—who had also been interested in buying the Mille Crag Bend—called Litton to see if he was willing to sell. When the old man refused, Dugald urged: "Well you know, Martin, you ought to do something good with that boat. It belongs on the river, not sitting around drying out." Martin must have given some thought to Dugald's words. After the younger man's death, he took his advice and gave the dory to Mary, a woman whose wisdom at the oars he has publicly praised. Mary feels it is a gift from Dugald too.

What I do not know, as we make our final preparations to put onto the river, is that we are carrying Dugald's ashes with us. Our boatwomen discuss where they will be laid to rest. Mary finally chooses the spot, and in some side canyon along the river's winding course she and Elena deposit them at the place he loved, where friends may come to visit.

The Ticaboo is being rowed by Cindell: small, wiry, a high school physical education teacher from Tucson. This is

Cindell's first time rowing a dory the length of the Colorado through Grand Canyon. She stuffs our last camp chair into the cross hatch, and my eye lights on a large arrangement of flowers resting on her dory's bow. An already fading sunflower anchors the bouquet.

This is Cindell's thirty-third birthday, someone tells me; the flowers are from her husband Roger. They usually row together. But this boatwoman—like the others—jumped at the chance to join our all-women's trip. The arrangement arrived at the dory warehouse in Flagstaff just before we were due to depart.

And this is not the extent of Roger's flare for romantic gesture. On our first night out, when we pull in at 19-1/2 Mile Camp, I notice that Ote is visibly relieved. She and Cindell are married to brothers, and Ote is the only one of our group who is in on the plan. As soon as the dories are tied up, she walks her sister-in-law one hundred yards or so to a tree at the back of the beach. From one of its branches hangs a small plastic zip-lock bag containing an elegant turquoise ring. Cindell never wears her wedding band on the river, afraid she may lose it in a flip. Her Roger, by now a few days further down river, has left this delicate replacement. We've managed to reach it before the ravens.

But we are still at the beginning of our journey. The women finish packing their boats. Stephanie and Nicole each command a large yellow rubber baggage raft; their helpers are Jenna and Denise. We make our first of many human chains to help load dry bags, sleeping kits, and other paraphernalia for 16 days of life along the river's banks. Everything that goes in must come out.

The Colorado's guides do an extraordinary job of protecting her sands and groves, side canyons and trails. More than once I have seen a boatwoman or man bend to pick up a cigarette butt or scrap of paper carelessly tossed by someone with less respect for the earth, putting it in a plastic bag to be carried out with the trip's trash.

Our life jackets are being fitted now: low and snug. They bear the names of local animals or places. Each of us will remember "Pallid Bat" or "Canyon Wren" or "Nankoweap," so these life-saving devices may remain with us and always fit as they should. We are almost ready. After Jano rounds us up for final introductions and a few last-minute safety tips, we group up four passengers and one guide to a dory and put onto the green water.

The river has been running relatively high at 27,000 cubic feet per second (cfs), issuing from under Glen Canyon Dam at a volume and speed that washes some of her rapids out and makes others larger, less predictable.

The Dam is one of man's many attempts to dominate and control the West. It was authorized by Congress in 1956, completed in 1963. Beyond erasing forever magnificent Glen Canyon, it has changed the Colorado from the raging current rowed by Powell in 1869 to the quasi-controllable river it is today. Only during the flood of 1983, when the water peaked at 92,600 cfs, did the river approximate what it must have been like before Glen Canyon dam was built.

We are finally on our way. And now the stories begin—about rock strata, sediment, water and wind: how the Canyon came to be. Stories of the ancient Basketmakers who first inhabited this place, of the Anasazi and more recent Hualapai, Havasupai, Hopi, Paiutes, and Dineh (Navajo). Stories about Powell, Stanton, and others among the early white explorers. The men who first ran this river—in scows, motor craft of various kinds, eventually rafts and dories. And the very few women linked to Canyon history.

The first women were the old-timers' wives and daughters.

Although the legends and books do not focus on them, many made enormous sacrifices for the river and shared fully in its early exploration. Then came a group of Hollywood models. Requisites were beauty and an ability to swim; they were hired by the first companies to glamorize the river's commercialization. Finally, several generations of boatwomen made their way onto the Colorado.

Georgie White was the first, a generation with a single name. For 40 years she worked as the only woman on this stretch of the Colorado, until male resistance began to crumble before female skill—and will. Then came Marilyn, Liz, Suzanne, Connie, Ellen and others: the second generation of Colorado River women. We are traveling with women of the third generation. They are still pioneers.

"Was that a rapid?" "No, just a riffle." Nervous or relieved laughter can be heard from boat to boat. "How long have you been rowing? Was it hard to break into the man's world of dories?" Our questions come, uncertain at first, the boatwomen's words also tentative, feeling us out.

Then, as the days unfold, the old stories emerge, tales told by river guides who add a bit each time they repeat a particular history or adventure, incorporating their own imagination or some newly acquired information.

There is the geology and the botany of Grand Canyon, how the same huge barrel cactus we saw on yesterday's hike can be seen in a hundred-year-old photograph made on the Stanton Expedition of 1892. There are tales of the Big-horn Sheep, the lizards and snakes and hawks and wrens. Our guides are experts in all these fields; their love for where they are taking us giving them an edge in the sharing.

And there are the human stories: what really happened to the three men on Powell's first expedition who gave up on the endeavor and walked out at what is now called Separation

Canyon? Were they murdered by Paiute Indians, as the plaque in their honor claims? Did they die of thirst and hunger somewhere along the nonexistent trails? Or were they murdered by Mormons who believed them federal agents, a version that has gained credibility with the recent surfacing of old letters? The old racist version is giving way to an acknowledgment of what really must have happened.

Then there were Glen and Bessie Hyde, honeymooners who went down river in a wooden scow in 1928. The few who saw them along the way said the trip was his idea; she was clearly unhappy, being prodded along by her publicity-seeking husband. Why was their boat discovered intact? Why were no bodies ever found?

I remember a boatman on my first river trip, back in 1995. He in turn told me about another boatman, a Grand Canyon Expeditions crew member named O'Connor Dale. It seems O'Connor and his group were sitting in a circle after dinner one night, on one of the Colorado's quiet beaches, and he was telling the Bessie and Glen Hyde story. Suddenly a woman in her eighties stood and walked to the center of the circle. "I'm Bessie Hyde," she announced.

The age was right, some of the details too. The woman was later questioned by reporters and others, but proved unwilling to reveal what had happened to Glen, or how she had walked out of Grand Canyon. Mute testimony to what can happen when a man tries to force a woman to do something she doesn't want to do. Or was it?

There are plenty of stories about Georgie White, or Georgie Clark, as she was later known. Her first experience on the Colorado included swimming a portion of it with a friend. In the mid fifties she devised a way of linking three big pontoon motor rafts—Georgie's G-rigs they were called—in order to take large numbers of people down river at a price they could afford. She was the first woman to run the Colorado commercially, and she demystified the experience, making it accessible to thousands.

But on this trip the stories that most vividly resonate within me are the ones about our own boatwomen, their ordinary and extraordinary lives. These stories are harder to come by; the women tend to talk little about their accomplishments. As we begin to know one another, though, their lives come into focus.

Each woman who has wanted to take a dory through Grand Canyon has had to row baggage or cook for these trips an average of six years before being entrusted with a boat and passengers. Ote started rowing in 1976; Elena, Mary and Jano in the 1980s. Cindell has rowed baggage for years; this is her first commercial dory experience. Of the 30 or so companies that run the Colorado, only two run dories (the rest use oar-powered or motorized rafts). Women may cook and cook and never get a boat.

Jano, Mary, Ote, Elena, and Cindell. Physically, in their personalities, age-wise, in terms of what they do off season, even insofar as temperament is concerned, these women are uniquely different one from another.

Jano is quiet, observant, a writer of short stories. With a fresh and provocative collection, she has just earned her Masters degree at Northern Arizona University. Here on the river her leadership style is strong yet collective, encouraging participation and mutual respect.

Mary is the artist; she has designed some of the company's promotional materials as well as many of the motifs we've seen throughout the community that so deeply appreciates images from this land. On our trip Mary teaches the women who are interested how to make baskets from willow and tamarisk roots. "Not bad ..." she proudly admits a Hualapai woman said of her own first attempt.

Ote, the oldest, is mother to two teenagers, and a kind of mother as well to these women who are her sisters at the oars. She knows the name of every tree and flower, speaks with pain of her Mormon childhood, dotes on her own children—her daughter will later join us for our last day and a half on the river. Ote takes out a tiny watercolor set and paints every changing Canyon light. She laughs about her early years as a hippie, but credits the river with saving her from the death of substance abuse.

Elena, the public health nurse, is currently between jobs. She is our trip's unofficial geologist and anthropologist, identifying fossils and sharing with us what little is known about the cultures that once inhabited these deltas and cliffs. Sitting in camp one evening, she will offer a provocative format for helping us to understand a time line so vast its meaning is easily lost in terms like millions or billions.

"Imagine the history of Grand Canyon as the hours in a single day," she begins. We listen as she describes the great uplifts and faults taking place between midnight and dawn. Native peoples inhabit this land during the early morning hours. Powell's expeditions arrive in the afternoon and we come along just seconds before midnight. We smile with Elena, in possession of one more piece in the puzzle.

Cindell speaks of how, when she's not teaching or rowing with her husband, she helps him in his glass blowing business. They are looking at land in the coal fields of southern Colorado, a place where the fuel for their art may be cheaper. We take to calling Cindell The Little General; despite her small physical size, her instructions issue explicit, forceful, not to be confused. It is Cindell who insists we observe five minutes of silence as the last glow disappears from a distant edge of rock. It is also she who, having donned bright green felt ears and slippers, prances among us after we make the difficult ascent to Elves Chasm.

Can women row dories? In this tradition-bound community, the question once challenged the women as well as the men. For years the answer was not the off-hand "of course" that it is today. But dory people now agree that women make up in finesse what they may lack in strength. "We learn to read the water really well. Each of us develops a style that works with our body. And then, we've had all those years of practice," Mary laughs.

Yes, these women are different but there is something unmistakable that links them. Something besides their love for the river, their deep knowledge about Grand Canyon. I listen to their stories. How Elena did her undergraduate work at Reed, then discovered the current and watched—as if in third person—as it changed the direction of her life. Even when it became clear to her that she needed a more dependable career, and she want back to school to become a nurse, she refused to give up her summers down here.

Stephanie's father gave her a Grand Canyon river trip for college graduation. She hiked in at Phantom and ended up alone in Jano's boat. "That was it," she says, with a slight smile. Stephanie's toothbrush, peeking up through a small loop on the front of her life jacket, is like some fanciful signature to her quiet but confident demeanor. Nicole and Jenna are teachers off-season; rowing, for them, seems a natural continuation of the teaching/learning process. It is Denise's first time on the river.

Cindell talks about how much she enjoys showing young people how to use their bodies; she never places her students in competition with anyone but themselves. Because of her size, she knows about physical disadvantage. Before our first major rapid she warns us she will get up on one knee, having found her own innovative way to put leverage and power behind her small solid body.

Jano and Mary I know from my experience on the Colorado two years before. Jano was leading her first dory trip then. It is with her help that I have gotten this adventure together. Our friendship has centered around her writing and my attempts to urge a sixty-year-old body into shape; we have traded mentoring and encouragement. Watching Mary handle a dory is like watching a ballet. Now, rowing her own boat she exudes a delight that extends her ready grin.

None of these details, though, reflects what makes these women seem a breed apart. No, it is the solidity of their under-lying self-confidence, the sense they embody that if you love something you just naturally go after it. And if you go after it you will do it well. No doubt is visible in these muscular arms, as they guide their boats through the water. No ostentation, either, no bravado or risk for the sake of risk. It is a confidence not easily found in my generation, and noteworthy even among much younger women. It reflects a knowledge of real power's most intimate sources.

In the course of our 16 days on the river, one of our group loses her finger-hold on the face of a vertical stone wall. She falls. Stephanie, who has been spotting for her, does not hesitate to throw herself into that fall, rolling at least ten feet and suc-cessfully protecting the woman's head.

Immediately these professionals, all of whom have had to pass a 40-hour course in wilderness medicine, do a thorough neurological evaluation to document the accident and deter-mine whether its victim will be able to continue the trip. Their watchfulness and expertise turn what could so easily have been a fatality into simply a bad scare.

All but one of the baggage rafts have run Crystal now. Two dories have sustained rock damage and will be mended by their boatwomen when we reach an accessible beach. All that remains is for that last raft to come through.

Suddenly, there it is. And then those of us watching from the rocky shore look on helplessly as it rises above the current and flips like a slip of paper in slow motion, coming down bottom-up upon the waves.

We can see Stephanie's and Nicole's bodies. One woman is clinging to the raft, the other rushes by some 100 feet before it. They are being carried through the churning rapid at more miles per hour than any of us wants to contemplate. The raft, now a lump of gray instead of its familiar yellow, careens between the rocks.

Ote's dory still bobs alone in the first of Crystal's eddies. We shout down to the boatwomen who have tied theirs up in the second eddy far below: "A flip," we yell, "there's been a flip!" "Shit," I later learn is Jano's first response, "I've got to get to those women."

With two passengers in her boat, she wastes no time pulling into the current. No one quite remembers how, but she is there as the two terrified members of her crew come hurtling towards her. She positions herself and, one after the other, pulls them into the Animas. Then she manages to grab the overturned raft and bump it to shore with her boat.

But this is only the most important part of this rescue. When a dory flips, it is easy to right. Two or three moderately strong women standing on the bottom, arching their backs and pulling on the flip line, can accomplish the task. We have been coached several times in this, have been given explicit training in how to proceed should our dory succumb to an angry wave.

When a baggage raft goes over, it's a very different story. The fully-loaded hulk of rubber is awkward and extremely difficult to return to its upright position. Now the gray mass sits defiant, our lashed-on gear hidden beneath it in the water.

More quickly than any of us could have imagined possible, we have brought the raft alongside a rocky part of the shore.

Not really a beach, but we had no choice. A few of us stand in the numbing 48-degree water to keep the wooden boats from crashing against the sharp obstructions or each other. Quickly, deftly, the boatwomen rig a series of ropes and pulleys; a rise of jagged rock affords a certain angle of maneuverability.

With more time to struggle with the rigging, twenty-some-odd women would have been enough. But a raft trip has stopped to offer assistance. With their power and ours it only takes a half hour to right the monster. Everything tied on is still there, wet but none the worse for its long soak. Relieved, we make our way a short distance further down river, where we will have lunch as the women whose dories have been damaged will pull them ashore and plug their holes.

Later that evening I ask Jano: "On a mixed trip, what would this day have been like?" "The men would have taken over," she tells me, laughing but with an edge of seriousness in her eyes. "The work would have gotten done of course. But we would have been pushed aside. That's the way it is. When there are men around, women just don't get a chance to deal with the problems that arise."

But neither is this the end of the event. Women have our own ways of handling mishap and fear. Jano gathers her crew on a secluded part of the beach, giving the two women who flipped their needed opportunity to debrief, vent, cry, be held. She makes sure they understand it was not their fault. In Grand Canyon, boats flip every day. And Crystal is one of the places where that most often happens.

A quality these boatwomen share is their deep devotion to passing it on. They aspire that each passenger not only experience Grand Canyon to its fullest, but come to know her own potential—previously unclaimed strengths, a trust in her body, new powers of observation, the ability to make connections in this harsh desert terrain.

"The one piece of advice I can give you is: go slow." That's Jano in Flagstaff the night before we depart. "Go slow. Look. Listen. Pay attention."

Like precious gifts these women give us the unequaled beauty of a magical fern-covered slot or the way out of a lifetime of vertigo. They do not offer these experiences lightly but neither do they over-dramatize them. Their job is to teach us how to acquire them for ourselves. It is not by pushing or extolling that they impart what they know, but by watching, listening, and being present—always—to offer a hand or point out a foot- or finger-hold. I master narrow ledges and challenging heights, one boatwoman in front of me, another behind—with just the right amount of gentle urging or physical support.

Not even the cooking is irrelevant. Our guides also give us the more mundane pleasures of a trip like this: delicious dinners prepared by each in turn. Perhaps starting with crackers and brie, smoked oysters, or fresh shrimp still cold from its storage below deck. There is chicken or homemade pesto or salmon steaks or beef, with plenty of veggie burgers and tofu for the vegetarians among us, or those with dietary requirements. And for a special treat, a carrot or cheesecake baked over coals in the heavy Dutch oven.

After a full day and a dinner like this, we tend to turn in early, eager to put down our sleeping mats, crawl under a light sheet and watch the now waning moon illuminate one more amazing skyline. The darkening night floods with uncountable stars, larger and brighter than the ones back home. The big dipper is always there, a familiar beacon. Shooting stars whiz by above a dark silhouette of cliffs.

Night or day, each vista is unexpected and more moving than the last: wild, filling us with the sense of our smallness as it paradoxically gives us back the memory of who we are. Gradually, we begin to come to this knowledge of self, divested of whatever baggage we've left behind.

We need less, appreciate more. Dropping into a slot canyon was a challenge we didn't think we'd meet, but did. Scaling a difficult stretch of rock another. We delight in the little bats that circle above us as we sleep, look closely at the Ringtail Cat tracks appearing at first light around our camp, marvel at the legions of tiny frogs.

The river becomes our companion, friend, source. We filter and drink its water, wash clothes in its eddies, bathe in its shocking temperature, feel its current against our skin. Many of us have taken to walking nude from water to individual campsite—those who might not have done so before as well as those for whom such casualness comes easily. Our guides, too, relax as they bathe, hug one another in strong demonstrations of friendship, enjoy the easy freedom of movement women's space provides.

We passengers are very different: Judith, Jan, and Cynthia with years of hiking experience. Brave Liz, consistently pushing herself to new limits. Jane recording light and scale on each page of her watercolor pad. Barbara building her rock stacks. Pat capturing human gesture in her portraits. Alice stopping to do Tai-Chi before a sudden waterfall. Yeshi putting herself in constant flesh contact with nature.

Pratibha has overcome her fear of water, the word "horrifying" giving way to the word "thrilling" in her lexicon. Lisa mourns her father's recent death, and begins to heal. Elana ponders the new space around her. Dorothy nurses a badly traumatized shoulder (after our trip, she learns it is fractured) even as she continues to help the rest of us. Kathleen does it all. Jennifer, at 25 the youngest among us, seeks adventure while remaining attentive to the more complex needs of those who are older or less able.

On our last night, Jaswant generously removes her turban

in order to show us how she winds it on, and what it means to her. Bobbi has fixed all equipment that was broken. Edella quietly continues to make herself available when dishes need to be washed or lunch fruits sliced. Patricia is good-natured about her badly bruised thigh. And I continue my own ongoing struggle against years of physical inactivity.

In a matter of days, the boatwomen have made it their business to see each one of us. They have learned our physical and emotional limits, and worked to help us stretch—unobtrusively, so that we do not know we are being worked with, except perhaps in retrospect.

Before the journey, one or another of us might have said we were running the Colorado for the excitement of the rapids or the beauty of the Canyon, for the opportunity to spend 16 days beside walls of rock that are at once ethereal and massive, translucent and imposing, gold orange red and deep violet in moonlight or brilliant sun. We might have said that we wanted to get away or be in nature or commune with four billion years of life.

What we didn't know was that we would be given the empowering gift of ourselves. This is what these boatwomen offer, each from her unique experience. These women who regularly spend time away from lovers and well-paid work to transport people to the center of the earth—where, if we have looked and listened, we will have found the greatest gift of all: a new belief in our untapped capacity to be and do.

CHAPTER TEN

Giving How?

We are sitting at the gate, two hours before departure. This time it's my son who is leaving, going home to his wife and three children in Montevideo. For the past week we have spent unusual time together. He came to Albuquerque, to attend a meeting in his field. It was he who had to decide who among his colleagues should go, and at first he intentionally chose someone else so as not to appear to be taking advantage of the fact that his mother also lives here. His colleagues had to insist he make the trip.

We grabbed odd moments—an early morning conversation before he climbed into his rental car and drove off down the hill, a late night dinner after a day of meetings, both of us fighting to stay awake. Then came the weekend, over much too soon. And this Monday morning farewell.

We sit beside one another, awkward, sad. He looks at me. "I have trouble buying things for myself," he admits. It is an hour and a half before they will call his flight. He is 36. We have checked one suitcase and a large box; a much-used bag, pushing the carry-on limit, sits at his feet. Gregory's comment seems casual, an obvious reference to the large amount of shopping he's managed to fit into the time we've had together, and to his inbred disdain for attending to—or even noticing—his own needs.

I remember the sparse contents of his suitcase when he'd unpacked the week before. Now he carries stair-step sizes in Polartec children's shirts, warm jackets for a season now loosening its hold so far below the equator, electronic equipment for his engineering colleagues, homemade bread. Almost nothing for himself.

If the comment is casual, its echo inside my head is not. My senses awaken as his words settle, with slow-motion intensity. I too have had trouble buying for myself, as if I didn't deserve what I want, or even what I need. Worse, I know I have gifted—especially early on—to get others to like me. If one finds it difficult to buy for oneself, could it mean one has trouble accepting love? If this is true, the love one offers must surely be suspect as well.

It's been years since Gregory and I have had the luxury of uninterrupted conversation, the special communication that once characterized his childhood and adolescence, my single motherhood, particularly before his sisters were born. Once we talked about anything and everything, finished one another's sentences, stood together against every threat.

Then came adulthood. Marriage. First child. Second. Third. And more time zones between us than fingers on a hand. There was always a grandchild who demanded—and got—his or her father's attention, always one more interruption to the continuity. Wonderful children, I wish they all lived closer and we could know one another better. Still, today my son and I lament the impossibility of meaningful conversation more than we are able to coax from letters, emails, occasional calls or yearly visits.

This has been a good one. Despite long meetings, there was time for a day trip to Bosque del Apache, the bird refuge south of Socorro. We talked against a backdrop of thousands of Sandhill Cranes trilling and beating their great wings to the rhythm of their ease of place. And our connection seemed to mirror that ease of place: each where he or she needs to be at this time in our lives, each also enjoying the company of the other. A couple of relaxing hours in a hot tub under New Mexico's night sky. Even time in the car, on our way from computer shop to Indian market, proved a fertile ground for exchange.

But when Gregory says "I have trouble buying things for myself," I recognize a sudden angst of my own, wonder how my son came to this particular denial, ponder the choices he must make as he struggles to live his life. I think of my own parents, their gifts of thousand-dollar checks alongside their annoyance if I forgot to reimburse them $3.29 for a bottle of milk and dozen eggs or their insistence on my accepting a similar amount when it was I who had run the errand for them. How anxious the contradiction always made me.

What we pass on. At this moment in my life I frequently feel myself balanced, like some tenuous bridge, between what my parents gave and took away and what I in turn give and take from my children. Will they experience this same strange balance between how I have mothered them and their own parenting?

Gregory's "I have trouble buying things for myself" elicits my glance at his dark Levis, worn almost through at the knees, awkward beneath his only suit jacket. He follows my eyes, grins. We laugh. Then: "How much does a watch like that cost?" He is looking at the Swiss Army timekeeper on my wrist. "I don't know," I try to remember, "Maybe $120. It's a great piece of machinery."

"I think I'll look for one of those; there'll be plenty of duty-free shops on my way home. I want to get Laura a watch. Hers has been broken for a year." Gregory goes on to explain that he promised his wife a gift a month, its monetary outlay equal to the amount saved on the cigarettes she no longer smokes. "It's been six months now, and I haven't made good on my promise."

To anyone listening to this conversation between my son and me, the topics would seem banal, chit-chat. But we know we are talking about important issues: value, worth, incentives, promises, how we want to treat those we love and the ghosts that often prevent us from doing so. Most of all, we are talking about a system of values. How it endures or changes from generation to generation.

I think about these values. And I think about growth. How, when we come to understand that certain behaviors hurt us and hurt those we care about, we can change our behavior simply because we want to. I think about how we make those choices, what they cost, and what they offer us in terms of relief, fulfillment.

I remember the Cuban years, after our escape from Mexico in 1969. Gregory wasn't yet nine; he would celebrate his birthday the day after my arrival. And I would travel halfway around the world to reunite with my children and the man who was then my partner.

Cuba, in the late sixties and early seventies, meant rigorous food rationing. Nothing taken for granted: one egg a week, three-quarters of a pound of meat, a pair of shoes a year. My son and I took pride in this egalitarian distribution of goods. We loved knowing our ration of potatoes or milk was the same as that consumed by someone in a remote part of the country. Our family asked for the national ration book rather than the special one enjoyed by foreigners. Participating on the voluntary brigades—to pick coffee, weed vegetables, harvest sugar cane, or wherever hands were needed—filled us with socialist pride.

Still, when friends visited the island they often left an extra pair of Levis, a half-used bottle of shampoo, a tube of toothpaste. If I knew the person and felt comfortable enough with the request, I might ask for shoes for the children, or photographic paper for myself. I remember a friend who once brought a single can of V-8 for my daughter Sarah; she was wild about the vegetable juice. Later we got wind of a complicated story: people were boycotting the company that produced the product and our friend had hesitated to cross that picket line of political correctness. In the end, imagining my child's longing, she had opted to buy and bring it down.

Another memory surfaces, another friend. We had been in Cuba for almost ten years by this time, and I hungered for my root culture of hamburgers, French fries and, yes, most desired of all, ketchup. Someone who knew about my longing visited the States and returned with a day-old semi-squished hamburger wrapped in wax paper inside her purse. It had not been discovered by customs, and reached my eager taste buds little the worse for the trip.

Much more recent images surface behind my eyes: the televised faces of children among the wandering refugees in Rwanda and Zaire. Thousands left behind when their parents were forced to flee. The desperate pleading of those children imprints itself upon our consciousness. We know that our newscasters fabricate skewed stories, the real ones often indecipherable beneath the disinformation.

Yet hunger is always simple.

What does it mean that my son and I have or do not have trouble buying things for ourselves, when dreams of equitable distribution died with socialist struggle and nothing we can do or say brings back that sense of possibility? "I love buying things for other people," he says now. Can Gregory imagine where my memory has taken me? "I get a real thrill out of getting this for this one, that for the other ..."

"I know," I agree, "but that can be problematic too." In recent years I have reexamined my persistent need to shower loved ones with gifts of all kinds. Genuine delight when eyes brighten, features break into broad smiles. And its flip side: that dull double take—too often repeated—when expectations aren't met. The friend who stops writing each time I send her pictures of her daughter. Another who cannot accept a gesture of generosity, and pulls away in response to even a small gift. The ritual of certain holidays, the giving they demand becoming more and more rote, formalistic. Feelings of emptiness as we take stock of the losses produced by giving—or its uncertain counterpart.

Last year my partner and I decided not to buy Christmas presents. Neither one of us are Christians, and we hate the way the holiday has been commercialized. Only the grandchildren would continue to be recipients of our giving. With adults in the family, the exchange had taken on a sense of increased obligation: they will give us such and such, we must reciprocate...What to buy for the person who "has everything?"

On the other hand, I have always loved crafting offerings for those I care about: a photographic print, a few lines of a special poem, the card that's just right for a particular sensibility or occasion. A meal. A call. A visit. Gregory has told me about his youngest son, how he saves allowances and money gifts, invariably spending such bounty on his sister or brother. I think of the way my father's generosity primed me to seek what is real in my own culture of giving. And how a sharpened consciousness continues to help me refine its contours with my own children and others.

An airline official picks up her hand-held mike and begins to call the flight. We stand and put our arms around one another, my son and I. His lean and eager 6'3", my 5'4" diminished by age but just as eager. For a few moments we hold one another: the greatest gift.

—Albuquerque, 1995

CHAPTER ELEVEN

What's in a Picture?

We've all seen the pictures: poster-like reproductions proudly displayed on the walls of Palestinian homes, many of those homes half destroyed by Israeli bombs. A young man's or young woman's face takes on the camera lens with calm defiance. Often the youth holds a weapon of some sort. Symbols of organized resistance alternate with writing we are unable to read. Although we may not be able to decipher the words, we know these are the images of suicide bombers, young men and more recently also young women who strap explosive devices to their bodies and go forth to detonate those devices on Israeli buses or crowded city streets.

Everything about the way in which these images are fed to us implies fanaticism: an act impossible to understand, much less condone. Along with the martyrdom, there is the loss of innocent life. Because we cherish peace, we cannot fathom this sort of act. But it is not our rejection of violence alone that prevents us from understanding. Our inbred racism and fear of cultural difference also make it easy to label the act.

We are told these young people believe their acts of martyrdom will lead them to a heavenly banquet table, to seats at the right hand of Allah, their God. But how can we know what they believe? Some may indeed hold such expectations; others may simply feel that, faced with generations of Israeli encroachment upon their lives, they have no weapon but themselves.

If we are willing to look beyond the easy headlines and biased superficial press, we will learn that only the most radical fundamentalists, those men who fly planes into buildings or are otherwise intent upon destroying whole nations, have faith in the promise of an afterlife of heavenly reward. Much as in our own Christian fundamentalism, where people believe in The Rapture—an event in which the saved will be taken to live with God and those who are not saved will be left behind—extremist beliefs exist in every one of the world's major religions. They characterize and define fundamentalism. Most committed young people who sacrifice themselves anywhere do so because they have been conditioned to believe it is "the right thing to do."

More serious and far more dangerous, the suicide bombings are being used to justify the ongoing occupation and aggression by Israel of the territories upon which Palestinians have lived for thousands of years.

Let us stop for a moment and consider some facts.

All wars claim innocent victims. The Afghan farmer and his family, blown away by a U.S. bomb, are innocent. The U.S. ground soldier, eliminated by "friendly" fire, is innocent. The Iraqi child who will not grow up because years of U.S. declared and undeclared war has starved her to death, is an innocent victim. So are the thousands of Palestinians dying while defending their land, and the hundreds of Israeli citizens who happen to be where a suicide bomber does his deadly work.

At this writing close to one thousand members of the Israeli army, some of them officers, have refused to do combat in the occupied territories. They love and are ready to defend their homeland, but are no longer willing to wage war against innocent Palestinian civilians. These men have learned from history; unlike the German soldiers during World War II, they will be able to tell their grandchildren: "Although it was difficult, although it cost us, we said no."

War **only** leaves innocent victims, which is why war will never put an end to war.

Now let us consider the issue of fanaticism. To use one's

own body as a weapon of death is a desperate, and yes perhaps also fanatical response to occupation. Is it any more fanatical, though, than sending any young person into battle, sending him or her off to murder other human beings—in the name of combating communism, keeping the world safe for democracy, preserving national security, or waging a war against terror?

Just as each of the major religions has its fundamentalist fringe, so does every culture have men and women willing to sacrifice their lives for justice. Desperation is common currency when all David has is his sling and a stone against the most modern of war materiel.

Here in the United Sates, homes on Holloman Air Force Base in southern New Mexico or in Arlington, Virginia also have portraits on their walls. These may be black and white, in solemn frames and devoid of the undecipherable script. But they too show the faces of young men and women prematurely dead. Their deaths occurred on battlefields in Afghanistan, Iraq, Bosnia, Panama, Vietnam. The parents grieve, and yes they are also proud.

No one here would imply that these young North American soldiers were fanatics, or that they were crazy to go to war. We know they went to war because their government told them it was an act of patriotism, that they were needed in the fight against communism, terrorism, or whatever perceived "evil" was being used, at the time, to define the enemy. The young, the poor, the least educated or informed, have always provided the bodies to the generals who sit behind desks. These young men may kill innocents just as the suicide bombers do, though the latter's target is spoken of here as collateral damage. In either case, the dead are just as dead.

What differentiates the Palestinian suicide bomber from the young U.S. recruit who enlisted out of poverty, confusion, or a blind belief in what his leaders told him was his patriotic duty, is a culture different from our own; and a desperation bred of generations of occupation condoned and even aided and abetted by much of the world.

Let us not fall so easily or become so quickly bogged down in racist disparagement of what we may consider another's cultural excess, when we have so much such excess here at home. Let us demand an end to war—**all** war—so that no young man or woman, whatever his or her religious belief or culture, must die and take others with them for interests not their own.

—Spring 2002

CHAPTER TWELVE

Language as Weapon[1]

My generation grew up on the adage "Sticks and stones will break my bones, but words will never hurt me."

This disrespect for language—its meaning and impact—has made the muddling of our social relationships much easier to accept or ignore. Vacuous phrases such as "I didn't really mean that" or "it just came out" taunted my childhood, giving me to understand that what one said didn't really have much bearing on how one wished to be perceived. My time and culture taught me that how things seemed was much more important than how they really were.

The empty phrase "I'm so sorry"—uttered by CEOs explaining their ill gotten wealth vis-à-vis the lost livelihoods of downsized employees, insurance companies denying lifesaving claims, Catholic bishops forced to revisit their obscene protection of pedophiles, or politicians trying to defend reversals of campaign promises—is no longer believed by most. Yet it continues to claim its place in social discourse. Too often it gets the speaker off the hook.

Within the intimate, supposedly safe context of family life, parents too often mimic the distortions, half-truths and outright lies of the larger society. "This hurts me more than it hurts you" is prelude to much too much abuse. Secrets "protect a family's honor" even as they destroy a child's future. Well-meaning adults utter phrases such as "I just want you to be happy," "I only want what's best for you," or "You'll be the death of me yet," without regard for how their words impact upon their child's self-esteem and future ability to function. Those who don't mean so well may say "Come on Bitch, you know you want it."

Commercial advertising is one place where this distortion of language has grown particularly flagrant. On millions of television screens, words and images join forces to push exaggerated implications, faulty reasoning, and false promises about an ever-greater range of products and services. Whatever the small print, this misuse of language elevated to a science or art form has us believing this automobile or that exercise machine will make us younger, thinner, more successful, even happier. "Ask your doctor if Nexium (or Zoloft or Zantex or one of dozens of other brand name medications) is right for you." Our healthcare is now thoroughly driven by the pharmaceutical and insurance companies. For both, manipulation of language is essential to growing profits.

It is in the international arena, however, that this well-crafted distortion is being used most dangerously to co-opt our thought processes, secure our allegiances, and promote our willingness to go along with policies that will ultimately do us all in.

Consider the "war on terror".

Decades, indeed centuries, of foreign policy that privileges U.S. greed over the lives and well being of others, depends upon getting us to believe we are "fighting for democracy," "working for the greater good," or "doing what's right." Patriarchal war-mongering, racist concepts of difference, and ideas of Manifest Destiny have been important to the promotion of these policies. Language lies provide the mortar that holds it all together.

Take the Arabic word *jihad*. Since 9/11 our politicians and press have translated this word to mean holy war, more specifically a holy war waged against anyone who is not Muslim or of the Islamic faith. No matter that this is not its meaning. Muslims, as dismayed as the rest of us at what a group of Islamic fundamentalists did on September 11th, 2001, have explained again and again that *jihad* does not mean what the thought-shapers claim it means.

A most accurate and moving definition was given by Mariane Pearl, widow of murdered journalist Danny Pearl: "Jihad is the name of a process that can be undertaken successfully only by a courageous person. A jihadi fights with himself or herself in what I, as a Buddhist, think of as a personal revolution," Pearl wrote. "It doesn't involve demonstrating in front of TV cameras or murdering innocent people. It is a slow and difficult process in which one seeks to overcome fears, prejudices and limitations to defend justice and [...] allow our personality to expand and blossom so that we can fully contribute to society at large."[2]

In the language currently wielded by our government officials, "collateral damage" describes the death of innocent civilians. "Rebuilding Afghanistan" means keeping control of that nation and its people. Support of Israel's genocidal war against the Palestinians is articulated as "working towards a solution in the Middle East." "Waging the war against terrorism" may mean anything from toppling a democratically elected government to dropping bombs followed by food packages on children. Or keeping lists of the books U.S. citizens check out of their public libraries here at home.

Language is important because it is through language that we exchange ideas, do battle with one another's beliefs, identify ourselves and name what we are willing to do to defend our earth and justice for those who live upon it. Language gives birth to attitude, policy, and action. In order to understand one another, we must listen to the real meaning of one another's words, rather than to the intentionally misleading translation offered up by those who intentionally mislead.

If we do not stop and pay attention to the language we use, sticks and stones and nuclear weaponry and yes, also words, may yet break our bones and obliterate life on our planet.

CHAPTER THIRTEEN

Culture of Intrusion

At the stoplight, the woman in the SUV to my right stares straight ahead, the small cell phone pressed to her ear, her attention—who knows where?

To my left, an older but more creatively appointed vehicle—what we call a low rider here in the Southwest—pulls up and the indistinct rumble I'd noticed seconds before engulfs me in a battering sound experience: all windows down, pounding heavy metal shared with everyone within two city blocks. Its beat threatens to shake me and my compact car loose from our own reverie.

I need to find out if my friend's plane is arriving on schedule. By the time the airline's automated menu has gone through its paces, I should have left for the airport five minutes ago. I used to take refuge in pretending that I had one of those old rotary phones, allowing me to wait on line for a human voice. These days that wait—whether in order to speak with someone about a service needed, complain about a service rendered incorrectly, or tell someone my water has suddenly gone off and I don't know why—is most often accompanied by the last music I'd ever want to hear, and—you guessed it—the loudest! As well as a periodic recording that assures me: "Your call is very important to us, please stay on the line..."

An exception to the above: whenever I want to buy something over the phone. The perceived intent to consume still grants me the privilege of immediate human contact.

As if these automated noises weren't irritating enough, there is always the written variety. Commenting in an email to a friend about the current crisis in the Catholic Church, my pressing the "send" button elicited one such message: "The content of this email may be offensive to its recipient; are you sure you wish to send it?"

What, now I've got the language police looking over my shoulder! Must be the word "pedophile." Well yes, as a matter of fact, I **do** want to send my message. I think my recipient is capable of discerning my meaning without taking offense. But it seems my email server has cuter questions up its electronic sleeve. The next time I press the "send" button, the automated warning mocks: "Your message should have its mouth washed out...if you get our drift."

I am supposed to find this humorous?

Ours has become a culture of intrusion, a culture of extraneous noise and sensory bombardment. Or, contemplated more analytically, a culture in which boundaries are being shattered in the interests of corporate greed. Even individuals have acquired the sense they have every right to intrude upon another's space, safety, quiet or comfort.

Loud as in decibels, or loud as in confusing. Louder, to the U.S. ear, has long been considered better, more intelligible or effective. It's become a truism that U.S. tourists abroad believe that if they speak English more slowly and louder they will be understood. And have you ever noticed that many TV commercials are ratcheted up a few decibels? This must be in an effort to reclaim the attention of those viewers who press the mute button or flee the room during those ever-longer interruptions of the programs they watch.

Cell phones stuck to ears in moving automobiles, restaurants, airports, shopping malls, and on streets. Conversations I have no interest in hearing, other peoples' business pressing in from all sides. Others' taste in music—loud and louder—entering my every pore. Automated responses to unasked questions, or to questions just slightly different from the ones I am trying to ask.

High volume music. Screams. People talking loud, on their cell phones, inches from my ear. A screech of tires. A blasting horn. Shouts. Thuds. Bells. Whistles. Whirs. Cracks. Slams. Buzzers. Hollers. Shrieks.

Noise pollution, sensory pollution—in addition to the pollution of air, water, food, what passes for news, the insistence that we consume without thought to need, and all the other assaults upon our senses—has reached a level I can only equate with a new type of pain. Its deafening assault is in direct relation to its numbing lack of meaningful content. And it takes our attention from all that to which we should be paying very close attention indeed.

At sixty-seven, I admit that this noise pollution affects me in ways it doesn't appear to affect the young. In fact, my forty-three-year-old son, a university professor, notes that his students and younger colleagues seem to **need** this extreme noise level: "When things get too quiet, they turn the volume up," he says. "They require a certain level of sound to be able to function."

This frightens me. That young people need an increased level of meaningless noise, while we older folks are quite literally being drummed out of those places we once could inhabit in peace, seems an odd commentary on contemporary culture. Have we created a culture of intrusion? What has become of the quiet in which all of us, young and old, could once listen to the wind, distinguish a birdcall, contemplate silence, or simply think?

And how will our humanity evolve if we no longer have access to that personal (highly political) space?

CHAPTER FOURTEEN

Stop Rape[1]

I hope my words will be a point of departure for some good discussion here tonight. There's a lot I want to say. Some of it may parallel your own thoughts, but I hope that a few of my comments will move you to look at some shop-worn assumptions in new ways. My understanding of rape may be unfamiliar to you. Perhaps you will disagree with certain of my ideas. But if we can listen to one another we should all come away with something of use.

Okay, then: rape. What is it? An act, a sexual event gone wrong, a crime? If a crime, is it always committed by a man against a woman? Whose word defines what rape is and what it is not? Does an unwanted sexual demand from a husband or partner fall into the same category as a violent assault by a stranger? Must there be physical brutality for an act to be considered rape? Does rape only conform to the definitions offered by our legal statutes, medical literature, or social norms? How have our notions of rape changed throughout time?

I should say, right off, that all of these are rapes and that rape is certainly a crime, whether or not society defines it as such. But as I see it, what we commonly consider to be rape—that is, any sexually-focused forced assault by a perpetrator against a victim—must be viewed within a much broader context. Societies based on greed and the acquisition of power, societies that enable a few to become wealthy by exploiting great majorities of their people, societies that are racist and misogynist, societies that misuse and abuse the earth we live on, the air we breath and the water we drink—such societies are engaged in continual acts of rape.

The rape of a single woman, even the rape of groups of women (such as in recent situations of armed conflict in which rape has been elevated to the category of war crime), must be understood in this context. The rape of the environment, the rape of our political world, the genetic engineering of seeds and food, and the sexual violence waged against women and children are linked in ways we are only beginning to understand. All these violations have as their common denominator an abuse of power.

Both patriarchy and capitalism are systems based on rape. The tacit acceptance of each of these acts makes it easier to accommodate them all. This, plus the low social and economic status of women, is the reason the rape of a woman by a man is not yet really taken seriously in our society.

In the late sixties and early seventies, women in what has since been called the Second Wave of Feminism, began once again to see ourselves differently from how our mothers and grandmothers saw themselves. There was a First Wave of women struggling for their rights, the movement of the early years of the century just ended. One of the ways patriarchy disempowers us is by obliterating our history. So I hope those of you who do not know about Susan B. Anthony, Elizabeth Cady Stanton, Sojourner Truth, Lucy Stone, Matilda Jocyln Gage, Jane Adams, Eleanor Roosevelt, Margaret Sanger, and so many other brave foremothers, will learn about them now. Knowing our history helps us know who we are and can be.

But as I was saying, in the late sixties and early seventies, women—many of them inspired by those earlier sisters—once again took up the banner of women's rights. Suffrage and jobs had been on the agenda for some time. Now women were looking at sex roles, reproductive rights, and abuse and self-esteem issues. Quite simply, we began to believe that we deserved integrity. That dignity was our due. That we had a right to choose service rather than accept its imposition. In the late sixties and early seventies this knowledge became collective once more. It launched a movement.

Movement, community, collective effort: these are the necessary prerequisites to social change. Only by working together are people able to move beyond that cop-out phrase: "Well, that's just the way things are." Among the unquestioned way things were for women in this country before a feminist analysis rekindled the rage that made change possible, incest, rape, battery, workplace harassment and other forms of violence against women were pandemic but endured in silence. This means that women of all ages, social classes, races and conditions were abused in large numbers and as a matter of course; but most women saw this abuse as something natural to their lives, their "cross to bear" if you will. And men were conditioned to believe abusing women was their right.

This pandemic abuse of women continues today, of course, and the patriarchal male conditioning as well. I do not mean to imply that we live in an entirely different world. Quite recently, as a matter of fact, a non-scientific but newsworthy poll on American campuses revealed a significant number of young men who said they believe that in certain circumstances rape is justified. Worse, more than a third of those polled admitted they would rape a woman if they knew they could get away with it! We must sit up and take notice when at this dawn of the 21st century young men say they see nothing wrong with rape.

But let us make sure we agree about what constitutes rape. *The New Bodies Ourselves* tells us that: "Rape is any kind of sexual activity committed against a woman's will. Whether the rapist uses force or threats of force is irrelevant. Men use different kinds of force against women, from pressuring us for a goodnight kiss, to withdrawal of economic support from wives, to using weapons. Rape is always traumatic. When we are raped, survival is our primary concern and we protect ourselves as best we can. Some women choose to fight back; others do not feel it is an option. If you were raped and are now [listening to] this (...), you did the 'right' thing because you are alive."[2]

This definition is pro-woman and generally useful, but I question its narrowness, the way it seems to float out there removed from the larger social context. I feel it is important to keep in mind the ways in which the rape of a woman or a child is linked to and made possible by the way we take for granted the rape of earth, air, water, food, different identities, public spaces, the killing of civilians in foreign wars, and human dignity itself.

I also question the use of the term sexual activity. While it is true that rape violates a woman's genitalia, it is not sexual activity. Rape is a crime of domination. The rapist does not want sex, he wants power. Rape, like other crimes against humanity, is always about power.

The Second Wave of Feminism's great achievement was to make visible what was invisible. Bringing rape and other manifestations of woman abuse out from behind closed doors made it possible for us to get together and share our stories, publicly discuss violence against women, put the idea that rape is wrong clearly out there on the public agenda. What twenty years ago was experienced as private shame, something women frequently believed we had brought upon ourselves or even deserved, has become something we can talk about among ourselves and with others.

The "personal problem" became the social phenomenon. Violence against women was named, defined. It was wrong, we affirmed, and must be stopped. And a new solidarity was born, one in which women could begin to see one another as sisters rather than competitors vying for male attention. In this new solidarity, the bitterness of individual oppression became a shared and righteous anger.

This change went deeper than the simple recognition of our common pain, however. The new feminism produced new analysis. Scholarly essays and books appeared and, perhaps more importantly, the mass media began carrying articles that helped change our popular perception about woman abuse. Women's Studies programs were initiated on campuses across the country. Conferences provided forums for discussion. Serious research was undertaken. Patriarchy began to be understood as a system, one in which men retain power, among other things by controlling women.

It would take a while before this feminist analysis would be sharpened beyond broad generalities. It would also be a while before the interaction between gender and other categories— class, race, sexuality, age, culture—would begin to be adequately explored. But an understanding and an energy had been unleashed.

In these years a feminist consciousness about rape was raised. Rape began to be understood as one of patriarchy's most blatant and pervasive crimes, and also one of its most protected. Today, although better defined and in certain scenarios dealt with more effectively, rape continues to be rampant and go largely unpunished. It is acknowledged as a crime, but the way it is handled mostly tells us that it is not taken seriously.

Think of what this means. Any one of us when we leave here tonight might fall victim to the crime of rape. If we survive—and many victims do not—what we choose to do about it will depend on whether we are sure we will be believed, whether we feel we can go through the often humiliating process of reporting the crime, whether we are willing to commit ourselves to facing our assailant in a court of law, in short: whether we are emotionally willing to be raped again. Even for those who are not murdered by a rapist, distinctions are made between remaining a victim and becoming a survivor. Achieving the latter status is not always a choice.

I consider myself fortunate to have lived through these years of important change. When I rage at how much remains to be accomplished, I remind myself that when I was growing up rape was still barely whispered, if spoken about at all. Women and girls who dared break the silence were automatically asked what we had done to provoke our assailants. Those of us who physically survived a rape experience were dispensed with as lucky to have gotten through it, with little or no attention to the psychological or emotional trauma that often plagued us for years. Men and boys who raped were almost never punished. "Boys will be boys" was the popular refrain. As I say, women of my generation are fortunate. Young women today benefit from our victories and are in a position to push the struggle further.

I'd like to share a personal story. I was in high school in the heavily restrictive fifties. Like many young women in small towns across this country, I longed to date the captain of the school's football team. One day, he did ask me out. After the proverbial movie and milkshake, we and the other couple we were with drove out onto a dirt road in the loneliness of the foothills east of Albuquerque. Immediately my football captain hero began ripping at my clothing, pummeling my body, attempting to force himself upon me. He clearly believed this was his right. Nothing was said. The other young woman must have thought I was putting on a good show of resistance, or maybe she was too occupied to notice.

I fought and screamed. No one paid attention to my protests. Finally, I remembered something my father had told me: aim for the point of least resistance. I did and managed to get out of the car. Crying, fumbling at my torn clothing, I ran toward the city lights. I ran and ran, then walked. When I reached my parental home in the early hours of the morning, my anguish woke my mother and she got up to ask what had happened.

My mother was loving. She cared about her kids. But she was unable to extradite herself from the ideology of the times. Because my date had not succeeded in vaginally penetrating me, she did not consider my experience a rape. "Go on to bed," she told me, obviously relieved, "nothing really happened. Get some sleep. You'll feel better in the morning." Indeed it took me decades to understand that event as rape, and begin to deal with its residual trauma.

Let us look for a few moments at rape in the United States. I haven't been able to find a Bureau of Justice definition for rape, but according to its 1997 statistics, a woman somewhere in this country is raped every two minutes. This means that during this evening's keynote, some fifty women will have suffered this crime. In 1996, 307,000 women were the victims of reported rapes, attempted rapes or sexual assaults. Between 1995 and 1996, more than 670,000 women were victimized in these three categories. And these figures reflect only those rapes or attempted rapes that were reported.

Most are not. A National Crime Victimization Survey carried out by the U.S. Department of Justice that same year tells us that only 31% of rapes and sexual assaults are ever reported to law enforcement officials, less than one in three. This makes rape the most underreported of all crimes. The most common reasons given by women for not telling anyone that they were raped are, one, the belief that it is a private or personal matter and, two, fear of some kind of reprisal from their assailant.

This is a particularly interesting aspect of the crime of rape, and one that reflects the ways in which the patriarchal culture has conditioned women to follow a course of action that effectively protects their aggressors. A woman's socially induced shame, embarrassment and fear conspires against her. Our mostly male officials—legislators, law enforcement officers and judges—frequently refrain from prosecuting rapists out of their own inbred fear (conscious or unconscious) that in the long run targeting offenders may prove dangerous to them. The rapist thus enjoys the tacit protection which is built into the fabric of patriarchal society.

It is wrong to assume that women are most often raped by strangers. Because it is so commonly tolerated, rape is a crime of familiarity. A 1994 Bureau of Justice report on Violence Against Women reveals that approximately 68% of all rape victims know their assailants. More than a quarter are raped by husbands or boyfriends, roughly a third by acquaintances, and 5% by other relatives. Again, these statistics reflect only the third of all rapes that are reported.

A portrait of contemporary U.S. rape, from the same 1994 study, further indicates that one out of every four reported rapes takes place in a public area or parking garage, most occur between the hours of 6 p.m. and 6 a.m., almost half the assailants are under the influence of alcohol or drugs, and more than one quarter use a weapon. In almost half these assaults the victim sustains injuries other than those inflicted by the rape itself, and three-fourths of female victims require medical care.

The young are particularly vulnerable. Half of all rape victims are under the age of 18 and one in six is under the age of 12. In these studies, teens between the ages of 16 and 19 were three-and-a-half times more likely than the general population to be victims.

I know how boring it can be to dwell on numbers. These statistics are important only because they give us an overall view of who is most likely to be raped. They are only useful if we use them to convey an idea of what it is like to be a woman in this country today. Fear of rape causes vast numbers of us to be afraid to go out at night, afraid when alone with men—even men we know—and especially afraid if we are young.

Rape also follows the country's racial breakdown, showing similar statistics as those of the population as a whole: about 81% of all rape victims are white, 18% are black, and 1% are of other races.

While nine out of 10 victims are women, it's important to mention that men and boys are also sometimes targeted by this crime. In 1995, according to the previously mentioned study, more than thirty thousand males over the age of 12 were victims of rape, attempted rape or sexual assault. (Recent acknowledgment by the Catholic Church of the vast numbers of sexually abusive priests whose victims have tried for years to get Church authorities to believe their painful stories, undoubtedly account for some of these. MR, 2003).

Poverty too is a factor. But we must be careful here. We must be very clear about the fact that people who live in poverty are not raped because they are poor, but because they have less power. Although rape crosses class, race and cultural lines, government statistics tell us that those with a household annual income under $7,500 are twice as likely as the general population to be victims of this type of crime.

So much for government statistics. What about the statistics provided by privately-run outreach and advocacy programs? Are they any different? First I would like to say that most U.S. cities today have Rape Crisis Centers, one of the feminist movement's most positive contributions. These centers usually have 24-hour hotlines. Trained advocates accompany rape victims to police stations and hospitals, offer counseling, and do preventative education and outreach in the schools. Some of the larger centers also work with offenders. The importance of this work cannot be over-estimated.

Due to the increased public consciousness that rape is a crime, many programs and hotlines now claim that the overall incidence of rape is down. RAINN (Rape Abuse and Incest National Network) reports that between 1995 and 1996 there was a 17% decline in rape, attempted rape and sexual assault.

RAINN points to the fact that more and more survivors are speaking out publicly, thereby helping to lessen the stigma long associated with victimization Their witness encourages others to speak. Advocates, prosecutors and survivors are working together in states across the country, sometimes achieving changes in laws and statutes. Celebrities are taking a public stand on the issue.

Such statistics are useful to our general understanding of the severity of the situation, but again I caution a degree of skepticism. I would argue that with less than a third of all rapes being reported, even this 17% decline demands closer scrutiny. It is subject to a number of other factors, and shouldn't be taken out of context.

There is the emphasis on punishment to be considered. What might constitute just punishment for the crime of rape? Do we want longer prison sentences, mandatory therapy, public service? What about chemical castration or the death penalty? Is it productive, or even right, to respond to violence with violence? Should rapists who have served their time be allowed to live in areas where no one knows their history?

An FBI Uniform Crime Report for January-June, 1999, credits the convicted rapist's increased probability of going to prison for an 8% decrease in rapes reported to the police during the first half of 1998. This report lists the greatest decline in the Northeast and Midwest, with smaller drops in other parts of the country. The FBI further signals a several-year trend in this regard. From 1997 to 1998 it shows reported rapes down 5%.

The National Center for Policy Analysis (NCPA) also points to punishment as a deterrent. A study by this organization claims that the probability of going to prison for rape has increased by 20% since 1993. This may help explain why rape reports have decreased 17% over that same period. Again, however, we must keep in mind that the FBI and other government agencies do not produce their statistics in a vacuum. Each study is carried out in its own ideological framework, emanates from certain preconceived ideas of what rape is, and responds to particular interests. Who pays for these studies? Whose interests do they serve? Remember, law enforcement in this country has defined rape very narrowly, and it is not yet taken seriously in our society as a whole.

Should punishment be our main or only recourse where violent crime is concerned? Should it be combined with re-education? Should popular education campaigns and programs receive more funding? Reading government-produced statistics and analyses, one notes an almost exclusive emphasis on punishment. It's not that different from the current ideas about crime in general: build more prisons but don't allocate funding for youth programs, drug rehabilitation or education.

Let's look at punishment a little more closely. The good news seems to be that a rapist's expected sentence tripled from 1980 to 1997. The bad news is that the expected sentence for a forcible rape is still only 128 days (up from 39 days in 1980 and 99 days in 1993). By comparison, the average sentence for robbery is now 59 days, and for murder 41 months.

These statistics lead to the conclusion that sexually assaulting a woman in this country, if it is prosecuted at all, still brings punishment more in line with burglarizing property than with taking a life. And yet we know that rape can forever affect a life, leaving great emotional trauma in its wake. It can cause HIV, AIDS, other sexually transmitted diseases. It can lead to unwanted pregnancy. The prevalence of rape strikes terror in great numbers of women. It has robbed us of our innocence and spontaneity. It has made us afraid.

Some of the most useful research being done today is in the area of Post-Traumatic Stress Disorder (PTSD). Women who have been victimized by rape and other forms of abuse frequently suffer from a disorder similar to what we once called shell shock: a condition common to those who have been to war. Some form of this disorder has literally become pandemic among American women. Surely we need an overall approach to the question of violence against women that takes this into account. From preschool up, in the family and in every social institution, we must begin to educate males to respect females and females to respect and defend themselves.

As with other types of crime, I would argue that education and advocacy are infinitely more effective than punishment. There is no hard evidence that rapists, even after doing time, will not rape again. In fact, there is considerable evidence to suggest that rape is a social disease and that rapists are sick as well as criminal.

We must educate the population at large that all violence and domination is wrong. Rape is a particular type of crime, but it is also a symptom of a more generalized situation, one in which societal violence is condoned and indeed encouraged. Consider the numbers of movies, TV programs, hit songs and commercials that project violence as something virile, glamorous, exciting. (Consider the Bush administration's preemptive strike policy, and its glorification of violence against other peoples. MR, 2003)

We must educate men to understand that rape is not their right, and develop effective ways of working with offenders. We must learn to listen to the woman who has been raped, believe her story and commit to keeping her safe. We must educate women that we do not bring this crime upon ourselves, and that sexual assault is never our fault. In the areas of date-or marriage rape, we must teach women that we have the right to say no,

and that no always means no. We must train women who want
to be trained in self-defense. And we must provide real advocacy for all victims of assault.

So much for the statistics. The numbers are important, but
the language of poetry more powerful. In the mid-seventies, poet
and novelist Marge Piercy wrote Rape Poem, vividly evoking
what rape and the fear of rape mean to women and how the social
acceptance of woman abuse as something normal and pervasive—
"boys will be boys, men will be men"—shapes women's lives, even
twisting our concept of love. I want to read this poem, because it
so eloquently portrays a period not often remembered. And
because in so many places it remains relevant today:

Rape Poem

There is no difference between being raped
and being pushed down a flight of cement steps
except that the wounds also bleed inside.

There is no difference between being raped
and being run over by a truck
except that afterward men ask if you enjoyed it.

There is no difference between being raped
and being bit on the ankle by a rattlesnake
except that people ask if your skirt was short
and why you were out alone anyhow.

There is no difference between being raped
and going head first through a windshield
except that afterward you are afraid
not of cars
but half the human race.

The rapist is your boyfriend's brother.
He sits beside you in the movies eating popcorn.
Rape fattens on the fantasies of the normal male
like a maggot in garbage.

Fear of rape is a cold wind blowing
all of the time on a woman's hunched back.
Never to stroll alone on a sand road through pine woods,
never to climb a trail across a bald
without that aluminum in the mouth
when I see a man climbing toward me.

Never to open the door to a knock
without that razor just grazing the throat.
The fear of the dark side of hedges,
the back seat of a car, the empty house
rattling keys like a snake's warning.
The fear of the smiling man
in whose pocket is a knife.
The fear of the serious man
in whose fist is locked hatred.

All it takes to cast a rapist is to be able to see your body
as jackhammer, as blowtorch, as adding-machine-gun.
All it takes is hating that body
your own, your self, your muscle that softens to flab.

All it takes is to push what you hate,
what you fear onto the soft alien flesh.
To bucket out invincible as a tank
armored with treads without senses
to possess and punish in one act,

to rip up pleasure, to murder those who dare
live in the leafy flesh open to love.[3]

Good poetry does not simply tell us things, it allows us to
experience them. Think, for a moment, about the line "rape fattens on the fantasies of the normal male". What more vivid
evocation of the fact that in a society rooted in greed and domination, where to be a man so often depends on exhibiting brute
force, on taking what one wants regardless of the consequences,
the act of rape can enter the fantasy world of even the most
"normal" male.

Piercy's poem brings back a time when it was common and
acceptable for the raped woman to be asked if she enjoyed it,
what she did to provoke the attack, why her skirt was so short.
It evokes the context in which the rapist might be your
boyfriend's brother or some other familiar figure, acquaintance,
friend. It makes palpable the ways in which women are deprived
of our simple right to a solitary stroll through beautiful country
or on a city street at night. It describes the status quo in which
women must fear not cars but half the human race. The end of
the poem proposes a solution: if we can learn not to hate ourselves, we will stop being victims of rape.

But this is only part of what we need to do. Certainly self-
love is necessary to the healthy self-image and self-confidence
that would shun aggression and abuse. But loving ourselves
alone is not enough. To say it is, is like saying it's up to us: blaming the victim once again. It is necessary that we see society for
what it is and make a common front against the violence on
which so many of our relationships are based.

We need communities of struggle capable of launching educational campaigns, fighting for effective legislation, and creating
support networks for abused women and their children. We need

police precincts with trained personnel, personnel that understands that rape is a crime and does not re-victimize its victims.
We need legislators who are not so invested in self-protection
that they cannot take woman abuse seriously. We need nothing
short of a change in social consciousness, so that mothers are able
to educate our daughters to expect and demand a different sort of
relationship: one of dignity and respect.

We need the ongoing and important work of women's
studies and gender studies programs, so that new generations
may be trained in areas vital to their growth. We need women's
centers where gender issues may be discussed and problems
addressed.

Over the past twenty or twenty-five years we have come a
long way towards educating around abuse issues, signaling rape
as a crime, encouraging women and girls to report it, and even
penalizing the perpetrator—as long as he is not protected by
power. We also have a long way to go. The next step in fighting
pandemic woman abuse is, I believe, coming to terms with the
fact that rape and other forms of abuse are about power.

We desperately need a new analysis of power.

Abuse of any kind is always about power, how it is wielded and misused. How a skewed distribution of power is accepted in our society; and not only accepted but defended. I am convinced that the next stage of struggle against rape, battery,
incest and other forms of violence requires that we think about
power in new ways. We must analyze the routine abuse of power,
figure out why and how power continues to be corrupted, and
take serious steps towards changing its gendered disbalance.

I am going to be extremely forthright tonight. And I want
to suggest some connections. Permit me, for a few moments, to
talk about other forms of power inequality. I will return to
woman abuse later, and I hope you will see the links.

Many of us have worked to bring about greater social justice. Some in this room may be veterans of the various social justice movements—here and in solidarity with other peoples of the world. Some, perhaps, have just engaged with one or more of these struggles. Still others belong to the youngest generations, searching for ways to make your own contributions, your own lives more meaningful and whole. I am sure that many of you are looking for ways to link your personal experience with these larger struggles.

Some believe economics define the greatest contradiction; certainly economic justice is basic. Others may prioritize race, sexual politics, or even the psychological or the spiritual. Sadly, in our common history the majority of those who call themselves progressive have trivialized, even disregarded, the needs of the individual, while the majority of those involved in more personal struggles tend to ignore the importance of economics and class. In this mutual alienation, the very concept of justice is obliterated.

The one thing that those who think in terms of the individual and those who think more collectively have in common, has been our failure to look at patterns of domination within our own communities or movements. This failure vitiates all our struggles, inevitably tainting their possibility for success. And it has been overwhelmingly true where gender domination is concerned. We tend to focus on a single issue, unmindful of the fact that what oppresses one oppresses all.

Am I only a woman and nothing else? Am I only poor? Am I not also a worker? Indigenous or of a particular ethnicity or culture? Parent? Student? Poet? Mother? Lesbian, gay man, transgendered or transsexual person? Do I experience the world from a specific vantage point of age? Do I have a disability that affects my life? Am I a victim, a survivor or perhaps even, in certain situations, a perpetrator?

Perhaps the most effective way of seeing the perpetrator in

others is by recognizing it in ourselves. It may be easy for us to affirm we have never been guilty of the particular crime of rape. But if we understand rape as part of a general culture of domination, few of us can say we have never participated in or profited from that culture. What about the racist, homophobic or anti-woman joke? What of our good-natured or embarrassed laughter when such a joke is told in our presence? Who can say he or she has never laughed at such a joke? Or absolutely always challenged a bigoted or disrespectful comment?

Gender discrimination crosses class, race and cultural lines. It is rife not only in our government, corporate world and dominant society, but also within our movements for social change, and in our private lives. Women are more than half the population. We have made progress in the articulation of our subjugation—in the more intimate contexts of incest, rape, battery, and workplace harassment as well as in the more public arenas of health, education, job accessibility, advancement and wages.

What is not discussed, not even in most social change communities, is the way in which domination over women, and their use and abuse, represent a power inequity that shapes society as a whole, and hinders our efforts to change it. And this inequity is everywhere taken for granted (actively promoted or declared a "necessary evil"). Male political figures, whose rhetoric covers all bases, think nothing of maintaining strict control over wives, daughters and women colleagues. More astonishing, this control is often explained away, justified or covered-up by the women themselves.

Oppression does not hurt the oppressed person alone. The oppressor's humanity, too, is diminished in the oppressive attitude or act. Abuses of power stunt the powerful even as they humiliate or destroy their victims. We must stop thinking of rape and other forms of woman abuse as a woman's problem. They are societal problems.

Gender equality is an area in which the rhetoric has long been a part of the discourse—everywhere from the United Nations Declarations on Women's Rights to our own government decrees and in the programs put forth by a variety of movements for social change. But the reality, at all these levels and in all these arenas, falls grossly short of the rhetoric.

Powerful men are not the only problem. For this is not about individuals, but about a system. Patriarchal conditioning is such that we all allow powerful men to hold onto their power. It is almost an automatic response. We may read lots of theory, understand on paper how power is distributed and how the unequal distribution of power affects our lives. But when it comes to taking concrete steps towards changing the power disbalance, we often find ourselves relinquishing power to a man simply because he is a man. This is where good theory comes up against daily practice. We must unlearn domination much as we unlearn racism or any other practice that is socially unhealthy.

Women and children, especially female children, have long been victimized by this system of domination, as have a variety of othered groups—and the earth itself. Men who have built themselves up through the abuse of power will continue (figuratively or literally) to rape air, earth, water, social and political structures, and individuals and groups that either stand in their way or threaten the secrets, silences and lies that protect their status. Men of different political persuasions will make a common front against such threats. And women who have achieved a measure of political power by playing the patriarchal game, will often continue to side with such men.

My hope is that we will be able to keep a reexamination of power in the forefront of our debate. For our current and future movements to have a fighting chance, we must set our strategies as well as our voices against all forms of domination: from the abuse of an unwilling body by someone seeking to control it to the abuse of weaker groups by the strong and smaller nations by the superpowers.

The sexual abuse of a child, the rape of a woman, the exploitation of a people or invasion of a nation, the destruction of earth, water, air: all are interconnected. All are the result of power corrupted and misused. Only by deciphering this inter-connection can we begin to unravel the terrible knot of power that holds us, imprisoned, in its grip.

—January 2000

CHAPTER FIFTEEN

Women and Resistance

Cuba and Nicaragua[1]

I'm going to begin with a short poem. It was written by Cuban poet Marilyn Bobes in the mid 1970s. Marilyn was born in 1955 and grew up with the revolution. It shaped her, and shaped her woman's sense of self—that complicated woman's sense of self so filled with promise and sacrifice and sudden unexpected obstacles. "Pitiful Role" reflects the promise and also the poet's dissatisfaction with the sexism that continued to exist two decades into Cuba's revolutionary period:

Pitiful Role

Poetesses, they said,
shall be modest
and devious
and small.
Although light on their feet
their imperfections will make it impossible
for them to fly.

But if one happens to tap
the right word
—the proverbial burro playing a flute—
everyone will exclaim *that woman's a lot of man,*

never *that poet's some woman!*
(Women, born in that shadow
where only slaves and masters live.)

And then they'll have to find a way to shut her up.[2]

Women and resistance. It's an age-old story, and one which in our lifetimes has taken some surprising turns; offering lessons as heartbreaking as they are inspiring. Over the past three decades, Latin America and the Caribbean have been scenes of particularly intense political struggles, struggles in which women have defied religious, secular and cultural limitations, risked everything, won some pretty amazing battles and also suffered a number of painful setbacks. I will talk about the cases of Cuba and Nicaragua, two countries in which I have been privileged to live for extended periods, working alongside their women, sharing their dreams and grieving their losses. These are exemplary histories.

Cuba

Cuban women inherit their strength from the rigors of slavery, years of colonial imposition and a tumultuous road to independence that is unique in today's world. The Cuban revolution claimed victory in 1959. A number of courageous women took part in the struggle against the dictator Fulgencio Batista, a few even held mid-level administrative or political positions in the government that replaced him. But women were allowed to join in combat only during the last few months of the war. And after it, despite increased educational and job opportunities, they occupied few roles in which real decision-making could be exercised.

The new government established the Federation of Cuban Women (FMC), a mass organization which would deal with so-called women's issues from that time forward. Right here we have a problem: when terms such as "women's issues" or "women's problems" are used to define the situation of more than half the population, a root misconception shapes the way women's place in society is understood. This root misconception makes a real gender analysis impossible. Remember, we're talking about the late 1950s, early 1960s. Within the international Communist movement, this was the analysis of the times.

The FMC mobilized vast numbers of girls and women from the age of 14 up, eventually claiming a membership of 85% of the country's female population. From the beginning, the organization labeled the feminist theory then beginning to emerge in the United States and some of the European countries as a form of "bourgeois deviancy."

Nevertheless, the Cuban revolution, and within it the FMC, made some very positive changes in women's lives. In the first years, ambitious projects enabled women working in prostitution and domestic service to retrain for other jobs. Fifty-nine percent of the 100,000 teachers in the 1960-61 literacy campaign, and 55% of those who learned to read and write in that campaign, were women. Because the Catholic Church was not as predominant in Cuba as in the rest of Latin America, the right to abortion and access to other aspects of reproductive health were won early in the Cuban process.

Within the first two decades of revolution the female workforce more than doubled. By 1981 almost 60% of all urban women between the ages of 20 and 45 were working outside the home, and this percentage was even higher in the rural areas. Between 1970 and 1981, the proportion of urban women of childbearing age with a secondary education also more than doubled, from 30 to 61%.

Over 400 million women in the world today are illiterate, and over 100 million girls never go to school; not a single one of these is Cuban.

These facts, and others too numerous to mention here, are tremendously impressive. Yet they do not by themselves project the exuberance, passion, and relief Cuban women felt during those years—nor the excitement and gratitude those of us on the outside experienced as we witnessed a political process that seemed dedicated to building a more just society. We had such hope!

Even today not all of that hope has been dashed. Despite overwhelming external pressures and more than a few internal mistakes, elements of revolution continue to be present in Cuba. They can be felt in a scenario that includes ongoing economic stress, collective exhaustion, and some obvious setbacks. But I don't want to talk about what the Cubans did right or wrong, what the successful projects were and what policies may have created further problems. Rather, I want to focus on what I perceive as a root inability, or unwillingness, to look at the issue of power; and how I believe this inability or unwillingness has kept women from achieving real agency.

For many years, we who support the Cuban revolution avoided any sort of critique. Who were we, we reasoned, to criticize another country's way of solving its problems—especially if we were convinced, and we were, that it's government was determined to find solutions to those problems in its own way and in line with its own history and culture. If we came from the country whose government remains so intent on destroying the Cuban revolution, we were even more hesitant to criticize. With discipline, we accepted the dictum that speaking publicly about some of the issues that concerned us would only fuel imperialism's propaganda machine. Wasn't it better to concentrate on the positive? Some of us did challenge policies we felt erroneous, but we did so privately with our Cuban comrades. We felt, and continue to feel, that Cuba's great accomplishments cannot be underestimated. We would defend the revolution, period.

Since leaving Cuba in 1980, I have gone back on brief visits a half dozen times—all in the 1990s. Despite my deep sadness at the many losses, each time I have returned from the island I've experienced a lifting of the spirit almost impossible to put into words. The Cuban people continue to exude a sense of purpose, dignity gained and justice sought.

Today we can see that the Cuban revolution offers a picture that pretty much reflects the gains made in most legitimate struggles for social change: important strides in the basic areas—literacy, education, work, healthcare—but a refusal on the part of the revolutionary government to look at gender and power as these intersect in the new society. Even as we applaud the more than four decade history of a government that has stood firm against ferocious odds while constructing a life that is arguably better for the majority of its citizens, we must lament its inability or unwillingness to take the problem of power seriously.

The fact that one man and his mostly male associates have been in control for all these years clearly has a lot to do with the problem. Nowhere are men eager to relinquish privilege.

But Cuban women, like women everywhere, yearn for freedom, the freedom to live to their full potential. In 1993 a group of respected women journalists got together, moved by the continuing denigration of women in mass media and by the increasingly uneven weight borne by women under Cuba's current economic crisis. These weren't upstarts or revolutionary newcomers. Mirta Rodríguez Calderón, the group's most visible presence, was a respected Communist Party member who had been a part of the revolution from its inception, even serving prison time for her activities against Batista. When she began meeting with other like-minded women, she held a responsible position on the editorial board of Cuba's most important news magazine.

The group called itself MAGIN: an old Spanish word meaning intelligence and inspiration, talent and imagination, the power of the image. For three years these women developed a gender analysis of Cuban society. They countered inferior or denigrating images of women in the media and held workshops for those they called communicators; not just journalists but anyone whose profession put her or him in daily contact with the public: doctors, nurses, librarians, social workers, teachers, lawyers.

These workshops examined the Cuban reality from a gender perspective. MAGIN's work had a far-reaching and extremely positive effect. Yet despite the fact that the organization never tried to compete with the FMC, the official women's organization fought it every step of the way. In September 1996, MAGIN was dissolved by decision of the Central Committee of the Cuban Communist Party. The excuse given was that the United States was trying to infiltrate Cuban organizations and this women's group might be vulnerable.

MAGIN continues to live in spirit, and none of its core members have emigrated. But Mirta and others have temporarily been forced to live and work outside their beloved country. They have suffered repression in a society where we could not admit, didn't want to believe, repression existed. Afro-Cubans, young people who may not have steady jobs or do not conform to an unspoken code of dress or behavior, even just Cubans who spend too much time (sic) with tourists, also routinely suffer police harassment.

The Cuban revolution had a viable project for a country heavily burdened by colonialism, neo-colonialism, dependency, poverty, and all their byproducts: traditional morality, racism, sexism, and heterosexism among others. Early programs achieved impressive successes in the areas of public health, education, and social welfare. Cuba's population became one of the healthiest and best educated in the hemisphere, if not in the world. In a moving display of internationalism, the Cuban revolution also gave generously of its human and material resources to peoples less fortunate. But dependence on the United States was in some important ways replaced by dependence on the socialist bloc, and when that bloc dissolved Cuba faced a sudden reduction in markets and aid. And, as in many such situations of external pressure, the space for internal struggle was also reduced.

Of equal importance, the Cuban Communist Party had developed and consolidated an authoritarian leadership model, one in which a single man and his close associates have maintained solid control for more than four decades. Many cutting-edge ideas about power and human relationships—principle among them, feminism and a gender analysis—have been kept at arm's length. The FMC leadership, following the example of the revolution's male leadership, fears displacement and rejects ideas they feel threaten them, as in the case of MAGIN. As a result, while life has improved for the Cuban people overall, little ideological work has been done to change long-held attitudes, prejudices, and roles.

After almost half a century of revolutionary change, Cuban women are better educated, healthier, have more access to reproductive services, and can aspire to better jobs. But they cannot aspire to real decision-making or the power that would enable them—or their brothers—to take a profound look at power in Cuban society.

Hard times always reinforce traditional values. During the past ten years of extreme economic duress, women have borne the brunt of what the Cuban government calls the Special Period in Peacetime. Shortages of raw materials have shut down production lines, sending many more women than men back into the home. Women also endure the stress of trying to feed their families and keeping their laundry washed when faced with shortages of food and cleaning supplies. A heightened tourist trade has opened the door to massive prostitution and other levels of hustling for younger women tired of the long haul or seduced by luxury items. A significant number seek marriage to foreigners as a ticket out of the country.

Authoritarianism, an unwillingness to turn power over to the younger generations, a defensive attitude born of the nation's forced isolation and the ongoing threat of U.S. destabilization, have conspired to produce an irrational fear of in-depth discussion and change. This fear has taken its toll. Open discussion cannot be turned on and off like a faucet. The next round is inevitably tainted by self-censorship and general social disenchantment. Unfortunately perhaps, the freedom to make mistakes is a necessary ingredient to the ability of successive generations to experiment, analyze, and produce viable solutions to the problems of their lives.

The next few years will undoubtedly see a changing of the guard. Fidel Castro will either die or step down. Where Cuba goes from there will depend upon how power is distributed, what sort of restructuring takes place. Cuba-watchers observe events on the island, diverse factions within the Diaspora, U.S. policy with regard to Cuba, and the U.S. business community—always eager to profit from the Cuban market.

What will this change mean for women in Cuba? They have gained enough and learned enough through the history of their revolutionary experiment, that it is reasonable to assume they will be prepared to build on the achievements of these years. But repression also claims energies and interrupts the natural flow of ideas. Those of us who love Cuba anxiously await the next chapters.

Nicaragua

The Sandinista revolution came to power almost twenty years after the Cuban victory. These twenty years—1959 to

1979—are important because they witnessed the powerful upswing in mid-twentieth century feminism internationally and the historic upheaval within the Catholic Church known as Vatican II. Both movements profoundly informed the changes experienced by women in Nicaragua.

The largest of the Central American countries, Nicaragua has long suffered U.S. intervention. Full-scale invasions took place in 1853, '54, '94, '98, 1912 through '25 and '26 through '33. For a couple of years a North American, William Walker, was actually appointed president of the country by the United States government of the time. As a result, Nicaragua's anti-imperialism and an anti-U.S. sentiment among the population have been intense. Augusto César Sandino led his rebel army to victory over the U.S. Marines in 1933, only to be murdered almost immediately by the first in the long Somoza family dynasty—itself put in place, backed and supported by the United States. Women were unusually prominent in Sandino's campaign, and would play extraordinary roles half a century later during the struggle against Somoza.

At first, as with many such experiences, the modern day Sandinista women were mostly the sisters or girlfriends of the men. Soon, and strikingly, they were also the mothers. But by the early seventies, women played real leadership roles. At the end of the war it was a woman field commander who led the famous retreat to Masaya and another woman who directed the battle that liberated the city of León, forcing the dictator to flee and making victory possible. The FSLN (Sandinista National Liberation Front) managed to stay in power for ten years. During that decade (1979-1990) women held a number of important political positions. Still, much of the promise implicit in the roles women held during the war eroded with an ever-tentative peace.

Women headed several ministries, including the Ministry

of Public Health during its period of greatest success. The world's first National Police Chief was a woman; she spent several angry hours telling me the indignities to which she was subjected during her five-year tenure in that position. In Nicaragua, after the Sandinista victory, women said they would never go back to a pre-revolutionary subservience to men. Yet all sorts of subtle and not-so-subtle pressures forced them to do just that. The claim that "women who fight alongside men won't easily return to the domestic sphere" gradually gave way to the same old equation of men leading and women assuming positions that looked good on paper but represented little real power.

Like the Cubans, the FSLN established AMNLAE—a broad-based women's organization to handle "women's issues." And again, one of the biggest mistakes was considering equality a woman's issue rather than one important to society as a whole. Nicaraguan women thought they were avoiding what they considered their Cuban sisters' errors. Rather than a mass organization, they quickly came to conceive of AMNLAE as a movement, one with a certain degree of flexibility, capable of inserting itself wherever needed. But, like the FMC, AMNLAE never achieved autonomy; it remained tied to the FSLN and manipulated by that organization's male leadership. Many Nicaraguan women called themselves feminists. Without organizational autonomy, the feminists' hands were tied.

Just as in Cuba, during the Sandinista administration life for the Nicaraguan poor improved. People learned to read and write. There were follow-up educational programs. Public health services became available to people in remote areas, and what had once been one of the poorest and most disease-ridden of the Latin American nations began to show improvement in dealing with curable diseases, attending to women's reproductive health, decreasing infant mortality and increasing life expectancy.

The United States, however, wasn't going to allow anoth-

er progressive (usually translated as anti-imperialist) government on this continent, and even before the Sandinistas took
power the Reagan administration began orchestrating the overt
and covert operations which would eventually cost it its life. By
1990, it was over. Hundreds of thousands of U.S. dollars, the
illegal funding and training of counterrevolutionary troops, a
propaganda war and all manner of diplomatic maneuvers succeeded in defeating the FSLN at the polls and installing a pro-
U.S. government which, interestingly enough, had a woman as
its figurehead.

Six years later, Nicaraguan voters moved even further to
the right and elected Arnoldo Alemán, an arch reactionary
from a slightly modernized version of Somoza's Liberal Party. In
2002, Alemán's vice-president Enrique Bolaños won a six-year
term. In each of these elections Daniel Ortega was the FSLN's
candidate, and in each he won a lot of votes but not enough to
defeat his opponent. Of course the United States has continued
to pour large sums of money into making sure Ortega cannot
win. But the struggles within the FSLN itself have also contributed. Ortega and his power group have successfully prevented any other candidate from opposing his candidacy.

It was after the first Sandinista defeat that Nicaragua's
independent women's movement took off.

Nicaragua's feminists were angry. Two events exemplify
that anger. The first had to do with their betrayal by the political organization to which they had given their all. The FSLN
brought great numbers of women into public life. It raised their
political awareness and feminist consciousness. But whenever
they explored solutions that were perceived as threatening male
control, the party wrested power from the women in some specific way. Sometimes it was by ousting a woman from a particular leadership position. At other times it was by tabling a long-
overdue policy shift or de-funding a program. Many of today's

independent feminists acknowledge the party's role in their political development, but are looking for new and more truly democratic forms of political organization.

The second event took place in March of 1998, when Zoilamerica Narváez, Daniel Ortega's step-daughter, held a press conference and accused the FSLN's maximum leader and ex-president of the country of having sexually abused her over a period of 19 years. Towards the end of the Sandinista decade, a number of those valiant young guerrillas had fallen into the traps of greed, ostentation and misuse of public office. But nothing rivaled the power of a young woman, herself a respected political cadre, standing before a microphone and revealing her own personal history of horror.

Not only had Ortega forced Zoilamerica into ongoing sexual submission, he went so far as to try to convince her that meeting his perverse need was her "revolutionary duty," that her special task in the struggle for social change was keeping him sexually satisfied. It took electoral defeat, and the fact that her stepfather was no longer her country's president—an undisputed symbol of power, both domestic and political—to free this young woman to the point where she was able to go public with her story.

Ortega has refused to respond directly to his step-daughter's accusation. As an ex-president he continues to enjoy parliamentary immunity, so she has been unable to take him to court in Nicaragua.[3] He and President Alemán entered into a pact which protected them both, and the FSLN as a party has expelled any member who dares broach the subject of Zoilamerica's accusation. Her courage, however, has brought the issues of incest and sexual abuse to the forefront, and the independent feminists as well as a group called Men Against Violence Against Women have been supportive of her stand. And early in 2002, after more than a year of consideration, the Inter-American Human Rights Court in Washington, D.C.

agreed to hear Zoilamérica's case.[4]

In the years immediately following the FSLN's first electoral defeat, during the government headed by Violeta Barrios de Chamorro and since, many Nicaraguan women who had swallowed rude blows to their integrity as women and kept silent because the party came first, began speaking out about what they had endured. They honored the FSLN for its heroism and for its role in their political education, but no longer saw their first allegiance to men who so clearly refused to share power.

During the 1990 electoral campaign, Daniel Ortega ran on a blatantly macho ticket; he described himself as *El gallo enavejado* (The Fighting Cock with Knife Unsheathed). More than one woman told me that one cock at home was quite enough, thank you; she wasn't about to vote another in as president. The FSLN's failure to embrace feminism and develop a gender analysis of Nicaraguan society was one of a number of reasons for its loss of political power.

I traveled to Nicaragua as part of an all-woman mission to observe that country's 1996 elections. We met with a group of women who had organized across party, class and cultural lines to put forth a minimal agenda for women's rights. Of the 24 presidential candidates, only Alemán refused to sign the women's 9-point agenda.

Thirteen years after the Sandinista defeat, Nicaragua is once more deeply mired in the poverty and desperation it knew before the victory of 1979. Unemployment is among the highest in Latin America. Health indexes are lower in every area: reproductive health is almost non-existent, curable diseases are once again epidemic, life expectancy has gone down and infant mortality up. Sex education is no longer a part of the public school curriculum. Class divisions are more evident than ever, and all that remains of the revolution's impressive projects is the memory that those dreams once seemed possible. Soon, as generations succeed one another, even that memory will fade.

But in the midst of this otherwise desolate panorama Nicaraguan feminists have become a coherent and impressive force. A force to be reckoned with, not only in Nicaragua but globally. Feminist thinkers like Sofía Montenegro and María López Vigil have given us analyses useful far beyond Nicaragua's borders. Feminist institutions have produced extraordinary work.

With the defeat of the FSLN, all progressive social programs were rolled back and a series of non-governmental organizations stepped in to promote healthcare, anti-violence work, sex education, anti-bias work with youth, AIDS education and advocacy, gay and lesbian outreach and much else that died when the Sandinistas were voted out of power. These NGOs, which are under constant government attack, are almost exclusively run by women. While resisting official harassment, facing dwindling international funding and struggling with the everyday difficulties implicit in making anything work in the context of a bureaucracy-heavy underdeveloped country, some of these organizations are doing stunning work.

One example is *Puntos de Encuentro* (Meeting Places). *Puntos* is a highly successful institution that produces a monthly magazine distributed to every corner of the country and reflecting the concerns and activities of women in the most remote places. *Puntos* has a number of outreach and advocacy programs for women and youth, among them a summer camp for young people where the most sophisticated diversity and anti-bias work is carried out.

But *Puntos*' most visible endeavor these days is its weekly television sit-com, *Sexto Sentido* (Sixth Sense). The show is a sort of Nicaraguan "Friends," broadcast on prime time by the country's most important commercial channel. The diverse and well-defined characters in *Sexto Sentido* deal with the usual range of issues: relationships, work, and family; but they also struggle with one of the characters accepting his gay identity; a woman being raped, her resulting pregnancy and subsequent decision about whether or not she should get an abortion; personal independence; AIDS; drugs; political impunity and other complex issues. An episode that highlights one of these questions is often combined with a public service spot urging viewers dealing with the same problem to get in touch with an organization or institution that can help. *Puntos* itself sometimes publishes 50 or 100,000 copies of an informative brochure around one of these themes, and distributes it free nationwide.

This is one example among many of how Nicaragua's feminists, disillusioned with politics as usual, are attending to the areas of social and political need abandoned when the FSLN betrayed its own history of struggle to become just one more in a tired inheritance of bourgeois political parties.

Our Rage

Longtime supporters of the Cuban revolution, and many in the solidarity movement who still rally around the FSLN in Nicaragua, argue that feminists—within those countries and outside them—expect too much from social change movements that barely had a chance to get off the ground, or were forced to prioritize their own existence against the terrible obstacle of U.S. intervention. Why harp on women's rights, they argue, when the well-being of a nation hangs in the balance? And why expect perfection from these struggling governments when women in the United States have such a long way to go before we gain anything resembling parity with men?

For years those of us who have raised these issues—and in my case I admit to having done so hesitatingly for a very long time, only in the past decade coming to question some of the basic precepts—for years, I repeat, many of our revolutionary comrades have considered us self-interested at best, unwitting voices of counterrevolution at worst. Do I expect political experiments plagued with the problems that Cuba or Sandinista Nicaragua have faced to be perfect? Of course not. Do I have a right to demand that a government that says it defends all peoples live up to that claim? I think so.

Expecting Cuba, and Nicaragua when it had the chance, to consider gender equality an integral part of social change should be as elemental to revolutionary thought as class struggle and issues of diversity. And this isn't only about rights for a particular group, but about power as a political category. Until those intent on creating a society based on justice are willing to examine the problem of power, nothing will change. Until those in control of the economy, political power and social relationships, prioritize an analysis and reassessment of power—and act to insure its equal distribution—revolutionary projects will remain truncated and vulnerable.

The 1989 disintegration of the socialist bloc still holds lessons for those of us interested in building a more just world. No one can deny the powerful role of international capital in bringing the experiment to its knees. But neither should we ignore the complex internal problems evident in each of the socialist experiments. A failure to look at gender has not been the only mistake revolutionary movements have made. But their almost universal failure to deal with a just distribution of power, best exemplified by an unwillingness to situate half the population in its rightful place, has been an area where the fear of losing privilege has led to the loss of much else.

Here's to the women of MAGIN, convinced of the basic rightness of the Cuban revolution but working—now behind the scenes—to insure that women will also be its beneficiaries. Here's to Nicaragua's independent feminist movement, so filled with courageous, tireless and brilliant women determined to salvage the real meaning of *sandinismo*.

I want to close by reading another poem. This one is "Lineage" by Nicaraguan poet Daisy Zamora:

Lineage

I ask about the women of my house.
Since childhood I've known the history of my great-grandfather:
Scientist, diplomat, liberal, politician,
father of numerous and distinguished offspring.

But Doña Isolina Reyes, married to him
from fifteen until death, what was her history?

My maternal grandfather graduated Cum Laude
from the University of Philadelphia
and his thesis, dated 1900, is still preserved.
He oversaw the construction of many kilometers of train track,
and only sudden death shattered his dream
of extending the railroad all the way to the Atlantic Coast.
Nine sons and daughters mourned him.

And his wife Rudecinda, who gave birth to those children,
cared for and breast-fed them, what do I know of her?

I ask about the women of my house.

My other grandfather was a patriarch
who sheltered the entire family with his shade
(including in-laws, cousins, distant relatives, friends,
acquaintances, even enemies).
He committed his life to expanding a patrimony
everyone squandered after his death.

And my grandmother Ilse, his dispossessed widow,
what was left for her but to die?

I ask for me, for them, for the women of my house.[5]

Listening to the Message

Y*ou must go back and tell the people that this is the Hour. And there are things to be considered.*

> *Where are you living?*
> *What are you doing?*
> *What are your relationships?*
> *Are you in right relation?*
> *Where is your water?*
> *Know your garden.*
> *It is time to speak your Truth.*
> *Create your community.*
> *Be good to each other.*
> *And do not look outside yourself for the leader.*

This could be a good time! There is a river flowing now very fast. It is so great and swift that there are those who will be afraid. They will try to hold on to the shore. They will feel they are being torn apart and will suffer greatly.

Know the river has its destination. The elders say we must let go of the shore, push off into the middle of the river, keep our eyes open, and our heads above the water.

See who is there with you and celebrate. At this time in history, we are to take nothing personally. Least of all, ourselves. For the moment that we do, our spiritual growth and journey comes to a halt.

The time of the lone wolf is over. Gather yourselves!

Banish the word struggle from your attitude and your vocabulary. All that we do now must be done in a sacred manner and in celebration.

We are the ones we've been waiting for.
                    —The Hopi Elders, Oraibi, Arizona.

I have been pondering this message from the Hopi Elders. I have read it many times over, inevitably placing myself and my life inside the meaning I cull from its instructions. I have read it to others or asked them to read it, watching their faces as they do, listening for their responses.

Is this spiritual advice, religious (divinely-inspired, mystical or symbolic) and so not applicable to those of us who did not grow up Hopi, don't really know the Hopi vision of our world, or are leery of anything religious? (I should say, for the record, that while I am deeply spiritual, at this point in history I find religion—all religion—abhorrent. It's claims and demands seem to me to be at the root of so many of our attitudes of superiority, prejudices, misconceptions and crimes against humanity—as well as imposing hierarchical structures and blinding its adherents to certain historical truths.)

That which is sacred is not necessarily constrained by religion. In cultures rooted in place and attuned to the rhythms of the seasons, where need and not greed governs the most important life decisions, and consensus outranks competition as the preferred method for making decisions, that which is called sacred is much more than an arbitrary set of beliefs. In such a culture, to do something in a sacred manner is to do it with a pure heart: responsibly, seriously, with full knowledge of its impact. The spiritual and the secular are of a piece.

I also read a political subtext into the Message from the

Hopi Elders. Perhaps this is because in my world vision everything is political—even as it may also be spiritual, practical,
intimate or general. I understand my particular storyline as a
strand in the story of humankind. Today many of these strands
are frayed, floundering, broken. The fast-flowing river, so great
and swift that it makes many of us afraid, is an image I can readily embrace.

But there are questions.

The statement that stops a number of the people I ask to
read this and tell me what they feel, is the exhortation that we
take nothing personally, least of all ourselves. "What does that
mean," a friend asks, "how can we **not** take ourselves personally? And how can we avoid taking personally the ways in which
our planet is being destroyed, the rampage of war waged in our
name, the rollback of so many hard-earned rights, our children's
visceral sense of insecurity, and our responsibility to struggle for
change? What's more, what possible reason could we have for
failing to take these things personally?

I read this part of the message differently. I do not believe
the Hopi Elders would urge any of us to retreat from our place
on the forefront of the struggle for planet wellness, or relinquish
the responsibility we share to make things right. I read the
admonishment not to take ourselves personally as imploring us
not to get stuck in the self-centeredness that fails to understand
we are all in this together, must pull together, work together,
risk ourselves in the current of that fast-flowing river that so
often threatens to drown us in its chaotic current. The river
runs. Whether we like it or not, whether or not we understand
it, we are caught in its flow.

But then there's the part about banishing the word struggle from our attitude and vocabulary. Struggle has been my
cherished companion, a rush of energy embracing knowledge
and intention, feeling and commitment. Struggle has filled me,

made me proud. (Is it this pride, perhaps, that we are being asked to shed?) It is through struggle—with others, with myself—that I have learned that misery and ignorance are not natural to the human condition, that change is possible, that there are viable alternatives to greed and domination.

It is through struggle that I came into my socialism and my feminism, became a writer, a poet, someone who uses language to express myself and affect the minds and emotions of others. It is through struggle that I gave birth to four children, raised them to understand my vision of the world, and then released them to follow their own. It is through struggle that I have remained curious, embraced my lesbian self, encouraged my partner's growth even as I ask that she nurture mine. It is in struggle that I stand up for what I believe is important, and continue to advocate for justice.

In struggle, I am who I am.

I want to understand what these Elders mean when they tell me to banish struggle from my attitude and vocabulary. Do I imagine I will forever have to strain against the forces bent on crushing honesty, twisting truth, destroying life? If so, what is my trade-off? What do I get in return for unending struggle?

Must the fact that the forces lined up against us have enormous power on their side mean that I have to push and push and push, not content until the monster stumbles or falls? Is not the smallest act of integrity also necessary to a world in which integrity matters? Courage means "the heart speaking." What if I stood perfectly still in my own power, my own ancient power? What if I made myself huge, like one must do when suddenly faced with a bear or lion or some other wild animal that regards one as a possible meal and has the obvious advantage?

As a young woman I embraced my era's struggles for justice with a passion yearning for its moment of bloom. From earliest childhood, dishonesty and unfairness elicited my rebellion. I refused to play the hypocrite's game.

Later my causes were more organized, collaborative: the stand against our nation's nuclear build-up, support for the Cuban revolution and the civil rights struggle in the U.S. south, fury against the U.S. war of aggression in Vietnam and its exploitative foreign policy elsewhere. Already an incipient poet, and immersed in the New York art world (where rejection of social hypocrisy and authoritarianism were as deeply ingrained as among the Beats and other rebel groups), it was easy for me to challenge a sterile, conformist society. Questioning mainstream political stances grew easily out of my rejection of the mores that shaped and stifled creativity in the United States at the midpoint of the twentieth century.

The anti-communist hysteria that had meant death and lingering devastation for hundreds of thousands at Hiroshima and Nagasaki,[1] induced neighbor to turn against neighbor here at home, produced a police state in this land, ruined creative careers and cost innocent people their lives, was bound to provoke its counterpart in a rush of protest and resistance, both individual and collective.

Born in 1936, I only vaguely remember Hiroshima, the end of World War II, the murders of Ethel and Julius Rosenberg. But I came of artistic and political age as the pendulum began to swing. My early poetry was influenced by the "art beyond politics" dictum, but it wasn't difficult for me to embrace a more Brechtian use of language. Everything, absolutely everything, was worth writing about. Injustice was as legitimate a subject as love.

Struggle became my way of life. What to do with that life, now, if I'm to banish struggle?

"We are to take nothing personally. Least of all, ourselves." It was during my New York years (1958-61) and later in Mexico (1961-69), that I began to gain a first-hand understanding of

late-stage capitalism, the ways in which the United States controlled the countries within its sphere of influence—through
deceptive investment, unfair trade, exploitation reminiscent of
the Middle Ages, diplomatic deviancy, military invasion, fear
tactics and the warning explicit in the knowledge that "he who
holds the power, calls the shots."

I took personally what my government was doing to
Mexico and other dependant nations, not because I was a target
of its corrupt policies but because I lived among their peoples as
a privileged, white U.S. American. For too many years, when
faced with the evidence of my country's abuse of others, guilt
and shame were the only emotions I could muster. Neither is
useful; both immobilize.

Feminist thought and action burst upon the Western
political scene towards the end of the decade of the 1960s,
beginning of the '70s. "The personal is political," the
Movement's spokeswomen claimed, and I could understand—
intellectually at least—that this was true. Reading this Message
from the Hopi Elders back then, I might have argued not only
that we **must** take everything personally but that not to do so
would dilute our politics.

By this time my own history included a bilingual literary
quarterly that had become an institution.[2] We published the
most important poets then writing in Spanish and English, as
well as numerous younger artists who were yet to achieve recognition. Some of them made their first appearances in the pages
of our journal. We were part of a great explosion, a renaissance
of independent creativity. We looked beyond the current literary canon to oral tradition and poems from some of the indigenous cultures. Yet we gave voice to very few women, and many
of those we did publish would have felt honored to be told they
"wrote like a man" or that their work was "as good as any
man's".

Gradually or immediately—I cannot say which—feminism took hold of me with both hands. It lifted me, presented me with a mirror image I didn't like, and rearranged my priorities. I began to listen to women's voices, seek out poetry and other texts by women, and—most important—dig deep for my own woman's sense of self, my own voice. Only a few years after putting together an anthology of 15 young Cuban poets, for which "I could only find three women," I did the work necessary to producing another anthology, this one of 25 Cuban poets—all of them women.[3] We were there. We needed only to look for ourselves.

Or, as the Hopi Elders tell us, "We are the ones we've been waiting for."

My career as an oral historian dates from this time. Going to other women to learn about their experiences broadened my perspective and produced a long list of books,[4] but the changes in my own life—grappling with feelings of inadequacy with regard to the men with whom I was involved, breaking old patterns of subservience—shaped my most important involvements from that time forward. This profound shift in the way I saw myself and the world influenced personal relationships, how I raised my children, what I expected of others, in short: how I felt, thought, saw, heard, knew.

This was a long process of course. Ongoing, I would say now. It took years, for example, before I was able to fully get my head around the fact that despite my deep admiration for some of my century's great revolutionary leaders—Lenin, Mao, Ho Chi Minh, Fidel Castro, Agostinho Neto, Samora Machel, Nelson Mandela: all men—only those who relinquished personal power remain unstained. Like many women of my generation, I had to walk (and drag myself and crawl and stumble and leap) the distance between a consciousness of male power abuse and an understanding of the authoritarian nature of patriarchy as a system.

I was one of those Marxists for whom it took many years, inestimable loss (much of it deeply personal, because it had meant the deaths of comrades close to me), and the dissolution of socialism as we knew it, to arrive at an analysis that places gender and race and cultural contradictions up there with the contradiction of class. It was only when I began to understand the ways in which all these contradictions intersect and shape one another that I was fully able to consider the importance of environmentalism, non-intervention as a point of departure for the relations between nations, respect for difference, spiritual as well as practical insights, human and civil rights, and the need to take each of these issues seriously.

Around this time I was able to make another important connection. From earliest memory I had suffered from a phobia whose source I couldn't fathom. Feminist psychotherapy helped me trace this phobia to the experience of having been sexually abused by my maternal grandparents before I was capable of speech. Slowly, painfully, coming to terms with this buried memory enabled me to understand the fundamental connection between the invasion of a child's or woman's body by someone (usually a man) who abuses power, and the invasion of a small or vulnerable country by one that is larger or more powerful.

Abuse mirrors abuse. The same sort of issues are at stake, whether we are talking about individuals or nations. Only the degree differs, and this difference is meaningless to the victim. Seen from a power perspective, both are imbalances that remain socially or politically acceptable as long as authoritarian rule goes unchallenged. Until we question the behavior and call the offenders to task, the abuse will continue—in spheres ranging from family, church and community to the international arena.

Gradually, I have also come to a place where I can understand that humans, animals, plants, earth air, water are linked in cycles of birth, life, death and rebirth. Abuse of one affects us all. No longer can I scoff at my friend who wanted to save the seals when so many millions of children die of starvation. My world has grown to embrace the children and the seals.

I began to understand power. How it works. How it is abused. How the ways in which it is wielded affect us all: wielder and target, powerful and powerless. I came to see power itself as a political category, and realized that only by placing an analysis of power at the center of struggle can real progress be safeguarded.

I understand the Message from the Hopi Elders as a message about power.

"The time of the lone wolf is over." In the context of my experience, the lone wolf is the man (or occasionally woman) who places him or herself above the needs of others. He who grabs power and holds onto it—whether through self-designation, as leader or dictator, or via a process claiming to be democratic while bought with money or influence: whether by no election or skewed election, military or legal coup, bloodshed or maneuvering Supreme Court justices serving the interests of the man in question.

The lone wolf is the father who sexually abuses his daughter, the pedophile priest (or minister or rabbi or imam or guru), the soldier who massacres civilian peasants under guise of war, the terrorist who flies a plane into a building full of people. The lone wolf is the international terrorist who operates under some self-fabricated "law of God" and the president who goes on a rampage of war under pretext of defending one country's national security.

"The time of the lone wolf is over," the Hopi Elders tell us, "Gather yourselves!"

But how do we gather ourselves? How do we go about doing this, especially, if we are to banish the word struggle from our attitudes and vocabularies. For isn't struggle the only effective way we have of gathering ourselves, pulling ourselves together in great communal resistance to these varied but inter-connected abuses of power?

Perhaps it is a semantic problem, but I don't think so. I believe this is about content as well as form.

Maybe the answer lies in the last line of the Elders' Message: "We are the ones we've been waiting for."

"We are the ones we've been waiting for" implies, to me, that we must stop looking to heroes, to those larger-than-life-sized figures divested of human complexity, for example and answer. We must learn to think and feel, and to trust our deep-est instincts. To consider the evidence, make our own decisions and commitments.

Who among us would not choose life over death, sanity over insanity, beauty over ugliness, justice over injustice? Who among us does not want, desperately, to give our children and grandchildren a world that is safer, more ecologically sound, with less violence and misery? Of course there are always some who do not want these things, some for whom personal greed overrides all other considerations. But are they not a very small minority? On a level playing field, would they not be insignificant?

"We are the ones we've been waiting for" means each of us must risk everything for a viable future, "let go of the shore, push off into the middle of the river, keep our eyes open, and our heads above the water." It means that as we do what is right and just and kind and generous, in whatever venue small or large, we must take note of "who is in there with us, and cele-brate."

Celebration, in the tragedy of today's world, must surely involve knowing where we live, rooting ourselves in place and honoring and protecting that place. Knowing what we are doing, taking conscious responsibility for our actions and their effect upon others. Knowing our relationships, choosing them with care while favoring inclusiveness over elitism. Knowing where our water is and protecting its sources, for water will be tomorrow's most highly valued commodity, just as fuel and electrical power are today. Knowing our gardens means, among much else, being alert to the genetic manipulation and poisoning of our food.

As the Hopi Elders so wisely tell us, we must create community and be good to one another. Only in this way can we level the playing field, strengthen the hand of those who choose life, and isolate the minority that doesn't.

At this beginning of the twenty-first century, when our experiences of setback and defeat have made so many of us road-weary, disillusioned with forms of struggle we once trusted, and hesitant about committing ourselves to new efforts that may end as those others did, in deception and resignation, perhaps celebration **is** our only viable struggle. Celebration of what we have achieved and of life itself.

Let us celebrate our passions, our differences, and what joins us. Let us celebrate our dreams and the infinite strands of creativity and work that have taken us thus far. Let us celebrate every example of creative affirmation, every guarantee of freedom and every struggle that made it possible. Let us celebrate peace and do our part to sustain the conditions that make peace work. Let us celebrate the individual who is true and the family that loves and cares for its members (whether traditional, nuclear, extended, single or two-parented, gay or straight, religious or secular, born or chosen). Let us celebrate every collectivity in which the thinking and the feeling and the doing and the making are truly horizontal in their interaction.

I close my eyes and see the river. Fleeing sunlight hands the reflected white brightness of salt spills over to a full moon's radiance. Where water rushes past rock there is a seam: forever riveting my vision. There, where land and water touch, process calls, hums, shouts.

CHAPTER SEVENTEEN

A Dictator by Any Other Name...

The term dictator has been used in my lifetime to describe a range of political leaders. Certainly Hitler was a dictator, perhaps the first of whom I was conscious—and about whom there is fairly universal agreement. The term was used by some when speaking of Stalin, whose ruthless repression and murder of tens of thousands of his people blighted a system intended to facilitate the worker's state. The Western press routinely referred to Mao and Tito and other Communist leaders as dictators, yet even their enemies were forced to admit that they governed states in which raising the quality of life for the majority was an ongoing goal.

Fidel, dictator for a succession of U.S. administrations, might meet the standard if armed takeover and a lifetime in office were the only criteria; but what of Cuba's titanic struggle to create a more just and egalitarian society, its successful education and health reforms, and the fact that it has a generous history of sending technical and material aid to other developing nations?

Is a dictator, then, only one who comes to office through a takeover rather than via free elections? What other characteristics must he possess? (I say he, because almost all dictators have been men, a fact that reflects the gendered nature of power.)

My personal experience in Latin America enables me to speak of that continent's twentieth century dictators: Trujillo, Batista, Duvalier, Stroesner, Somoza, Bordaberry, Videla,

Pinochet: men who possessed all the characteristics of a dictator (illegal assumption of office, grabbing by one means or
another exaggerated executive powers, extreme brutality in the
social, political and economic spheres, and a focus on armed
defense of his regime at the expense of the welfare of its citizens).

Over time the term dictator has been used rather loosely.
I do not subscribe to this sort of careless naming. By the same
token it is difficult to convey—to a readership unfamiliar with
the reality—what dictators have done to human lives. I have
family and friends who bear the deep scars of this experience—
in Chile, Argentina, Uruguay, Nicaragua, Guatemala, South
Africa. Others have been lost, their lives cut short or rendered
unrecognizable by the brutality of dictatorial regimes.

My daughter-in-law's Uruguayan family survived their
country's dictatorship split down the middle: she and her sister,
both teenagers at the time, were forced into exile with their
father. Her brother, who had just been accepted into medical
school, stayed behind. So did his fiancée. As a result, for six
long years neither group saw or had telephone contact with the
other. There were no diplomatic relations between their homeland and the country where the exiled members had taken
refuge.

Recently, on a visit to Uruguay, I asked these men and
women if they would be willing to talk about what those years
had been like for each of them. It was a warm January night in
the Southern Hemisphere. We'd come from watching a neighborhood soccer game in which their children—my grandchildren—had taken part. They were willing, but there was a palpable tension in the air as sisters and brother and others settled
into lawn chairs under the beach house's ivy-covered portal and
began to retrieve memories long kept safely stored in silence.

That night I learned something about what dictatorship

can do, even to those who survive it in relatively good shape. I listened to the sister who hated having been forced to leave her country and to the brother who tried to recreate what it had been like never having been able to speak out. The fiancée, long-since wife and mother, explained how she'd completed a five-year degree in a career she didn't want, because dictatorship tainted academia, making honest decisions impossible. This was not a conversation about prison, torture or Post-traumatic Stress Disorder; I've had plenty of those as well. This conversation put me in touch with family separation and the subtler aspects of life under dictatorship, the less dramatic damage that nonetheless affects entire populations. It made vivid the way dictatorship can creep up on people, holding them in its grip until escape may no longer be an option. It made me see process rather than the horror of end result alone.

Few people I know agree with my contention that in the United States, here and now, we have a dictator for president. An aspiring dictator, perhaps a new sort of dictator, but a dictator nonetheless. Given U.S. hegemony and the nature of power in the world today, he represents incalculable danger for humans and the earth we inhabit. George W. Bush is a dictator in all but name, surrounded by a coterie of men and women as single-minded and devoted to their leader as the Goerings and Himmlers of the Third Reich.

Although Bush has assumed dictatorial powers, the United States is not a dictatorship. Not yet. We can still protest, and do so in great numbers. A wide range of opinions are expressed, although the administration encourages the more conservative which are consequently gaining in official currency. A discourse of messianic nationalism is not limited to Bush, but has been taken up as well by many in his government—even by Colin Powell, who some believed might prove to be a voice of reason. Lawmakers in general have been hasty in giving the Executive the power to make decisions that push the nation to focus on homeland security and defense while cutting back on infrastructure and social programs. It is a frightening time.

Faced with a dictator president, we still have that margin of freedom in which we may prevent a true dictatorship. And it is imperative that we do prevent it.

Dictatorship in the name of democracy: a 21st-century phenomenon. The United States calls itself a democracy. Despite Manifest Destiny, the making and breaking of foreign governments (many of them democratically elected) and similar expansionist policies, much of its history has been truly democratic. We have a liberal Constitution and Bill of Rights, a tradition of suffrage that has proved a model, struggles such as those waged for civil and minority rights that remain exemplary. But to earn the right to call itself a democracy, surely a country must meet the standards long associated with the term: honest elections, representative government, a genuine concern for its citizens' welfare, real meaningful freedom of speech, assembly and dissent.

Not only does our current president proclaim himself the global standard bearer for democracy, he has taken it upon himself to wage war in a number of places in defense of that representation. A powerful establishment media echoes his words. In the name of democracy Americans are being asked to pay for and die in wars thousands of miles away. No, not asked: forced. Those in favor of Bush's policies often proclaim "We support Our President and Our Troops," implying that those of us who disagree do not support the young men and women being sent abroad to kill and die. I resent this implication. I am appalled that so many thousands of young U.S. Americans are being sacrificed. True support for our troops would be bringing them home alive.

Increasingly, protest is considered unpatriotic. Flag waving takes the place of informed debate. Protest, although growing fast, also seems to be beside the point when it comes to affecting policy. Bush simply charges ahead with his storyline, at home and abroad. He has publicly stated that the United Nations is "either with us, or irrelevant," and that other nations must join his coalition in a war without end or they too will become irrelevant.

Let's look at how George W. Bush meets or fails to meet the most important definitions of a dictator.

Dictators assume power through coups, historically military coups. A country's powerful interests may feel threatened by a civilian president—sometimes socialist or populist or otherwise intent upon spreading the wealth—and sectors of the Armed Forces take over. Historically, these takeovers have been affected with more or less bloodshed, ranging from tens of thousands slaughtered to a brief skirmish in which a dozen or so may die. Frequently our own CIA has had a hand in engineering these coups—Guatemala, Chile, Congo, Panama, to name a few.

For many years within the United States, large personal fortunes or the ability to siphon public funds have determined who wins elections—at least to the most important state and national offices. These elections may not be classified as takeovers, but they can hardly be considered democratic; without spending millions you can't win. Still, the presidential election of 2000 cast democracy in a qualitatively new mold.

There seems little doubt that Al Gore ended up with more votes than George W. Bush. Later independent investigations show that the Republicans perpetrated all manner of electoral fraud. When this fraud didn't achieve the desired results, the matter was placed in the hands of the Supreme Court, a Court sworn to judicial honesty but largely appointed by interests for whom a Bush presidency was imperative. This then was a judicial, rather than a military, coup. George W. Bush became president via the decision of five out of nine Supreme Court justices. Immediately, he proclaimed his victory a "triumph of the democratic process."[1]

This use (or misuse) of language is one of the ways in which those who have usurped power in this country are able to manipulate large sectors of the population. We are told that our democracy is precious, that we must protect it and that the wars we are urged to fight are in its defense. Our highest officials warn us that a situation threatens U.S. national security, and without questioning the statement we are ready to fight the presumed threat, even when doing so means sacrificing our own freedoms, economic stability, and the lives of our young.

Since September of 2001, whenever people have begun to mobilize for job security, health care, prescription drug benefits for the elderly or other important domestic issues, the sudden revelation of a terrorist threat to our borders, transportation system or bridges has drawn the public's attention away from such concerns. Raising Homeland Security's color-coded warning from yellow to orange is enough to frighten people and make them compliant, even when such heightened security has almost always turned out to have been unnecessary. We are ready to fight, to die and to kill. And killing seems all the easier since we have been trained to consider those we kill non-persons.

We have been manipulated into believing that what we have is democracy. Every rousing speech, every media assumption, every commercial advertisement, many films, song lyrics and repeated images support this belief. So masses of people, tricked into accepting this misnomer, don't question the half-truth. This manipulation is also incremental in nature. As the population is coaxed or badgered into accepting each new piece of misinformation, the next is but a few degrees further along on the path of that which we have come to consider acceptable. The doublespeak is aimed at convincing us that caution justifies racism, tax cuts for the wealthy and consumer confidence will heal the economy, privatization translates into security, or making war will curb terrorism and bring peace.

Getting large numbers of people to accept his lies is vital for any dictator. Contemporary methodology is much more sophisticated than the brute force displayed more than half a century ago. On Kristallnacht in 1938, government-sponsored hordes raged through Nazi-controlled cities, physically destroying synagogues and Jewish businesses and homes. Following 9/11 here, official discourse was careful to pronounce itself against violence towards the Arab community; yet dozens if not hundreds of people of Middle Eastern origin have been murdered, their families victimized, their property destroyed. Perpetrators have suffered no significant punishment. This racial profiling and its tragic consequences are ongoing.

There are other uncomfortable similarities. The Nazis called up Jews and others and forced them to register; millions were sent to their death. Here, today, thousands of men of Arab or Middle Eastern origin have been summoned to registration centers, only to be summarily detained. Many of these men have been denied access to families or lawyers; in some cases their whereabouts are unknown. Will Bush stop at this level of gross injustice, or will we be able to stop him? Will he find it necessary to carry the repression to some "final solution"?

Dictators have additional characteristics. Essential among them is a blatant disregard for public opinion. At this writing, according to a number of polls 64% of U.S. Americans are against Bush's decision to invade Iraq. These people disagree with the president for a variety of reasons; some may believe in peace, others may believe in war but feel that the case against

Saddam Hussein has yet to be fully made; and there is a range of opinions between these two positions. Still, 64% of the population is a clear majority.[2] Even if this majority were to become 74% or 94%, I don't believe it would deter Bush's plans for war. Dictators forge ahead with their policies. It is inherent to the condition.

Because I believe that axes of political power represent complex economic and geopolitical interests, I am loathe to make too much of what many consider a classic dictator's psychological profile. Still, the term Napoleonic Complex—when speaking about a man of small stature who tries to make up for what he lacks in physical size through unchecked conquest—references a reality. Similarly, other physical and psychological characteristics, often traceable to a painful childhood or brutal parenting, can and do shape a person's adult life.

The noted Swiss psychotherapist and author Alice Miller has put forth a theory about why certain men become dictators: cold, calculating criminals unable to feel true compassion and uninterested in anything but personal power.[3] Miller explores the childhoods of Hitler and others, and notes that "the bodies of the executioners, torturers and the orchestrators of organized manhunts may have learned their fateful lessons very early and thus very effectively. What made respected members of society suddenly act like monsters?" she asks. What they have in common, she discovers, would seem to be brutal early childhood parenting.

Miller explains that "[P]resent-day neurobiological research makes it easier...to understand the way Nazis like Eichmann, Himmler, Hoss and others functioned. The rigorous obedience training they underwent in earliest infancy stunted the development of such human capacities as compassion and pity for the sufferings of others. They were incapable of emotion in the face of misfortune, such feelings were alien to them.

Their total emotional atrophy enabled the perpetrators of the most heinous crimes imaginable to function 'normally' and to continue to impress their environment with their efficiency in the years after the war without the slightest remorse." Perhaps this is the previously missing piece in our ability to understand the actions of the world's most brutal dictators, men like Duvalier, Somoza, Pinochet and, yes, Saddam Hussein. Now it seems we must add George W. Bush to the list.

But with Bush, the veneer of normalcy—even "compassionate normalcy"—is extraordinarily well developed. George W's father was Yale-educated, knowledgeable about global politics, and became President of the United States. His son, too, attended Yale—though he graduated with difficulty.[4] He tried a series of business ventures, most notably in oil, and is generally considered to have failed at them all. He is a reformed binge drinker who was primed for the role of world leader without ever having traveled abroad. When he first took office, his garbled pronunciation and one-line non-sequiturs quickly became national jokes.

Let no one be deceived, however. Our current president may be unsophisticated and lacking in intellectual depth, but he is shrewd and has shown that he knows how to surround himself with men and women as insidious as they are ruthless. Together, they are pushing forward a politics of domination in the domestic as well as international spheres. The enactment of certain laws, the promotion of carefully-chosen players, have been particularly useful in putting this politics in place. Central among these are the Patriot Act of 2001 and the Domestic Security Enhancement Act of 2003, a draft of which was leaked to the public in February.[5]

Bush's policies reach into our lives in a variety of ways. A Christian fundamentalist ideology allows for a discourse of "compassion" while shaping, controlling, punishing.[6] The first victims of these policies are environmental health and safety, privacy, poverty programs, public education and academic freedom at the university level, dissent, healthcare (Medicare and Medicaid, funding for public hospitals, women's reproductive health, prescription drug benefits, research not done by the major pharmaceutical and insurance companies, etc.). Public debate and dissent, and the right to privacy, are under violent attack. Anyone seen as "different," or as not complying with the Bush doctrine, is suspect. Abroad the victims are the established international bodies and all countries and peoples who get in the way of this administration's dream of world conquest.[7]

Dictatorship is about the abuse of power, power that is unchallenged, that has been elevated to a sort of omnipotence, whether through military control, via sophisticated mechanisms of manipulation, or by political blackmail. One wonders why so many otherwise intelligent men and women— Democratic and Independent members of Congress, intellectuals of stature, allied presidents, members of the UN Security Counsel—speak out against the Bush doctrine but with few exceptions fall into step behind the president when the hour for a vote or some other tangible form of support arrives.

It has become a truism to say that absolute power corrupts absolutely. Yet making the leap from speaking about the unauthorized and criminal exercise of power to calling a dictator by his name seems difficult for many to make.

In protest demonstrations on the streets of U.S. American cities one placard among many reads "Regime Change Begins at Home." It is past time we take this exhortation seriously. Impeachment would seem a logical next step.

CHAPTER EIGHTEEN

"Unsubstantiated Belief"

What We Assume as Truth, and How We Use those Assumptions[1]

My Random House Dictionary of the English Language[2] defines folklore as "a body of widely held but false or unsubstantiated beliefs." The Oxford English Dictionary[3] gives a slightly different but related definition: "The traditional beliefs, legends, and customs, current among the common people. The study of these." The class bias in the latter is obvious: the beliefs, legends, and customs held or practiced by "the common people" are suspect, somehow—and thus, perhaps, unsubstantiated or false.

As folklorists you are familiar with these definitions, familiar with them in ways—and with nuances—I cannot duplicate. And of course you know what folklore means to you. Before going further, I should make it clear that I do not believe you subscribe to these dictionary definitions; later I'll get back to the ways in which you yourselves describe the valuable work you are doing.

My comments here today will necessarily be those of a layperson. I will not attempt to enter your field or take on the range of issues it embraces. Yet I find connections. In my years of working as an oral historian, I faced some of the problems you face.

As a poet, a writer, thinking about your invitation to speak to this meeting I started by considering what the term folklore has meant to me, someone outside the field.

Folklore, or the folkloric—at least to the unspecialized ear—implies something exotic. Not necessarily unsubstantiated, but certainly other. There is the ever so slight aura of that which is legend rather than accurately-recorded history, superstition rather than scientific truth, a wisdom not easily quantified, the cultural practices or creativity prevalent among people who are different from ourselves. Often dramatically different.

Identification with mainstream society—white, owner class, formally-educated, elitist, generally male—builds upon our socially-conditioned racism and xenophobia to make sure we see the people who inhabit these categories as central, while relegating those of other races, ethnicities, economic status, gender identity, and religious or political beliefs to the category of marginal, i.e. other. Indigenous peoples everywhere seem particularly folkloric to the middle-of-the-road U.S. American.

Thus Judeo-Christian philosophy (or baseball, Fourth of July picnics, an easy-going "Come back and see us, honey!," and the Armed Forces of the United States) are mainstream, while the Navajo or Hopi belief systems, drums, spirituals, hip-hop, "Mi casa es su casa," irregular or guerrilla struggle, or not subscribing to a socially acceptable model of success, remain outside the mainstream. The free market and Wall Street represent economics as we know and live them, while barter or in-kind trade may appear folkloric. This tendency to judge other people and their cultures according to how like or unlike us we perceive them to be, sets the stage for behavior that may range from fearful and disdaining to immoral and even criminal.

There have long been two competing tendencies in U.S. culture, separate but overlapping folklores if you will. One is made up of the positive traditions of fairness, pride, rugged individualism, independence, democracy, freedom of speech and dissent, for which our nation has become a beacon—real or imagined.

The other is the sense of superiority and entitlement that produced such rapacious conquest going back to the 19th century and before (the U.S. takeovers of the Philippines, Puerto Rico, and Cuba, the building and operation of the Panama Canal, all the way up to the power it wields today through its control of the World Bank, International Monetary Fund, and World Trade Organization, to name only the major international institutions). This second tendency promotes the idea that we do not need to know about the rest of the world, understand or respect its cultures, or speak its languages. It disparages and sabotages such truly international bodies as the United Nations and World Court.

The Bush administration has built on this long tradition of perceiving ourselves as superior, entitled and all-powerful, and has taken great care to refashion our collective concept of what is real (acceptable) and what must be considered fringe (unacceptable). Flag-waving vs. a lack of patriotism, pro-life dogma vs. a reverence for all life, narrow family values vs. more inclusive family values, responsibility to the environment and our endangered resources vs. support for corporate greed, invasion of foreign lands and peoples as a way of "keeping the peace."

But our current predicament did not begin with the Bush administration. Its roots go way back. In the case of Iraq, for example, today's invasion and occupation was preceded by years of military aggression and economic sanctions which caused, among other horrors, the death by starvation of half a million Iraqi children. We needed rhetoric here at home that would make this aggression acceptable, and Democrats as well as Republicans placed such rhetoric solidly in the mainstream of our political discourse. The practice has been used by all stripes of politicians before and throughout Vietnam, Cambodia, Laos,

Guatemala, Nicaragua, Somalia—the list is a long one.

It is interesting to examine the ways in which certain values, beliefs and convictions survive, while others—no less "American"—are pushed aside. As folklorists, or simply as those concerned with a people's traditions, this question presents a vital challenge to us today.

Those of us who do not subscribe to the Bush/Cheney/Ashcroft /Rumsfeld agenda—policies based on information now clearly revealed as unsubstantiated—are increasingly threatened, marginalized, made to feel "folkloric." I realize that folklorists may find this use of the term too great a stretch. But I go back to the "body of widely held but false or unsubstantiated beliefs" being thrust upon us today, even as those who dare to question such beliefs are being made to feel that we are unpatriotic, outsiders, do not belong.

I am struck, in other words, by a careful and, I believe, intentional distortion in public discourse—and thus in meaning. If folklore is defined, at least etymologically, as "widely-held but false or unsubstantiated beliefs," why is the administration's rhetoric not considered folkoric?

One clue is the dramatic and astoundingly successful twisting of language that goes on in every venue, and has brought the U.S. public to a place where any new pill is believed to be the magic cure for a complex disease—as long as its advertising includes images of the young and radiant.

There is also a much more profound explanation. Following the late 1980s defeat of important socialist experiments—an identity crisis for progressive people everywhere—language and concepts such as class struggle or imperialism began to appear antiquated: in a sense folkoric. Whole generations of young people who grew up in the 1980s and '90s, no longer took these ideas seriously. But I would offer a word of caution.

The brutal implacability with which the Bush administration now rules the world may in fact bring about an unexpected reversal in this mindset. These concepts can no longer be considered antiquated, their truth is out there for all to see. Millions in the countries we attack are currently experiencing imperialist conquest. Millions here at home are living the brutal effects of class warfare. Who can predict what may happen when these millions, whose new consciousness comes from their own experience, decide to do something about the injustices?

Each of the administration's policy initiatives, whether they are aimed at increasing corporate profit at the expense of the environment or have to do with yet another blatant military takeover in another country of the world, is couched in soothing and reassuring (numbing?) terms. They are introduced with phrases such as "to streamline the process... to replace an archaic system... to provide greater flexibility... to bring balance back."

Just one example: Late last year the EPA announced new pollution standards for antiquated hog factories that had already polluted 35,000 miles of our rivers. Then EPA-director Christie Whitman introduced the new rules with the following totally unsubstantiated claim: "This is a major step forward to protect our nation's waters." Fine, except that the rules were bland and ineffective, and the "standards" weren't even mandatory. They were simply goals to be wished for. Each hog factory was to develop its own voluntary plan for controlling its pollution. The EPA's new "standards" even allowed each factory to keep its plan secret.[4]

I won't attempt to list the occasions on which the administration has misrepresented intelligence findings, suggested links between terrorist organizations that have no basis in fact, or lied about a presumed national security threat here or axis of

evil there. The current formula seems to be to use unsubstantiated or misleading information to frighten people, then go to
war to straighten things out. Once at war, it becomes traitorous
to ask questions. Patriots must rally round the Commander in
Chief.

Throughout the country, since the installation of this
administration and particularly since 9/11, we can point to
innumerable coercive measures, including but not limited to
the curtailment of public discourse, extreme racial profiling,
repression against those of Middle Eastern origin, thousands of
illegal imprisonments and deportations, jobs lost, and subtle
and not so subtle changes in education.

Here in Albuquerque four public high school teachers
were fired this year for refusing to remove anti-war posters from
their classrooms. They had encouraged their students to debate
the administration's decision to attack Iraq, and had displayed
student work featuring both pro- and anti-war opinions. They
were told to take down only the latter. When they refused, they
lost their jobs.

Many people are fighting back. Librarians across the country have quietly and not so quietly been refusing to turn over to
the government lists of the books people read. Six hundred U.S.
Armed Service families with sons or daughters currently serving
in Iraq recently responded to the president's reckless "bring 'em
on" challenge by holding a protest at which they demanded
that Bush bring the troops home now.[5]

But avenues of protest are also closing. Attorney General
Ashcroft's avid list-keeping most recently targets federal judges
whose decisions appear too often to be "soft on crime."
Judgeships and other powerful positions are going to men and
women who support the administration's conservative agenda.

We should not doubt that an orchestrated campaign to get
U.S. Americans to think alike—to join a mainstream, yet

unsubstantiated, view of reality—is underway. To those who suggest I exaggerate, I say they might find it useful to study the mechanisms by which a nation of Germans was prodded to take its historic anti-Semitism to previously unparalleled levels of genocidal crime.

In *The Mass Psychology of Fascism*, visionary psychologist and social analyst Wilhelm Reich dissected the problem of mass psychology: "[t]he economic and the ideological situations of the masses are not necessarily congruent," he warned. "[thus] the examination of society must be of a twofold nature... To use a simple example: if workers who are starved because of low wages strike, or steal bread, their actions result directly from their economic situation. The striking or the stealing out of hunger need no further psychological explanation. The ideology and the action are appropriate to the economic pressure. Economic situation and ideology are congruent. In such cases, reactionary psychology attempts to show the allegedly irrational motives of the striking or stealing; such attempts always lead to reactionary explanations.

"In social psychology, the question is exactly the reverse: What is to be explained is not why the starving individual steals or why the exploited individual strikes, but why the majority of starving individuals do *not* steal and the majority of exploited individuals do *not* strike. Socio-economics, then, can satisfactorily explain a social phenomenon when human thinking and acting serve a rational purpose, when they serve the satisfaction of needs and directly express the economic situation. It fails, however, when human thinking and acting *contradict* the economic situation, when, in other words, they are *irrational*."[6]

As we attempt to dissect the mass psychology used by the current administration as it succeeds in getting ever larger segments of the population to accept what only a few years back would have been unacceptable, we would do well to consider this way of looking at mass psychology in the period leading up to the entrenchment of German fascism.

Especially during the first weeks and months of his administration, I heard more than a few Bush critics label him folk-loric—for his obvious lack of sophistication, inexperience abroad, unfamiliarity with other peoples and their cultures, or butchery of the English language. His mispronunciation of simple words like nuclear (nucular) raised eyebrows or became the inspiration for a whole new brand of political humor.

I admit that at first I too engaged in such banter. Perhaps it functioned as a sort of collective escape valve for our mounting anxiety, as we realized that a bloodless coup had been perpetrated upon us and we were now trapped in a situation from which escape seems less and less possible.

Soon, however, I realized that this down-home manner and talk made the president seem more like "one of the gang," familiar and likeable, folkloric in a very different sense. After all, who cared if nuclear had become nucular? What the new administration was doing was surely more important than how it spoke.

Yet language was also being manipulated in much more subtle ways. And this manipulation was, in fact, beginning to change the way many U.S. Americans see our role as the single world power, our relationship to other peoples within and outside of the United States, indeed our very identities—individual as well as collective.

As the President and Secretary of Defense repeated their assurances that Iraq's Saddam Hussein was linked to the tragedy of September 11, 2001, or that unnamed intelligence supported Iraq's possession of a program of weapons of mass destruction, and as we the people assimilated this body of widely held but false or unsubstantiated information—incorporated it into our belief system, as it were—a folkloric acceptance began to stand

in for thoughtful analysis, and a new era of double-speak consolidated itself.

Ours is an era in which we are urged to believe that pollution is protection, the thinning of our forests against threat of
wild fire is best achieved by uncontrolled logging, tax cuts for
the wealthy will give jobs to the unemployed, and unending war
will bring peace. Some concepts have been stolen from our lexicon: the terms revolution or revolutionary, for example, are
today more likely to describe advances in technology, or even a
new deodorant, than to evoke a struggle for social change.

Popular culture is a powerful tool, and dangerous when
wielded by dangerous political interests. It is no secret that
administration officials have met with the owners of Hollywood
studios to urge them to produce films with a particular slant on
a range of social and political issues. (This undoubtedly has happened before, but now seems an acceptable practice.)
Government pressure and outright censorship have been wielded with a heavy hand against a mainstream press that had long
prided itself on its impartiality. The lyrics of a popular song hit,
currently receiving a great deal of radio airtime, are based on
the assumption that Saddam Hussein was directly responsible
for the attacks on the World Trade Center and Pentagon.[7]

Assumption becomes reality in the public mind.

Even poetry—traditionally a poor cousin when it comes to
government attention and support—has recently been in the
spotlight in this context. But here the attempt at cooptation
backfired in a chorus of protest. Early this year, Laura Bush
invited poets to the White House for a Symposium on Walt
Whitman, Langston Hughes and Emily Dickinson. I wonder if
she or her handlers had any idea of the deep spirit of rebellion
these three poets represent. As her husband put the finishing
touches on his plans for a "Shock and Awe" attack on Baghdad,
a couple of the invited poets asked their friends to send poems

that speak for the conscience of their country.

In a matter of days, 11,000 such poems flooded the internet. Mrs. Bush quickly canceled the symposium. On February 12th, the date for which it had been scheduled, more than 200 poetry readings against the war were held throughout the country. A second round of readings took place on February 17th. And on March 5th the core group of what by then had become a new incarnation of Poets Against the War[8] presented to Ohio Democratic congresswoman Marcy Kaptur an electronic manuscript containing 13,000 poems by nearly 11,000 poets.[9]

Bush and company continue, unabashed, to twist language and tell half-truths and outright lies about the weapons programs supposedly operated by governments they wish to attack, and about a variety of other issues. Ex-president Clinton was threatened with impeachment for lying about an extra-marital affair. George W. Bush has lied about issues of vastly greater importance to our lives, present and future, and so far has gotten away with it.

Those among us who are not taken in by the 2 + 2 = 5 logic continue to speak out—though this has meant no small number of jobs lost, travel plans disrupted, and for some even detention without due process.

Where is reality in all this? Where is sham passing as reality? The representation of truth, when we do not have access to the complexities of our subject, can be extremely difficult.

I imagine that many of you, in your different involvements with folklore, face this question almost daily. I know I did when I was interviewing and then presenting the voices of Latin American women to my readers.[10] For the past several decades, in the oral history field, there has been continuous discussion about the role of the interviewer: who she is in relation to her informant, what class and cultural filtering inevitably takes place, and whether it is possible to compensate or adjust for this filtering in any meaningful way.

Not surprisingly—because feminist theory and practice are very much about understanding power relations—the most probing, honest, and to my mind useful contributions to this ongoing discussion have come from feminist oral historians.[11] One of the results is that good oral historians today begin by attempting to situate themselves with regard to the people whose stories they tell. A pretense at impartiality is no longer acceptable.

I would argue that this fictitious impartiality is not only unacceptable, it is itself a lie. We all have class and cultural origins that inform who we are, the ways in which we relate to others, our worldviews. We make choices, of course. We choose and reject and accept. Our life experiences change us, and we choose those changes with which we feel comfortable. Perhaps our work—if we love it, if it is a calling rather than simply a job—changes us most deeply.

We are living in a troubling, often frightening, time. Woman or man, Republican, Democrat or Independent, professional or laborer, poet, folklorist, teacher, health provider, postal clerk, student, or Army recruit: we cannot feel good about a nation spiraling downward in prolonged economic crisis, the loss of so many jobs, the explosion of violence in our streets and homes, a palpable loss of those traditional American values of hope, independent thought and tolerance, the increasing number of citizens without access to the very basics of life.

Especially, we cannot feel good about our unasked-for policing of the world. Or about the nightly news from overseas: selective or watered-down as it may be. To see the horror and fear in the eyes of so many young men and women, and to come to expect the daily reports of their deaths in a blatantly illegal war, has to affect us deeply.

I promised to get to your own definition of your work.

Many of you may be wondering just when I plan to do that. The American Folklore Society describes itself as "an association of people who create and communicate knowledge about folklore throughout the world. [Its] more than 2,200 members and subscribers are scholars, teachers, and libraries at colleges and universities; professionals in arts and cultural organizations; and community members involved in folklore work."[12] I can imagine that current events must either confirm your belief systems or prod you to revisit a number of your assumptions.

I am thinking not only of Afghanistan or Iraq, but also of a number of seminal events that have recently been shared by so many: the diverse rituals that marked the turning of the last millennium, the problem of how best to honor those lives lost on September 11, 2001, the destruction of Afghanistan's enormous ancient Buddhas by a ferociously dogmatic Taliban, the loss of so much cultural history when U.S. troops invaded Baghdad and bombed its venerable museum, and the violence which inevitably results when an invading army fails to understand the cultures of those it attempts to conquer.

Each of us, from our particular point of view and in our roles as professionals and communicators, has a responsibility to make this world a saner, healthier, safer place. Whatever your area of folklore study or interest, you are privileged to be dealing with the archetypes and expressive forms that together represent what is most unique to, and undying in, the human condition: our relationship to the earth and one another, our creativity, our cultural identities, the very imagination that makes a future possible.

With the current threat to the integrity of identity and imagination, this responsibility takes on a whole new dimension.

My plea is that each of us, in our diverse fields of endeavor, work to transcribe the cultures of others accurately, with humility and cultural sensitivity, even as we restore meaning and integrity to our own language. We must demand that our leaders use language responsibly, and that they safeguard the discussion and dissent so precious throughout our history. And we ourselves must nurture the discoveries in our fields and in others so that they, in turn, will be able to nurture a future welcoming to those coming after.

CHAPTER NINETEEN

One Precious
Moment[1]

I

Could we have imagined a world more rife with horror, more submerged in chaos, more blighted by injustice of all types, and more thoroughly hijacked by a single power-crazed administration than the one we inhabit at this beginning of the twenty-first century? Could we have predicted a world in which those who rule are so utterly consumed by greed, so power-hungry yet so protected, so careless and seemingly oblivious to the ways in which what they perpetrate today will affect all future life?

The arrogance and isolationism with which the George W. Bush administration has decided to formally renounce any involvement in an international criminal court, has declared it will no longer be bound by the 1969 Vienna Convention on the Law of Treaties, has refused to sign UN documents protecting women and children, and has continued to ignore the Kyoto accords on the reduction of greenhouse gasses, shouts a single message: We don't care.[2]

Who, even a few years back, could have imagined a government openly making vicious war against an already devastated land, while at the same time dropping food packages that look like land mines and asking school children to send dollar bills to their counterparts in that far-off country? This describes our invasion of Afghanistan.

The United States has a long history of such assaults, but until fairly recently the U.S. people still had the capacity to be shocked—so the operations were carried out covertly. Until fairly recently, today's images would have been discarded as absurd, even by those Madison Avenue experts whose job it is to convince us that any sort of absurdity is logical or sane; even now when information and disinformation are played as entertainment rather than news.

Perhaps those who have lived through holocaust, torture, lifelong deprivation or abuse, experience these questions as absurdly rhetorical. Perhaps it hasn't been as difficult for such people to imagine the world we have now. Perhaps only those for whom such questions are primarily intellectual are battered by astonishment, plagued by flashes of disbelief. And enraged at how criminality has become acceptable social behavior.

I know that I leave myself open to every sort of critique when I say that I dream a simple solution. Terrifyingly, beautifully simple. I suggest that if each of us were committed to a full measure of justice for every other being, and did our part as well to care for our earth, air, water and other resources, the problems that confront us would fade. That simple. But just that unlikely.

The perpetrators don't have the answers: those presidents and priests, CEOs and economists and generals. Despite their ever more sophisticated rhetoric, it is by now absolutely clear that they seek power for the few at excruciating cost to the many. Anyone who stands in their way is glibly termed "collateral damage."

Those brave men and women who struggle against the perpetrators—beginning with those who showed up in Seattle and Genoa and continuing with the millions around the world who are demonstrating against Bush's policies, those flocking one-hundred thousand strong to Port Alegre, or working for peace and an equitable distribution of goods and services in their own communities—wage the good fight. In terms of

power, they are horribly disadvantaged. Most target a piece of
the whole, and don't stand much of a chance when confronted
with today's hegemony—although some have recently suggested that we have a bipolar world once again: the Bush administration on one side and international public opinion on the
other.

I dream, sometimes, of a modern day Lysistrata, but much
more complete. Not a withholding of sex alone, but of any sort
of cooperation with those who are doing such a thorough job of
destroying our nest and all who inhabit it.

I say the simple solution is unlikely because it is clear to
me that what I perceive as obvious will not, cannot, come
about. It would require a child-like recognition, a turn of heart
and mind impossible for those who hold the reins, impossible
even for those who truly **want** such a change but can only think
in terms of globalization...the liberalization of markets...what
must be on the next agenda for this or that summit...how to
lobby or promote, coerce or convince.

And I say the simple solution is beautiful precisely because
of its simplicity, like the mathematician who describes a complex equation in which every question has been elegantly
answered. What is simple is too often overlooked. I am a poet
and it is as a poet that I write now.

Eyes that have seen too much and a disappointed heart
have brought me here, to this place where I can no longer listen to the raucous speeches, transparent lies and hollow promises. Before the massive demonstrations in the spring of 2003, it
had even become difficult for me to attend the rallies and vigils
of like-minded people; I feared my grief and anger would be co-
opted by agendas that were not my own.

More than 50 years ago, World War II tanks rolled over
crypto biotic soil on North Africa's fragile desert. The prints left
by those tanks are still there. It takes much longer than half a

century for those tiny organisms to regenerate, pull things together again, grow. If we don't start treading lightly, what we need to live will go the way of that damaged sand, vanquished by war materiel long ago replaced by ever more modern models. In Cuba billboards often bore the admonition: "If you know, teach. If you don't know, learn." Simple as that. Each of us doing our part on the world stage or in the relationship, family, community, workplace or school. This is the sort of simplicity I am thinking of: individually and collectively learning to see the other, reject concepts and ideologies that minimize the other's rights, and assume responsible stewardship wherever we may be. I didn't always feel this way. Not that many years back, in fact, I would have scoffed at such a seemingly simple suggestion. This, then, is the story of how narrow my original vision of who deserved a full crack at life was, and how that vision has changed. I want to explore my own social conditioning, and journey out.

II

I was born in 1936, which makes me 67 at this writing. From an early age, something—I still don't know exactly what—made justice important to me. My parents preached honesty and fairness, though as our family life unfolded I, like so many in every generation, came to understand that their ideas of honesty and fairness were limited by their own conditioning, prejudices and fears. I am a product of the North American middle class, privileged by race and disadvantaged by gender— as well as much later also by sexual identity.

My own early ideas of justice were limited too, of course. I thought about blacks as deserving better than what they got, but was almost completely alienated from the Mexican-Americans who lived downtown in my own southwestern city.

My friends and I referred to them as *Pachucos*. I imagined their greased pompadours held hidden knives. When, in my last year of high school I finally wangled a date with the brown-skinned captain of the other high school's football team, he tried to rape me. I had no Latino or Latina friends.

I have written elsewhere of my parents' refusal to rent a small apartment to a college friend of mine from Ghana. This was during my only year of college. My friend had been refused a room in the university dorm, and was having a hard time finding one off campus. I'd believed my parents' anti-racist rhetoric; my father contributed to the NAACP and the National Negro College Fund, and frequently lectured us about racial equality. I was sure a room they rented off their garage, currently empty, was the solution to my friend's predicament. I was shocked, then, when they argued property values and their fear that the neighbor kids might not want to play with my younger brother. I raged with self-righteous indignation, and didn't speak to them for several months. Still, I had as few friends of color as my parents.

My eastern mother and father were fascinated by the local Indians, and we periodically took old clothing out to the pueblos to trade for silver and turquoise jewelry. I was only vaguely uncomfortable with this practice, certainly didn't grasp the ugliness of bartering throwaway clothes for family heirlooms. I remember a warm afternoon at Santa Ana pueblo, eating melon at the adobe home of one of my father's colleagues from work. We never saw him or his family again. My father loved people— all kinds of people—and I believe we would have had more diverse friends had it not been for my mother's ultimate rejection of most of those my father brought around. In her inherited classism, they were never good enough.

My family also took us on great trips. Dad taught music in the public schools and had the summers off, so we boarded freighters to South America and listened to him read us *The Father Brown Stories* while picnicking in English poppy fields. Those journeys expanded my sense of the world, though I've wished our parents had been politically astute enough to be able to ask more complex questions about what life was like for the people we met.

In the nineteen fifties no one I knew spoke openly about homosexuality, so despite the fact that my aunt and her partner lived in Santa Fe and we visited them often, I was unable to think of lesbians and gay men as real. Homophobic and racist allusions and jokes were part of my parents' discourse, mild when compared to some, but still unexamined. When con-fronted, they denied the implications. They didn't think of themselves as racist, classist, or prejudiced in any sense. Yet my mother's response whenever I made a grammatical error—or fell into the New York accent that was my birthright—was always "You speak like a Brooklyn shop girl."

It took me many years to understand that this response was not only classist but also anti-Semitic. Just after I was born, my parents changed our surname from Reinthal to Randall. My repeated questions as to why, invariably brought answers like "Oh, it's easier to spell" or "We just didn't care for your grand-parents' values." It wasn't until after my father's death in 1994 that my mother admitted she had suffered anti-Semitic jibes as a young girl. "I never wanted my children to suffer like I did," she said. I knew that when my father got his college degree major U.S. universities still had quotas for Jews. If our parents had been able to share their pain and fear instead of lying to us, my early years at least would have felt a lot less confusing.

This brief reminiscence is meant to revisit my childhood and young woman's experiences with Blacks, Mexicans, Indians, Jews, and homosexuals. What of the non-human species? Roger was the Dalmatian given to me as a child. I remember loving him, and then losing him to the Second World War. For reasons I've never understood, my parents offered Roger to the war effort, promising he would be returned when the conflict ended. But instead of my dog, what we got was a letter explaining that he'd been trained to kill and was no longer considered safe as a child's pet. I remember a dull anger, accompanied by a promise to myself that I would never love another dog.

As a young woman I was seduced by the excitement of bullfights—first in Spain, then at the *Plaza Monumental* in nearby Ciudad Juárez, Mexico. I remember rooting for the very occasional bull whose courage and resistance earned him an *indulto* or pardon: thousands of units of Penicillin for his nearmortal wounds, followed by retirement to pasture. Pageantry and tradition justified, for me, the horrible cruelty of the sport. Much like the pageantry and tradition of the Catholic Church seem, to many in its hierarchy, to excuse protecting the priests who sexually abuse minors. In the bullring as in the Church, the issue is power.

Fortunately, in time I outgrew the romantic justifications.

Although I certainly couldn't have articulated it back then, I have come to understand that the justice I sought as a child was mostly for white men. I'm sure I believed I included women, since it was not lost on me that I am one. I'm equally sure I included people of color, without wondering why I only began to count them as friends when I got to New York in the late fifties.

Too easily I accepted the expectations and morality that placed me and other females in positions subservient to the men in our lives. Intellectually I also believed that men and women of other races or social conditions deserved their full measure of justice. Practically speaking, as a child I knew few people unlike myself.

As for other living things—animals, plants, the earth itself—I wasn't taught to cherish them. What we ate came from stores, clean, packaged, and disconnected from its source. Few I knew back then questioned how what we ingested was grown or raised, what hormones or other substances were added. Genetic engineering was an issue far in our future. Entering high school before Sputnik, I was led to believe that girls didn't need to learn science or math. Even a rudimentary interest in science might have sparked an engagement with the natural world, but that wasn't a part of my education—either at school or in my parental home.

Still, I saw myself as someone concerned with fairness and, within my limitations of class and color and culture, I was. As a young person I knew I would be a writer. Making the creative journey undoubtedly provided me with a context in which justice seemed a laudable thing. Would I have developed in the same way had I sought a career in business or politics? I don't know.

III

But I did know that I would be a writer. And I do know that I have actively worked for social justice all my life—continually stretching what that means to me and experimenting with how I might participate in achieving it. As an artist (poet, writer, photographer), I have grappled within several different political constructs, with how someone whose currency is the word, the image, the idea, can effectively contribute to a world in which justice defines who we are and how we treat others.

In my early twenties I spent several intense years in New York City, among the Abstract Expressionist artists who were seeking to invent an American school of painting, and among poets seeking authentic patterns of American speech. Some of these people were what our culture likes to call apolitical; process was more important to them than content, social or any other. But some—among them mentors Elaine de Kooning, Jerome Rothenberg, Joel Oppenheimer, Walter Lowenfels, Nancy Macdonald, Allen Ginsberg, Ammon Hennacy, Milton Resnick, and Pat Passlof—were always engaged with the important issues of their times. Those who didn't explicitly paint or write about those issues, organized, demonstrated, signed petitions, or stood at the barricades.[3]

Personally, at this time in my life I was decidedly less respectful of myself than of others. As a young woman, hungry for the intimate connection that might lead to what I then thought of as soul-mating, I allowed myself to be used by almost any man who showed an interest. Older women, including my mother, had been unable to offer me alternative models. And I'd been unable to develop one of my own.

I thought of myself as independent, because I lived alone, supported myself, made my own decisions. It was a mediated independence. Many although certainly not all of the young women in the New York art world of those years were "groupies," following and catering to the men rather than prioritizing our own creative visions. It is a heritage that still aches in me, and I wonder when our diverse cultures will nurture honesty over hypocrisy, enabling young women and men to explore their real needs with neither shame nor subterfuge.

But the work was also beginning to be central, and in important ways it showed me a way out. In those late nineteen fifties, McCarthyism still chilled our nation's creativity. Artists and writers I knew had been persecuted by the witch hunts, their lives broken. Others I knew only through their work, lost jobs, were imprisoned, gave or refused to give names. Fear stalked us all. Creative people were particularly vulnerable.

Career jobs—in the academy, on the important journals,

in museums and galleries—went to those artists who were politically safe. What saved us in the subsequent generations were
our rebellion and our talent.[4]

The Beat and Black Mountain poets, the painters and
sculptors who lived below 14th street, the earnest young men
and women inhabiting the unheated lofts and apartments with
the bathtub in the kitchen, rebelled against an establishment
we were only just beginning to define. A gut sense of fairness
and rejection of hypocrisy moved most of us more than the several political theories then competing for our attention. At least
this was true for me.

I left New York City in the fall of 1960. My painter and
poet colleagues and I were beginning to move in different directions. They remained in a world defined by art. I entered one
defined by art and politics. The lines were more fluid than this,
of course, but the emphasis was important. Years later, an old
New York City friend told me: "You coped by leaving, I coped
by staying."[5] She was talking about our lives as women and also
as political and artistic beings.

I went to Mexico, and quickly fell in with other expa-
triates from the United States and from several Latin American
countries. In New York I had become a single mother. With my
young son, I reinvented myself in a country it would take me
years to know and whose language I was only beginning to
learn. Never one to move away from a challenge, I threw myself
into the fray: late-night poetry salons in two languages, a politics of anti-imperialism, a Mexican poet I would soon marry,
and the dream of a bilingual literary journal that would become
a culturally rich and influential institution.

The decade of the sixties in Mexico put me in contact
with writers and artists throughout the world, all working
through their own personal and collective rejections of establishment conditioning. I learned that one could write or paint

or sculpt or dance or sing or make theater about anything that touched one's spirit, desire, rage. Not only that one could, but that one **had** to write about what was vital, what was integral to one's holistic sense of self.

Form and content had begun to merge.

Those were years of an extraordinary creative renaissance, one in which art and progressive ideas—political, economic, psychological, sociological—came together in new directions and forms. The man I married seemed the opposite of those free spirits I'd left behind in New York. But then, those men had only really felt free to fulfill their own aspirations, not mine. And neither they nor I knew how to talk about the problem. I mistook Sergio's possessive jealousy for love, at least for a while. It wasn't until he joined a cult that proclaimed quite unequivocally that women could not attain nirvana, that I began to understand how deep the woman-hate ran.

Our arrival in Mexico at the end of 1960, and the repression of the 1968 uprising that changed that country and me, became parenthetical bookends to a particularly intense period of my life. Sergio Mondragón and I married and had two daughters, Sarah and Ximena. We divorced in 1968, and the following year—with U.S. poet Robert Cohen—I had another daughter, Ana. We published *El Corno Emplumado / The Plumed Horn* for 31 issues, and it became one of the defining forums for the work of many upcoming writers and artists in North and Latin America as well as to a lesser extent throughout the rest of the world.

I was also growing in my ability to incorporate new human groups into my personal "family of man"—and I use the male-defined term here with intention. Long gone were the days when Albuquerque's downtown Mexican-Americans frightened me; my own family was now thoroughly Latin Americanized and I myself had become a hybrid—reading and speaking

Spanish as easily as English. The stones of the ancient Aztec and Maya civilizations became conscious reference points. I savored a dozen sorts of tamales, became addicted to *mole*.[6]

Spanish was and still is the language in which my children and I communicate. When a Texas Ranger on the U.S.-Mexican border made my husband the target of his racism, I seethed. When a shabby roadside restaurant on old Highway 66 refused to serve our Mexican family, I reacted violently: completely identified now with my loved ones and with the person I myself had become.

During this time, the Cuban Revolution also became an up-close and personal part of my life. I traveled to Cuba first in January of 1967, again at the beginning of 1968, and—when political repression finally made it necessary for me to flee Mexico—my family and I moved there in the fall of 1969. Cuba would be my first experience of socialism in action. "Marxism in Spanish," we called it, laughing. The revolution's first two decades were magical, transforming. Now I was able to stretch my concepts of justice further, and also take note of the challenges inherent in how one might go about exchanging the old stratified social patterns for new more egalitarian ones.

IV

Cuba initiated a new chapter in my creative life. By this time I had discovered feminism—its current incarnation spearheaded by women my age in the United States and Europe—and, as with all intellectual or spiritual discoveries, I began looking at my own life in this new context. Cuba and women are almost synonymous in my experience. This was a country that had fought against enormous odds for its independence and freedom, and I was eager to learn what that independence and freedom meant for women. My poetry—my writing in general—

became more consciously female, more rooted in and proud of my womanhood and with a gender-specific take on life. Now I wrote not only as a socialist, and as a hybrid North and Latin American, but also as a woman—of a particular culture, class and experience.

Speaking about my life, I have often summed it up by saying I was fortunate to have been in the right place at the right time. I know this is never only about good fortune, though. One must have the courage to grab an opportunity, and the fortitude to see it through. Still, there is no doubt in my mind that I was indeed fortunate to have lived in Cuba from 1969 through 1980 and in Nicaragua from the end of 1980 through the beginning of 1984: years in which I was privileged to participate in the making of new societies.

My children reaped the inclusive justice-oriented wonders (and sometimes also the excessive regimentation) of a Cuban education. I was supported in my desire to write about Cuban women: to learn an oral historian's skills, and to listen to women who had become the protagonists of their own lives tell the stories of those lives. Most important, for eleven years and as one more worker/mother/poet, I participated in all aspects of one of the great social experiments of our time. One that despite its problems and setbacks continues to be an example.

As a poet, I met other poets—Cubans and those from many countries of the world. I read Angolan and Palestinian poetry for the first time, and memorized some of Nazim Hikmet and Bertold Brecht's poems, all in Spanish translation. I learned to read César Vallejo in his original language-changing tongue. I learned about how creative people organize in a socialist society, joined discussions about the rights and obligations of artists, reveled in a culture that loves and respects creative endeavor and supports its writers and artists.

I value my participation in many of the official Cuban

artistic programs of those years. But one experience that stands out is an unofficial effort. During my last few years on the island, a dozen or so other poets and I met each Saturday morning at a place on the campus of the University of Havana known as *El Rincón de los Cabezones*–Big Head Corner. Beneath the grotesque busts of great (male) intellectuals, we read and critiqued one another's work. We called our workshop *El taller Roque Dalton*, after the great Salvadoran poet who had also been my good friend.

Although I was prone to incorporate into my living the lessons of whatever idea sparked my interest, there was often some distance between idea and assimilation. I still hung with mostly male poets and writers. I apprenticed to a male photographer. Male voices and visions had been overwhelming in the sections of *El Corno* Emplumado dedicated to Cuban work, as in the journal overall. Once in Cuba, my 1978 anthology of young Cuban poets included a couple of women in a mostly male selection.[7] By 1982 I understood the ways in which I had been shaped by my own prejudices, and made up for this with the first bilingual anthology of twentieth century Cuban women poets.[8]

I was also taking a closer look at my home life. When Robert and I met and fell in love in Mexico, he seemed very different from Sergio: a man consumed by an anguish he too often took out on me. By comparison, Robert seemed transparent: honest, capable, strong. Younger than I, he was more a product of the Hippie generation than the Beats, a smart New Yorker who read Wittgenstein, wanted an open relationship, and scorned those who were not like him. I left Sergio grateful to be free of that intense self-hate, and initiated the relationship with Robert eager for what I thought would be a more egalitarian, more intellectually and politically stimulating arrangement.

The problem was, I didn't yet know how to love myself. I didn't yet know who this woman I needed to love was. And I

was more and more deeply involved with revolutionary movements and organizations that shunned personal reflection. Self-
examination was perceived of as "bourgeois deviancy." For a
middle-class white woman like myself, it was only too easy to
push the personal questions down. Robert and I, like Sergio and
I, were linked by poetry, by our creative spirits and passion to
change the world. We loved our children. And we engaged in
the battles around household division of labor, monogamy vs.
non-monogamy, and the other issues that characterized our generation.

Like many in my children's generation, two of my daughters feel my struggle to make the world better for all children
prevented me from spending enough time with them. They
berate me for this much more than they do their fathers. Only
my son speaks of a fully satisfying childhood. My youngest
daughter feels she lacked a real childhood, knew what we her
parents "liked her to do—and they were all grown up things."[9]
How my generation of women who were involved in revolutionary struggle mothered, is clearly a sore point for our offspring—and for us. Although I am close to all my children,
regret and pain often accompany my own memories of mothering.

By the end of the seventies my life in Cuba had begun to
unravel. I had learned a great deal about how a small nation can
try to change its political, economic and social reality. And I
had learned, first-hand, about the obstacles. Some of the lessons, and many of the people, will be with me forever. I will
always be grateful for the ways in which Cuba embraced my
children and me, what it gave us, the audacity, dignity, courage
and creativity I witnessed.

At the same time, my rebellious nature had entered into
conflict with certain aspects of an authoritarian and essentially
male-dominated state. I had left Robert a couple of years before,

and was living with a poet, musician and ex guerilla from Venezuela, Antonio Castro. Antonio was a kind and gentle man: devoted, loyal. From an impoverished background and after five years in prison, his values were solid. But now this relationship too had played itself out. I accepted an invitation to visit Nicaragua during the last three months of 1979—to research and write a book about that country's women—and I returned to live at the end of 1980.

V

I went to Nicaragua with my youngest daughter Ana, who was ten at the time. My son and two older daughters elected to remain in Cuba, although Ximena joined us in Managua when she graduated from high school the following year. Some of the young Sandinistas, then making a revolution unnoticed by most outside of Central America, had spent periods of time in Cuba throughout the seventies, and several had become close friends. When we arrived in Nicaragua we had privileged contacts, and I found myself in on the ground floor of an experiment in social change that was vibrant and in many ways more open-ended than what I had experienced in Cuba.

In 1969, when I'd gone to live in Cuba, that country's revolution was already ten years old. It was set in many of its ways. Its socialism, although uniquely Cuban, was also inevitably influenced by the more classically traditional views of the international Communist movement, especially the privileging of class over any of society's other contradictions. This relegated women to a place where equality in education and the workplace were believed sufficient to effect lasting change.

When I went to Nicaragua, in 1979 to work on the book and at the end of 1980 to live, everything was new. Anything seemed possible. Nicaragua also bore the distinction of being a nation of poets. Artistic creativity is deeply respected there. Many of the poets and artists, as well as those men—and occasional women—in charge of the new government, were my friends. Many of the new government officials were also serious writers.

During my almost four years in Nicaragua, I worked at the new Ministry of Culture,[10] with the women's organization, with the Union of Artists and Writers, and for the FSLN's ideological department. I witnessed and was part of a multi-faceted artistic outreach. Women continued to be in the forefront of my concern, and I wrote several books about Nicaraguan women— as well as about Nicaraguan writers, and the unique relationship between religious faith and revolution, something that had not been part of the Cuba experience.[11]

My contact with Liberation Theology also changed me in important ways. I never became a believer,[12] but the progressive Catholic communities taught me that compassion and a deeper introspection about self were not in contradiction with the struggle to remake society. In fact, both are necessary to that struggle—if it is to address the needs of the whole community.[13]

Two decades separated the Cuban and Nicaraguan victories, two decades that were particularly important in twentieth century history. The 1959 victory of the Cuban revolution predated the revival of feminist thought and practice internationally (what some have called the second wave of feminism); it was also pre-Vatican II, the powerful movement for change within the Catholic Church. Both these events would exert important influences on the FSLN during its ten years in power.

Both these events were important, as well, in shaping women's experience. It is unnecessary to explain why this was true of feminism. Vatican II made a difference in women's lives because Christian culture and morality had conditioned and thwarted those lives throughout the Christian world, and a more liberal reading of the relationship between the Church and its people opened previously unheard of opportunities for women. In the ten years of Sandinista administration, a number of women achieved important positions; many more, while not center stage, literally made the revolution possible. Their stories amazed me. Their strength and apparent refusal to retreat into traditional women's roles had me—and many others—believing that life was changing for women in dramatic and irreversible ways.

Eventually, in Sandinista Nicaragua as in Fidel's Cuba, the men in power balked at women's attempts to have meaningful input into any decision-making that challenged the power equilibrium. Policies continued to privilege male power. I believe that the inability to look honestly at the issue of power was at least partially responsible for the 1990 Sandinista electoral defeat, just as it prevents the Cuban government from making structural changes that take a redistribution of power into account.

But this is an issue examined in other essays, and not central to the story I'm telling here.[14] For the purposes of this essay, suffice to say that some of the Nicaraguan women became important mentors to me: Doris Tijerino, Dora María Téllez, Sofía Montenegro, María López Vigil and others. Although they have lost much of what they fought so hard to build, their lives and views are compelling.

This is about my poet's consciousness and sensibility, how it developed in the various places I've lived and worked, and how it eventually led me to embrace all creatures, landscapes, and natural elements necessary to our survival. Shorter but equally intense work-related trips to Chile (1972), Peru (1973-74) and North Vietnam (1974) also profoundly influenced my creative and political consciousness.

VI

In 1984 I returned to the United States. I had lived in Latin America for close to a quarter century. I was exhausted, in need of reconnecting to my roots, and eager to understand how the various strands of my experience intersected in the woman I had become. Over the next years I would focus on the desert landscape of my youth, my new-found woman-loving self, psychotherapy that helped uncover an experience of incest in my early childhood, life without my children, and an almost five-year battle with the U.S. Immigration and Naturalization Service that ordered me deported because of opinions expressed in some of my books.[15]

This is when my world split open. Male-dominated organizations and institutions no longer limited my vision or sense of self. The U.S. women's movement, and within it a confident lesbian community, welcomed me home—to my country and individuality. The deep understanding of international political and economic domination, shaped and sharpened during my years in Latin America, remained indelible. To that I now added a merging of mind and body, a new openness to humans in all our magnificent difference, and an awareness of the importance of protecting resources I had long taken for granted. I touched a cultural taproot, long ignored, of language and image, sound and feeling. And there was the desert, the New Mexican desert of my youth, where as a teenager I had followed the wavy lines of Geological Survey maps as I explored earth, space, light, time.

I hadn't understood how much I needed this, my original landscape. Or how much reconnecting with it would lead me back to myself. My body was there, waiting to be used. I had never used it, not really: moving from shy and awkward teenager to sedentary writer. My lasting partner—a woman—slowly coaxed me into walking, hiking, biking. She never derided, always encouraged. And it was on the desert and in the mountains of New Mexico that I discovered not only my own muscle and reach but the Diamondback basking in the sun, the mule deer standing silent on the trail, the gift of a coyote bounding across the road, birds and bears and bobcats.

I often walk the foothills behind my home and look for the peregrines' nest in the rocks above. Like miniature primroses, small white flowers precede silken tassels on the Apache Plume: miracles in a time of drought. A single hedgehog cactus along a three-mile trail displays defiant red flowers. I wait for August, when the cholla forest will burst into fuscia bloom. Seasons of change on the desert.

I, who have always been impatient with domestic animals, have found I love all animals in the wild. Slowly, almost imperceptibly, my passion for justice extended to them—and to the plants they eat, the air they breathe, the clean rain they need to survive. Early spring's crimson bud on the claret cup. The story of rocks as they emerge from the earth, wear and change, travel downhill and become dust once more. The story of water in its similar—but much shorter—cycle: pouring from the sky, carving deep canyons, sustaining life and then vanishing upward in vapor and mist only to repeat its journey.

Had I been born, like Antonio, into a family that sought its sustenance from the land, that of necessity looked to rain and rock and soil and the animals that call these home, I might have learned much earlier that I am part of nature, and to care about the lives of all creatures and natural elements rather than prioritizing one species over others. Since I was not, I needed the luxury of time and age to learn to appreciate these other inhabitants. I remember a good friend, in the seventies, who was almost embarrassed to tell me she was going out on a ship to save the whales. Correctly, she assumed I would belittle her concern for whales when so many humans were besieged by hunger, violence, war. My friend died more than a decade ago. I wish I could tell her I finally understand.

During my first years back in the U.S., my immigration case also highlighted issues of artistic expression vis-à-vis love of country, an artist's rights and obligations, how the U.S. power structure perceives women, punishing those who challenge government policy and won't say we're sorry. I learned how one manages prolonged political struggle while maintaining one's integrity. I wrote a number of poems—published nine books, in fact—during those years in which I battled the INS. One poem speaks of the unique ways in which my immigration case brought these issues together for me:

Immigration Law

When I ask the experts
"how much time do I have?"
I do not want an answer
in years or arguments.

I must know
if there are hours enough
to mend this relationship,
see a book all the way to its birthing,
stand beside my father
on his journey.

I want to know
how many seasons of chamisa
will be yellow then gray-green
and yellow
        light
            again,

how many cactus flowers
will bloom beside my door.

I will not follow language
like a dog with its tail between its legs.

I need time equated with music,
hours rising in bread,
years deep from connection.

The present always holds a tremor of the past.
Give me a handful of future
to rub against my lips.[16]

VII

Seasons of chamisa. Desert flowers. These images were
finding their way into my poetry, along with the human stories
and the newer more complex emotions. With the help of good
lawyers, supportive family, and many many friends—artists,
writers, performers, political activists, unionists, religious people, women and men, lesbian gay and straight, academics, students and others—I won my immigration case in August of
1989.

Now I was free to remain in the country of my birth,
specifically among the red rock mountains, canyons and desert
of my adolescence. I began to notice and enjoy nature, and
explore my relationship to it. I found the love of a woman who
has been my partner for the past seventeen years, a love relationship posited on each encouraging the growth of the other, a
relationship that will endure. I had begun to deal with the scars
of childhood sexual abuse. I was growing old—if not gracefully,
at least with a welcome sense of wholeness.

This sense of wholeness, however, seemed to develop in the context of a rapidly deteriorating national and global political situation. Forced to wage my immigration battle under the Reagan and elder Bush presidencies, I remember wishing I had been able to do so under Carter. Now I understand that under the George W. Bush/Cheney/Rumsfeld/Ashcroft administration, I would almost certainly have been deported. Government policies that had to remain covert twenty years ago are now carried out overtly—and few have the courage to question their rightness, or even their legality. The wanton invasion of other countries and reversal of civil liberties here at home—both under the rubric of "fighting terrorism"—have become ordinary and acceptable to most U.S. Americans.

My heart weeps as each new day brings another lie, another war, another example of arrogance, abuse of power, deceit, greed run wild, and gross distortion of this system we continue to call democracy.

I used to believe that poetry could save the world. By save the world, I didn't mean in the Christian definition of salvation. I meant that poetry—the power of words, their energy and ability to ignite our clarity, tenderness or rage, our deepest feelings and most elevated intelligence—is capable of freeing us from complacency and turning us towards an understanding of what is necessary for our survival and healthy growth.

Can poetry save the world?

I don't know. The disintegration of so many dreams in 1989 and the failures within our own movements for social change have left me unsteady on my previously sure feet.

What I do know, what I know more completely than I have, is that one precious moment is capable of effecting a change of heart or will, of opening eyes or taking the wanderer by the hand. Of all our contemporary writers, Barbara Kingsolver may be the one who most accurately describes this moment of truth, most often occurring when we take time out from our rage or terror to notice the way creatures in nature go about their elegant business of life, love and the pursuit of a world that so often eludes us.

In her novels, poems, and essays, Kingsolver offers many such moments. I would like to close this reflection with one of them. After several pages in which she and her husband Steven Hopp describe searching the Costa Rican countryside for the scarlet macaw, they give us this:

> All afternoon we walked crook-necked and open-mouthed with awe. If these creatures are doomed, they don't act that way: El que quiera azul celeste, que le cueste,[17] but who could buy or possess such avian magnificence against the blue sky? We stopped counting at fifty. We'd have settled for just one—that was what we thought we had come for—but we stayed through the change of tide and nearly till sunset because of the way they perched and foraged and spoke among themselves, without a care for a human's expectations. What held us there was the show of pure, defiant survival: this audacious thing with feathers, this hope.[18]

Maybe this is the building block, the cornerstone with which we must continually begin, again, to create a lasting knowledge capable of bringing us face to face with our alternatives: embrace all creatures and elements or hasten the annihilation of all. That one precious moment, holding the beautifully simple answer. Poetry must become the word that saves—not for some mythical invention of afterlife or glory, but for the here and now of who we are and can be.

—Spring 2002–Spring 2003

CHAPTER TWENTY

Let America be America Again, Round 2

Let America be America again
                                        Langston Hughes

But was it ever? Perhaps for those
who roamed with buffalo and spirit song
before Vespucci came
bearing a name so foreign to their lives.
Perhaps for the families
pushing their wagons west
planting crude crosses
as they rutted heartland and rivers,
the challenge of mountains.
Already conquest was the national business,
raucous scratch to a country's underbelly
bleeding out in expanding circles
from the foreign object tossed in a sea of salt.

That poet who pleaded *Let America be America*
again, let it be the dream it used to be
was black and queer and knew how to sing
to all who live upon this land.
Could he feel, in the pain of a slave grandmother
the fireball that would one day consume

patients in an Afghan hospital,
or see Iraq—half children—
pulverized beneath American bombs?
In years that spanned Auschwitz, Hiroshima, Santo Domingo
could he have imagined poorly-fed guerrillas
routing the greatest war machine
or a U.S. dictator who would spread his smiling teeth
to swallow the world?

For America to be America
we might start by giving back the name
it grabbed for us alone,
stole from the nations of Central, Latin
and South America.
For America to be America
each of us might begin
by opening one ear to Langston's plea
and putting the other to the ground
where water shrinks in the aquifers
rocks move with gravitational flow
birds nest before flight
and small animals like those on every continent
await our next move.

—Spring 2003

CHAPTER TWENTY-ONE

Thirty Four O Two

Some believe many resisted
didn't support the final push
to ultimate conquest and death.
There are signs, they say,
like pieces of fresco on the ruins of a building
at the western edge of the continent
most likely to have radiated
final criminal intent.
Female figures of different colors
can still be seen embracing and at work.

Discrete groupings called themselves countries then,
spoke separate languages. On the eastern coast
of what some have called the southern land mass
at a place that may have been Port Happiness
in one of the tongues
most rapidly ceding to translation
there is evidence of a periodic gathering of peoples
a lingering energy our monitors classify
as continuing to pulse
through all the centuries of silence.

About a charred inscription, characters
as yet indecipherable,
we have conflicting interpretations.
Some experts from the patchwork continent
believe the marks mere ornament
while those from the land whose upper region

rises in endless horizon of sand
claim they remember. They remember.
Yet theirs is a memory scorned
by those writing the Table of Official Proof.

Only the unnamable is repudiated by all—
ancient carnage, three-dimensional
remnant of a great death.
Women. Men. Children. A breaking apart,
destruction so deep and vast no language can hold it.
We speak around but not of it,
walk its circumference, allude or refer
only by describing what it was not.
How to avoid its repetition is the work of high priests
though clandestine sages have lately taken up the task.

Recently discovered sites yield documents
bearing the pronouncements *we will not forget*
and *this must never be allowed to happen again*
—perhaps referring to other disasters,
earlier moments
when harmony ripped
beneath the weight of greed.
Some experts reject these findings
as incompatible with the terminal nature
of the main event.

Many who made it through The Fourth World
say we must join forces
in this struggle for survival.
A struggle, they say,
that demands we learn to control
earth air water

and other living beings,
harnessing these for the benefit of all.
They are busy developing and stockpiling
the weapons they say will keep us safe.

But a few believe it was just such domination
that led to the explosion,
the event which brought about
such poisoned atmosphere.
This divide between those who honor memory
and those who reject an element
invisible to the eye, unheard,
lacking in physical form or proof.

Those few who venture beyond the protective fences
will surely find the answer
or all will succumb beneath the weight
of reinvented wheels
trampling us under freshly turned earth.

—February 2003, on the threshold of war against Iraq

Notes

INTRODUCTION

1 I use U.S. Americans throughout this book to differentiate us from Latin Americans who are also Americans and resent our sole claim to the term American. Referring to ourselves as Americans is one more in a long list of ways in which, in our use of language as well as through our actions we evidence our isolationism and sense of superiority.

2 UN statistic, quoted on StandDown.net.

3 On October 16, 2002 Congress allocated $355.1 billion to defense, $37.5 billion more than in the previous year and more than in any year since World War II. ("Congress Sends Bush $335 Billion Defense Budget" by Reuters, New York Times, October 16, 2002). Forty-six percent of our taxes go to the Military Industrial Complex (Charles Sheketoff, Oregon Center for Public Policy).

4 Quoted in Nuremberg Diary by G.M. Gilbert (New York: Signet, 1947).

5 Quoted in "Paradoxes" by Eduardo Galeano, IPS News Service, October, 2002.

6 Sixty Minutes, CBS, September 26, 2002.

7 Not all Catholic clergy take such conservative positions. According to an October 15, 2002 article in the Evansville Courier & Press, Detroit's auxiliary Bishop Thomas Gumbleton is urging every parish priest to preach against Bush's preemptive strike against Iraq. Gumbleton is the founder of Pax Christi USA, the national branch of the international Catholic pacifist organization.

8 From "What Is Education?" In Context, A Quarterly of Humane Sustainable Culture, IC #27, Winter 1991.

CHAPTER ONE

1 An earlier version of this essay, "September 11, 2001: Positioning Ourselves in the Global Village," appeared in Mending the World, edited by Marjorie Agosín and Jean Craige, White Pine Press, 2002.

2 Beginning towards the end of 2001, a number of Israeli soldiers began refusing to fight in Gaza or the West Bank. "60 Minutes"

correspondent Bob Simon interviewed several of these Refuseniks as they are called in May of 2002. The men are loyal to Israel and willing to defend their country in any capacity except that of fighting in the occupied territories. Some have gone to prison for their stand, but the movement is growing.

3   President John F. Kennedy launched the Alliance for Progress in 1961 as a way of fighting communism. The idea was that if the peoples in the U.S. sphere of influence could better their lives, they wouldn't be so eager to try other political models. $80 billion in aid was offered to all the countries of Latin America, with the exception of Cuba, but these countries had to adopt the type of economic and social planning proposed by the United States. The Alliance for Progress trained local military and police in counterinsurgency methods. It introduced projects whose stated goals were to improve people's quality of life but which often produced more in trade for the U.S. than sustainable improvement in local economies. After much disgruntlement and corruption, the Organization of American States (OAS) finally disbanded the permanent committee that oversaw the Alliance in 1973. (Source: Columbia Encyclopedia, Sixth Edition, 2001).

4   Today's international lending is largely controlled by the International Monetary Fund and World Bank. Countries receiving loans must adopt rigorous economic measures that include central planning based on the capitalist model and drastic reductions in social services. Argentina and Uruguay are recent examples of countries that followed these instructions to the letter and spiraled into economic chaos as a result. Approximately 80% of the World Bank's funding is raised through the sale of public bonds (Beverly Bell, Center for Economic Justice). In April of 2002 a World Bank Bonds Boycott was launched by an international coordinating committee concerned with what the Bank's policies are doing to countries throughout the world. Many have signed on, including—in the U.S.—the cities of San Francisco and Milwaukee, the International Brotherhood of Teamsters and the American Postal Workers Union, the Calvert Group, and orders of Dominicans, Franciscan Friars, Sisters of the Holy Cross, and the Conference of Major Superiors of Men. More Information on the World Bank Bonds Boycott can be obtained at

bankboycott@econjustice.net.

5   Less than a week after 9/11, hate crimes against Middle Eastern men or men who looked like they were from the Middle East increased exponentially. In Mesa, Arizona a gas station owner was shot to death because he wore a turban. The shooter said he thought the man looked like the images of Osama bin Laden he had seen in the press. Murders, beatings, and harassment of other Arab or dark-skinned men followed (many with bull's eyes superimposed upon them). Hundreds have been documented to date.

6   Western news media, the only media trusted by most people in the United States, consistently underreports civilian deaths in Afghanistan. Marc W. Herold, Professor of Economics and Women's Studies at the University of New Hampshire, has been documenting civilian casualties and publishing his findings. On December 10, 2001 he released data showing that more than 3,500 Afghan civilians had perished under U.S. missiles and bombs. As the occupation continues, Herold periodically updates his figures. ("A Dossier on Civilian Victims of United States' Aerial Bombing in Afghanistan: A Comprehensive Accounting" at www.cursor.org-/stories/civilian_deaths.

7   "Dead Afghan Civilians: Disrobing the Non-Counters" by Marc W. Herold, Cursor.com, August 20, 2002.

8   Official declarations, such as this one by Secretary of Defense Donald Rumsfeld, are not all we have to worry about. The continued imprisonment without trial or access to lawyers of hundreds of Arab men in this country and Afghan soldiers and others at Guantanamo Base, Cuba, goes against all provisions of national and international law.

9   General Tommy Franks made this statement shortly after the August 7, 2001 invasion of Iraq.

10 First used in 1845, the term Manifest Destiny conveyed the idea that the rightful destiny of the U.S. included imperialist expansion. It was used to justify taking over a large part of Mexico, and many subsequent imperialist wars.

11 Since 9/11, we are incessantly encouraged to display the flag and sing the National Anthem. A year after the event, President George W. Bush declared the date Patriot's Day.

12 Kenneth Lay was the CEO of Enron who steadfastly denied any

wrong-doing when the giant corporation declared bankruptcy and thousands lost jobs, pensions, stock.

13 In "No War for Oil! Ken Silverstein makes a persuasive argument that the Caspian's energy reserves are not in Afghanistan but in Azerbaijan and Kazakhstan where the threat of radical Islam is small; that the Taliban, with its strong central government was actually better for the United States than the current and weaker Karzai government; and that the country, with its chaos and lawlessness, is singularly unattractive to U.S. business interests.

14 Lambda Legal estimates that at least 50 gay men and lesbians lost their lives in the World Trade Center. Eugene Clark, Larry Courtney's partner of almost 14 years, is engaged in legal action against Courtney's insurance company for denying him spousal benefits (Lambda Legal Press Release, April 22, 2002). Only the gay press has featured bios of the gay victims about whom there is information. Mark Bingham was a gay passenger on United Flight #93; along with the other more applauded passengers, he helped to thwart the plane's hijackers. Carol Flyzik was on American Flight #11. David Charlebois was the co-pilot of American Flight 377. Ronald Gamboa and his partner of 13 years Dan Brandhorst were on United Flight #175; they were traveling with their 3-year-old adopted son, David. Like these men and women, there are many others. One of the few openly gay victims to be publicly acknowledged is Father Mychal Judge, the New York Fire Department's Catholic chaplain who was killed while ministering to a fallen firefighter (The Advocate.com).

15 "Not In Our Name" is developing as one of the largest organized protests against the Bush agenda. The internet has vastly increased our ability to mobilize, raise money, and tell our elected officials what we think.

16 The Nobel Committee's statement reads: "In a situation currently marked by threats of the use of power, Carter has stood by the principles that conflicts must as far as possible be resolved through mediation and international cooperation based on international respect for human rights and economic development."

17 The William Joiner Center for the Study of War and Social Consequences, University of Massachusetts at Boston.

CHAPTER TWO

1   "Begging to Disagree," The Nation, January 7-14, 2002, p. 9
2   Liberation Theology, a progressive current within the Catholic
    Church, emerged after the Second Vatican Council was called by
    Pope John XXIII in 1962. It prescribed a gospel-oriented content
    for Catholicism and a more socially conscious orientation than
    that of previous papal encyclicals. Cardenal had used this new
    directive in his work with the Solentiname community. The more
    relevant theology also bridged the gap between Christians and rev-
    olution throughout Nicaragua and much of the rest of the Third
    World.
3   Successive polls produce more complex responses. A December
    12, 2001 New York Times poll, based on nationwide telephone
    interviews conducted with 1,052 respondents several days earlier,
    showed 77% feels it is okay for the government to hold non-citi-
    zens for up to seven days without charging them or to detain them
    indefinitely if they are believed to be threats to national security
    (18% disagrees); 72% believes government has a right to listen in
    on previously-privileged prisoner-lawyer conversations (22% dis-
    agrees); 64% feels the president should have full authority to
    change the Constitution (29% disagrees). But when respondents
    were asked how they feel about the government enacting strong
    antiterrorism laws that excessively restrict the average person's
    civil liberties, 45% were against such laws. And 50% preferred to
    see terrorists tried in criminal rather than secret military courts.
4   In an amateur video said to have been found by U.S. troops in an
    abandoned house in Jalalabad, bin Laden is translated by U.S.
    experts as saying: "(Inaudible) due to my experience in this field, I
    was thinking that the fire from the gas in the plane would melt the
    iron structure of the building and collapse the area where the plane
    hit and all the floors above it only. This is all that we had hoped
    for."
5   I am referring here to the Wen Ho Lee case. Wen Ho Lee was a
    respected nuclear scientist at the Los Alamos Laboratories in New
    Mexico, who was scapegoated by government over eagerness and
    racial profiling, accused of giving atomic secrets to China, and
    kept in solitary confinement for more than a year. Lee always
    maintained his innocence. Finally there was no proof to convict

him, and the authorities were forced to let him go. The judge apologized to him on the part of the government as well as the American people.

6   Harvey Cox recently wrote: "We quote Isaiah, not Joel. We talk about Rabbi Abraham Joshua Heschel, not Rabbi Meir Kahane. We favor St. Francis and his birds, not Torquemada and his racks. Alas, however, they are all part of the story." (The Nation Magazine, December 24, 2001, "Religion and the War Against Evil," p. 30).

7   This scene, one of many, is taken from the book *Warrior Marks: Female Genital Mutilation and the Sexual Blinding of Women* by Alice Walker and Pratibha Parmar (New York, Harcourt Brace, 1993).

8   There is mounting testimony of scenes like this one, from thousands of survivors of religiously based ritual abuse and/or the activities of illegal but politically protected white supremacist organizations such as the Ku Klux Klan, Posse Comitatus, the John Birch Society, and others. Details of this particular scene are from the 1988 Costa Gavras film "Betrayed" (Tom Berenger, Debra Winger), which was based on a true story.

9   In painting this picture I do not mean to emphasize Palestinian over Israeli terrorism. Reality points dramatically in the opposite direction. The State of Israel has answered stones with bombs (with 100 Palestinian lives lost to every one Israeli), just as the United States has answered Al Qaeda's terrorist attacks by destroying the entire country of Afghanistan. In both cases, State terrorism is overkill.

CHAPTER THREE

1   Public television, like public radio, is largely shaped by the administration in office, which has a number of ways—most of them economic—of influencing programming along political lines. There are a number of excellent programs on Public Television, and many that are not so good.

2   Jean·Paul Sartre, *Nausea* (1959).

3   "Women and Honor: Some Notes on Lying (1975)" in *On Lies, Secrets, and Silence: Selected Prose 1966-1978* (New York: W.W. Norton & Company, 1979) 185-194.

4   *This is About Incest* by Margaret Randall (Ithaca, New York:

Firebrand Books, 1988).

5   *Translated Woman, Crossing the Border with Esperanza's Story* by Ruth Behar (Boston: Beacon Press, 1993).

6   *Translated Woman,* 276.

7   "Writing in My Father's Name: A Diary of *Translated Woman's* First Year," by Ruth Behar, in *Women Writing Culture,* edited by Ruth Bejar and Deborah A. Gordon (Berkeley: University of California Press, 1995) 67.

8   "Writing in My Father's Name," 78.

CHAPTER FOUR

1   From the catalogue to the exhibition, "Return" by the Rumanian-American photographer Sylvia de Swaan, Munson Williams Proctor Institute, Utica, New York, 1995.

2   *The Mind of a Mnemonist: A Little Book About a Vast Memory,* by A. R. Luria (Cambridge, Massachusetts and London: Harvard University Press, 1987).

3   As I write this, a much publicized contest has just taken place between the world's chess champion and a computer. The computer won the first game but the human won the series. If a computer can beat a person at something as complicated as chess, does it mean the machine has reached the level of the human mind; or is it, after all, that human minds created the machine?

4   One healer blames cortisol, a toxin in the blood. He claims positive results from combining hormone therapy, stress-reducing techniques, and yoga. A more western approach uses experiments with the ever-victimized rat. Animals who are given complex new environments on a daily basis, actually grow more branches on the tree of veins in the brain. Their connections, or synapses, multiply. Those rats that are required to exercise on a regular basis grow more veins, leading to more blood (oxygen) in the brain. These are but two of many recent segments addressing memory loss on national TV.

5   Quoted in *The Education of a Woman: The Life of Gloria Steinem* by Carolyn G. Heilbrun (New York: Dial, 1995) 402.

6   Wilhelm Reich was a disciple of Freud's who parted company with the master and developed his own theories about energy. During the early years of the Russian Revolution, he studied the sexual

practices of Russian workers, resulting in a book called *The Sexual Revolution*. Others of Reich's books, such as *The Theory of the Orgasm*, *Character Analysis*, *The Mass Psychology of Fascism* and *Listen, Little Man* became popular in Europe and the United States in the 1940s and '50s. Reich developed something he called the theory of the orgone. Towards the end of his life his work was discredited and he himself went to prison for refusing to relinquish the claim that he could cure cancer and for generally refusing to conform. After his death, Reich's students branched out into three different schools, one of which was influential in developing current Reichian therapy.

7   The so-called False Memory Syndrome is discussed more extensively in Chapter 3.

8   *The Balkan Express* by Slavenka Drakulic (New York: W. W. Norton, 1993) 3.

9   *Seeing Voices, A Journey Into the World of the Deaf* by Oliver Sacks (Berkeley: University of California Press, 1989) xi.

10 *Ceremony* by Leslie Marmon Silko (New York: Viking Penguin, 1977) 2.

11 From "The Site of Memory" in *Inventing the Truth, The Art and Craft of Memoir*, 1987.

12 *The Man Who Mistook His Wife for a Hat* by Oliver Sacks (New York: Summit Books, 1985), 183.

13 "Larry Eigner, 68, Poet Who Saw The World From His Wheelchair" by William Grimes, New York Times, February 11, 1996, 22.

14 Meridel LeSueur, 1900-1996. Conversation with author.

15 An obvious example of this is the fact that women most often shoulder the care of elderly parents. Another is the late twentieth century phenomenon of lesbians taking on the care of those in the gay male community suffering from AIDS.

CHAPTER FIVE

1   In New Mexico a therapeutic foster parent is someone who has been trained to deal with severely traumatized children and takes them, through a State or private agency, until they are doing well enough to be permanently adopted.

2   For a provocative and very beautiful look at the variety of lesbian

families, in text, first-person narrative and photographic image, see *Women in Love: Portraits of Lesbian Mothers & Their Families* by Barbara Seyda with Diana Herrera (New York: Little Brown & Company, 1998).

3   Had I come out during the years of my immigration case, which I did eventually win, the government would have been able to deport me for my sexual identity rather than under the ideological exclusion clause. It was important for us to be fighting a First Amendment case—for freedom of expression and dissent. The sexual identity issue would have complicated this.

4   This was written during the Clinton administration. With George W. bush, a discussion of foreign policy must include the subsequent scenario covered elsewhere in this book.

5   After the April, 1999 tragedy at Columbine High, experts noted that popular video games like Doom not only desensitize young people to the idea of killing but also train them to kill with amazing deliberation and accuracy. The two Columbine students who massacred 12 fellow students and a teacher before taking their own lives, displayed an accuracy rate (death per bullet fired) twice that of the New York City police who months before had murdered an unarmed African immigrant.

CHAPTER SIX

1   "Now With Bill Moyers," PBS, August 9, 2002.

2   I was born in 1936 and grew up through our country's most deadening years of social conformity. After the Soviets launched Sputnik in October of 1957, the U.S. education system took a new look at how it was preparing students—girls as well as boys—to meet the challenges of the modern world. The generation immediately following mine were privy to improvements in the teaching of math and the sciences.

3   The Nation, May 30, 1994, reprinted in The Nation: The Century, An Alternative History, January 10/17, 2000.

4   Title IX was a clause in the 1972 Education Act stating that no one shall because of sex be denied the benefits of any educational program of activity that receives direct federal aid.

5   A lone congresswoman, Barbara Lee of Oakland, California, voted against giving George W. Bush immediate and far-reaching war

powers. Because of her courageous stand, she received death threats and was forced to hire bodyguards.

6 *Fireweed: A Political Autobiography* by Gerda Lerner (Philadelphia: Temple University Press), 2002. pp. 297-298.

7 This program is the Terrorist Information and Prevention System (TIPS), publicly launched by the U.S. government in January of 2002.

8 Reported on NPR's morning news broadcast, August 26, 2002. Among those behind bars at this writing, 46% are black according to AP on Line on the same date.

9 In fact, we do have the power to turn things around, but not by engaging in the sorts of activities urged upon us by our government. Mass mobilization and refusal to play Bush's game could force saner domestic as well as foreign policy.

10 August 11, 2002.

CHAPTER SEVEN

1 An earlier version of this piece was first published as one of the two introductions to *Sexual Harassment: Women Speak Out*, edited by Amber Coverall Sumrall and Dena Taylor (Freedom, California: Crossing Press, 1992).

2 This is a paraphrase.

3 Since Anita Hill's testimony, charges of sexual harassment have risen, incidents of punishment as well. Hill did write a book about her experience: *Anita Hill, Speaking Truth to Power* (New York: Doubleday, 1997). A book was also written to discredit her; its author later recanted, admitting he had been paid to produce it.

CHAPTER EIGHT

1 This piece was written in December of 2000, immediately following the judicial coup that sought to legitimize the presidency of George W. Bush.

CHAPTER TWELVE

1 First published in an earlier version on Znet on Line, July 14, 2002.

2 "The Public Life of Private Struggles," Mariane Pearl, The New York Times, April 19, 2002.

CHAPTER FOURTEEN

1 Keynote to have been given on January 27, 2000 at Florida Sate University Women's Center, Tallahassee, Florida. Delayed airline connections prevented my being able to deliver this address.

2 *The New Our Bodies Ourselves* (New York: Simon & Schuster, 1992) 135.

3 From *Living in the Open* by Marge Piercy (New York: Knopf), pp. 88-89.

CHAPTER FIFTEEN

1 Keynote speech, first given at the conference on "Women, Writing, and Resistance in Latin America and the Caribbean," Simon's Rock College of Bard, November 10, 2001. I have also given different versions of this address in other venues.

2 "Pitiful Role" by Marilyn Bobes is reprinted from *Breaking the Silences: 20th Century Poetry by Cuban Women*, edited and translated with historical introduction by Margaret Randall, Vancouver, B.C., Pulp Press, 1982. The translator has made some changes in the current version.

3 After several years hiding behind his parliamentary immunity, following Ortega's most recent loss at the polls he suddenly did take her to court. He wanted, he said, to "put this whole thing to rest." The judge was an FSLN member and Ortega's friend; she quickly threw the case out on technicalities. Once again, Ortega was abusing his stepdaughter, this time publicly and "legally."

4 Following this writing, the Human Rights Court did hear Zoilamérica's case. It asked the current Nicaraguan government to make retributions to Zoilamérica, not for the abuse but because of the obstacles it has placed in the way of her bringing her abuser to court. A money settlement has been requested. If she receives it, Zoilamérica plans on giving it to the foundation she has set up to aid victims of sexual abuse.

5 "Lineage" is from *The Violent Foam* by Daisy Zamora, translated by George Evans (Willimantic, Connecticut: Curbstone Press, 2002).

CHAPTER SIXTEEN

1 There were a number of reasons behind Truman's decision to drop atomic bombs on these civilian populations. Saving American

lives and making a statement against fascism weren't among them, since Germany had surrendered in May and Japan was already negotiating its defeat (it had surrendered Okinawa in June, and would do so completely eight and five days, respectively, after those fateful blasts). Demonstrating to the Soviet Union the immense power of the U.S. was certainly one of Truman's concerns, and many believe the Cold War was launched those fateful days in August, 1945.

2   *El Corno Emplumado* / The Plumed Horn was founded and edited by Mexican poet Sergio Mondragón and myself (Robert Cohen replaced Mondragón on the last two issues). It came out of Mexico City from 1962 through the middle of 1969, when repression shut it down. The journal averaged 200 pages per issue, and published some of the best writers on both continents, as well as many from other parts of the world and many who were unknown at the time but would later be among the best of several generations.

3   The first of these anthologies was *Estos cantos habitados* / *These Living Songs* (Fort Collins, Colorado: Colorado State Review Press, 1978). The second was *Breaking the Silences: 20th Century Poetry by Cuban Women* (Vancouver, B.C., Canada: Pulp Press, 1982).

4   *Cuban Women Now, Spirit of the People: Vietnamese Women Two Years from the Paris Accords, Doris Tijerino: Inside the Nicaraguan Revolution, Cuban Women Twenty Years Later, Sandino's Daughters, Christians in the Nicaraguan Revolution, Risking a Somersault in the Air, This is About Incest, Sandino's Daughters Revisited, The Price You Pay: The Hidden Cost of Women's Relationship to Money,* and *When I Look Into the Mirror and See You: Women, Terror & Resistance,* among others.

CHAPTER SEVENTEEN

1   For a thorough study of the electoral fraud of 2000, as well as an analysis of the Supreme Court's role in deciding the presidency, see *Supreme Injustice: How the High Court Hijacked Election 2000* by Alan M. Dershowitz (Oxford University Press, 2001).

2   Other polls are even more revealing. One, taken in February 2003, reveals that a majority of Second World War veterans are against going to war with Iraq. An inordinate number of retired U.S. generals, including Norman Schwartzkopf who led American troops

in the first Gulf War, advocate against this war. Within the CIA and FBI, as well, important segments have broken ranks with the Bush administration to say this war is a bad idea.

3 "The Political Consequences of Child Abuse" by Alice Miller, The Journal of Psychohistory 26 (2) Fall 1998.

4 In the early days of George W. Bush's presidency, he delivered the commencement address at his old alma mater. "To those who made A's and B's," he quipped to the graduating seniors, "I salute you. To those who made C's I say: you too can become president of the United States."

5 The Patriot Act, which in the aftermath of 9/11 and almost without discussion gained the support of an overwhelming majority of Congress, included the reduction of judicial oversight, made search and seizure easier, legalized wire-tapping, secret arrests, holding foreign prisoners without legal representation or trial, and much else. The Domestic Security Enhancement Act, if enacted, would push this neo-fascist control of the population a great deal further. The nonpartisan Center for Public Integrity in Washington obtained a draft copy and Bill Moyers scooped it on "Now" on February 7, 2003.

6 In "The United States of America Has Gone Mad," John le Carre writes in The Times of London (January 15, 2003): "Bush has an arm-lock on God. And God has very particular political opinions. God appointed America to save the world in any way that suits America. God appointed Israel to be the nexus of America's Middle Eastern policy, and anyone who wants to mess with that idea is a) anti-Semitic, b) anti-American, c) with the enemy, and d) a terrorist." This is but one very succinct description of Bush's use of biblical reference and fundamentalist ideology to shore up his doctrine.

7 The United Nations is clearly the international body with the power to check Bush's madness. Bush has repeatedly declared the UN "irrelevant" if it does not do his bidding. Despite the enormous power wielded by the U.S. administration, a number of UN Security Council members have stood firm against attacking Iraq before weapons inspection has been given a chance. President of the Center for Constitutional Rights Michael Ratner, in "A U.N. Alternative to War: 'Uniting for Peace'," ZNet Commentary,

February 8, 2003, writes: "In 1950 the Security Council set up a procedure for insuring that stalemates between countries would not prevent the United Nations from carrying out its mission to 'maintain international peace and security.' With the United States playing an important role, the Council adopted Resolution 377, the aptly named 'Uniting for Peace" in an almost unanimous vote. [This resolution] provides that if, because of the lack of unanimity of the permanent members of the Security Council ... the Council cannot maintain international peace where there is a 'threat to the peace, breach of the peace or act of aggression,' the General Assembly 'shall consider the matter immediately". This resolution has been used ten times since its adoption: after Egypt nationalized the Suez Canal in 1956 and to pressure the Soviet Union to cease its intervention in Hungary in the same year, among others. Ratner suggests it should be used now, to mandate that the inspection regime be permitted to complete its inspections and to delay the United States' war on Iraq.

CHAPTER EIGHTEEN

1   Talk given at the American Folklore Society's annual meeting in Albuquerque, New Mexico, October 11, 2003.
2   Second Edition, unabridged, 1987.
3   1991.
4   From "Under the Radar", an excerpt from the forthcoming *Thieves in High Places* by Jim Hightower. Hightower is a former Texas Agriculture Commissioner and author of *If the Gods Had Meant Us to Vote They Would Have Given Us Candidates*.
5   The "Bring Them Home Now" campaign was launched by Military Families Speak Out, Veterans for Peace and other groups, at a press conference at Fort Bragg, North Carolina on August 14, 2003.
6   *The Mass Psychology of Fascism* by Wilhelm Reich, first liberated edition translated from the German Manuscript by Theodore P. Wolfe, Masters of Perception Press, Bangor-Salinas-Sebastopol, 1970. pp. 14-15.
7   "Have You Forgotten" by Darryl Worley was number one on both the Country Music Charts and the Radio and Record National Airplay list, according to D. Perwaz of the Seattle Post-

Intelligencer ("If It 'aint Country it 'aint Music to Pro-War Ears," April 8, 2003). At the other end of the political spectrum, Natalie Maines of The Dixie Chicks was forced to apologize twice for her comment that George W. Bush had acted hastily in attacking Iraq. The group's single "Travelin' Soldier" plummeted on the charts when disk jockeys refused to give air time to "traitors"—also targeting Madonna, Mos Def, Sheryl Crow and others. All radio and TV stations have received Patriot Lists, indicating which performers should be promoted and which silenced.

8 An earlier and equally spontaneous generation of Poets Against the War was active during the last years of the U.S. War in Vietnam.

9 *Poets Against The War*, edited by Sam Hamill, Thunders Mouth Press/Nation Books, New York City, 2003.

10 Throughout the 1970s and '80s I published a number of books of oral history, or Testimony as it was called in Latin America, including *Cuban Women Now, Spirit of the People, Suenos y realidades del guajiricantor* (with Angel Antonio Moreno), *Doris Tijerino: Inside the Nicaraguan Revolution, Sandino's Daughters, Christians in the Nicaraguan Revolution, Risking a Somersault in the Air*, and *Sandino's Daughters Revisited*, among others.

11 I think particularly of Ruth Behar's seminal *Translated Woman: Crossing the Border with Esperanza's Story* (Boston, Beacon Press, 1993).

12 In an email from Timothy Lloyd, Executive Director, American Folklore Society.

CHAPTER NINETEEN

1 This essay was written for *Women, Writing and Resistance*, edited by Jennifer Browdy de Hernández, South End Press, Boston, 2003.

2 According to a New York Times article of May 5, 2002, almost all the world's democratic nations and all European Union countries have ratified the treaty to establish the International Court of Justice. President Clinton signed, but George W. Bush is retracting that signature, and this retraction is almost unheard of in the annals of international jurisprudence. Only Pakistan and China have neither signed nor ratified. Russia has signed and much later ratified.

3   These were early mentors. As my life unfolded, I have been fortunate to count others as well, among them Thomas Merton, Meridel LeSueur, Robert Creeley, Laurette Sejourne, Adrienne Rich, Audre Lorde, Susan Sherman, Ruth Hubbard, Dora María Téllez, Stan Persky, and Mirta Rodríguez Calderón.

4   I am not speaking here about my own talent, still embarrassingly incipient, but about that of many of my friends—who were already making names for themselves in the art and literary worlds of those years.

5   Hettie Cohen, writer and editor, once married to LeRoi Jones (later known as Amiri Baraka).

6   *Mole* is a rich sauce made of peanuts, chocolate, several different types of chiles and other herbs. It accompanies turkey or chicken for baptisms, holy communions and wedding dinners even among Mexico's poor.

7   *Estos cantos habitados / These Living Songs: Fifteen New Cuban Poets*, translated and with an introduction by Margaret Randall, Colorado State Review Press, Fort Collins, Colorado, Volume VI, Number 1, Spring 1978.

8   *Breaking the Silences: 20ᵗʰ Century Poetry by Cuban Women*, edited and translated with an historical introduction by Margaret Randall, Pulp Press, Vancouver 1982.

9   Quoted in the documentary film "The Unapologetic Life of Margaret Randall" by Lu Lippold and Pamela Colby, 2002.

10 The Ministry of Culture was headed by my old friend, priest and poet Ernesto Cardenal, who had been part of the birth of *El Corno Emplumado* in Mexico. Vice Minister of Culture was Daisy Zamora, another of the country's important poets who would later also become a good friend.

11 My Nicaraguan books are *Inside the Nicaraguan Revolution: the Story of Doris Tijerino, Sandino's Daughters, Christians in the Nicaraguan Revolution, Risking a Somersault in the Air: Conversations with Nicaraguan Writers, Gathering Rage: The Failure of Twentieth Century Revolutions to Develop a Feminist Agenda*, and *Sandino's Daughters Revisited*.

12 In my particular journey, I have come to reject almost all religious expressions, from the traditional to the New Age, from the conservative to the apparently liberal. I believe they privilege the

quasi-spiritual over the truly spiritual, cut their adherents off from a realistic world view, and perpetuate patriarchy which, in my mind, is at the root of our unequal distribution of power.

13 The faith component of many who made the Sandinista revolution was responsible, among other things, for Nicaragua's abolition of the death penalty.

14 See my own *Gathering Rage: The Failure of Twentieth Century Revolutions to Develop a Feminist Agenda*, Monthly Review Press, New York, 1992; and *Sandino's Daughters Revisited*, Rutgers University Press, New Brunswick, New Jersey, 1994; and *Cuba: Neither Heaven nor Hell* by María López Vigil, Epica, 1999.

15 For a detailed description of my immigration case, see *Walking to the Edge: Essays of Resistance*, South End Press, Boston, 1991.

16 First published in *Memory Says Yes*, Curbstone Press, Willimantic, Connecticut, 1988. Later included in others of my poetry collections.

17 If you want the blue sky, the price is high.

18 From *Small Wonder, Essays*, by Barbara Kingsolver, Harper Collins, New York, 2002. p. 59.

About
Margaret Randall

In 1985, Margaret Randall was ordered deported under the ideological exclusion clause of the 1952 McCarran-Walter Act after her writing was judged "subversive." After lengthy court battles she won the right to retain her citizenship. Randall is the author of over 100 books of poetry and nonfiction including *When I Look Into the Mirror and See You: Women, Terror and Resistance; Sandino's Daughters; Sandino's Daughters Revisited; The Price You Pay: The Hidden Cost of Women's Relationship to Money; Hunger's Table: Women, Food & Politics; Where They Left You for Dead/Halfway Home* and *Coming Up for Air.*